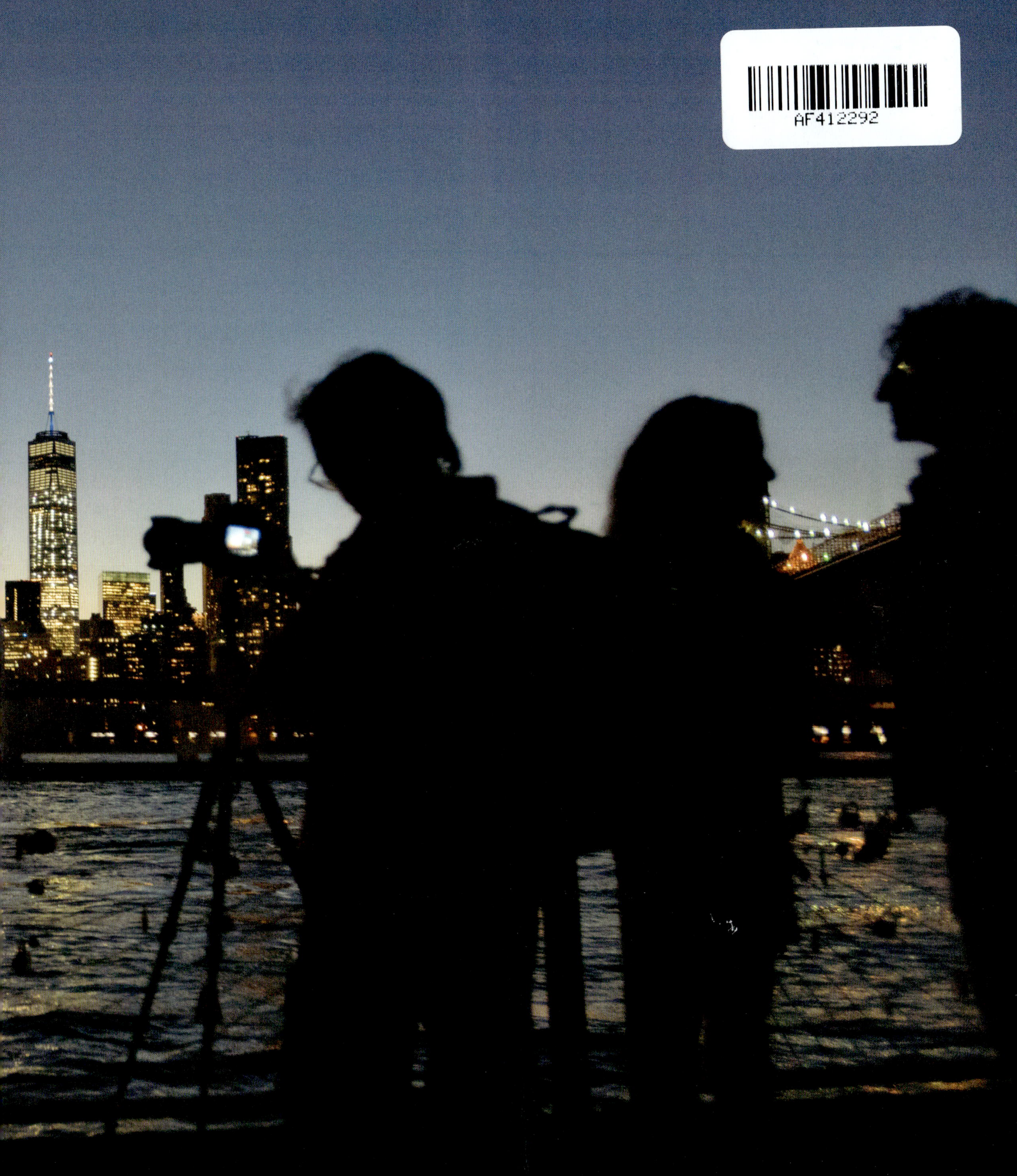

AF412292

Paris/NYC David Bacher

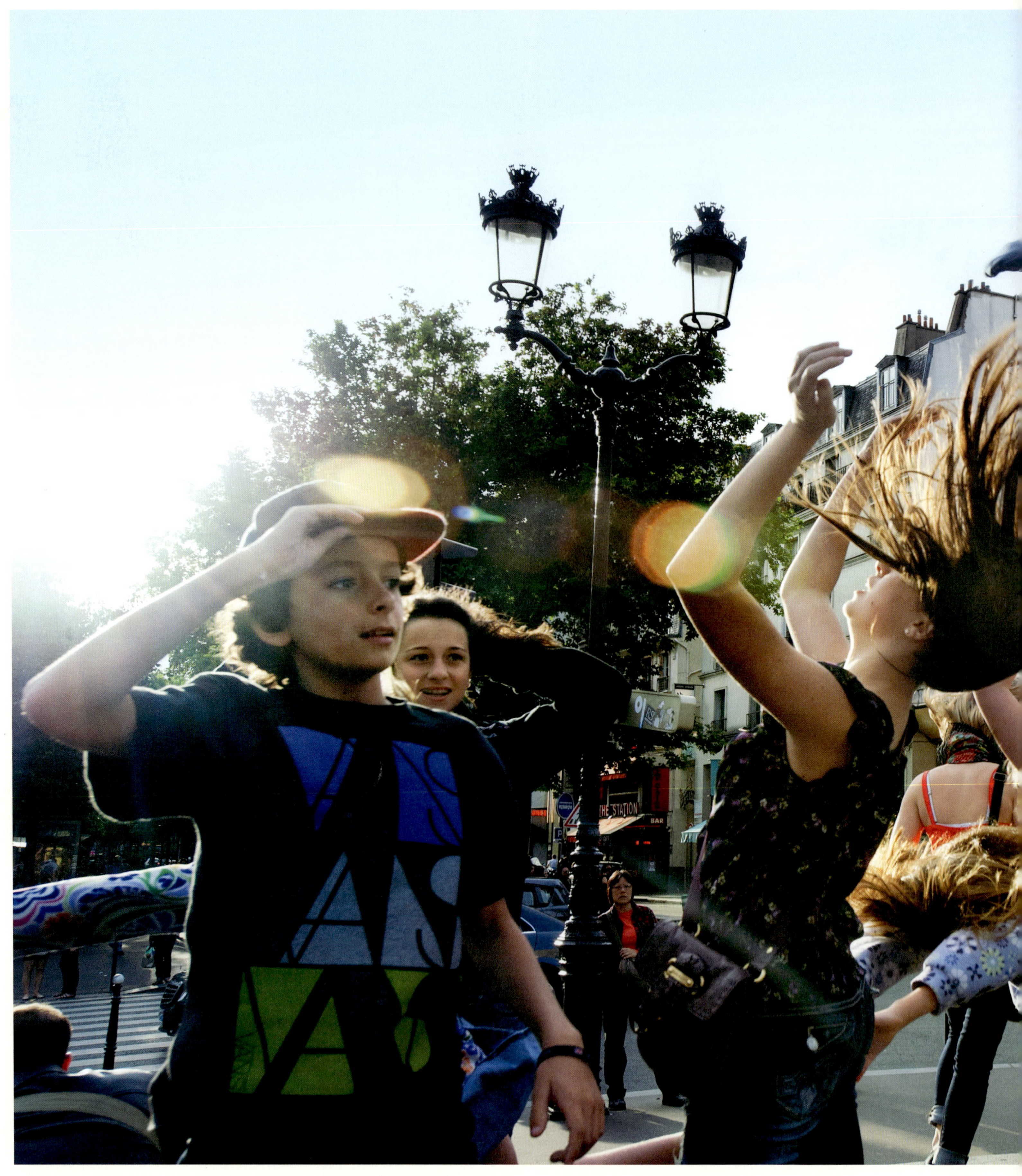

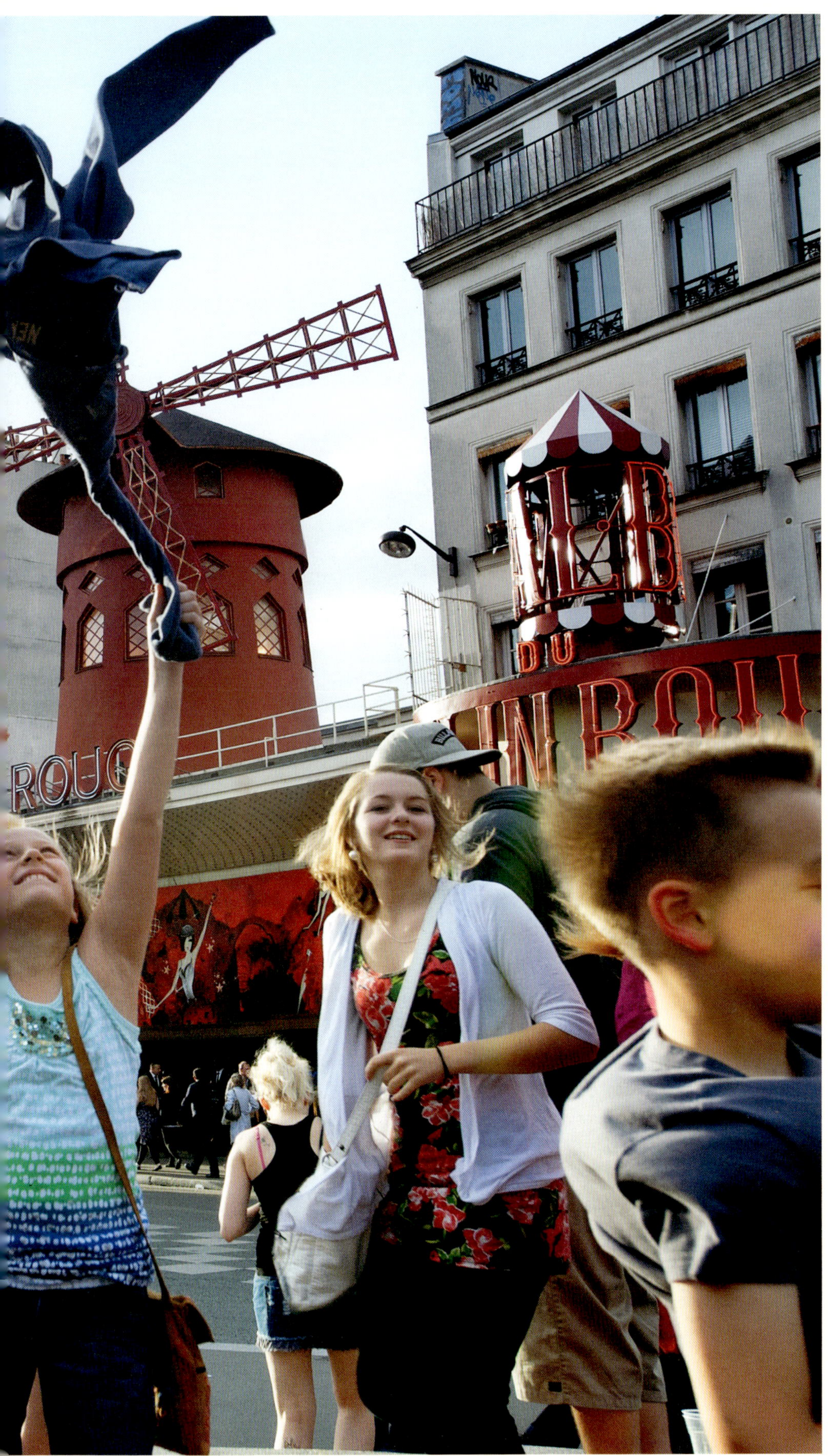

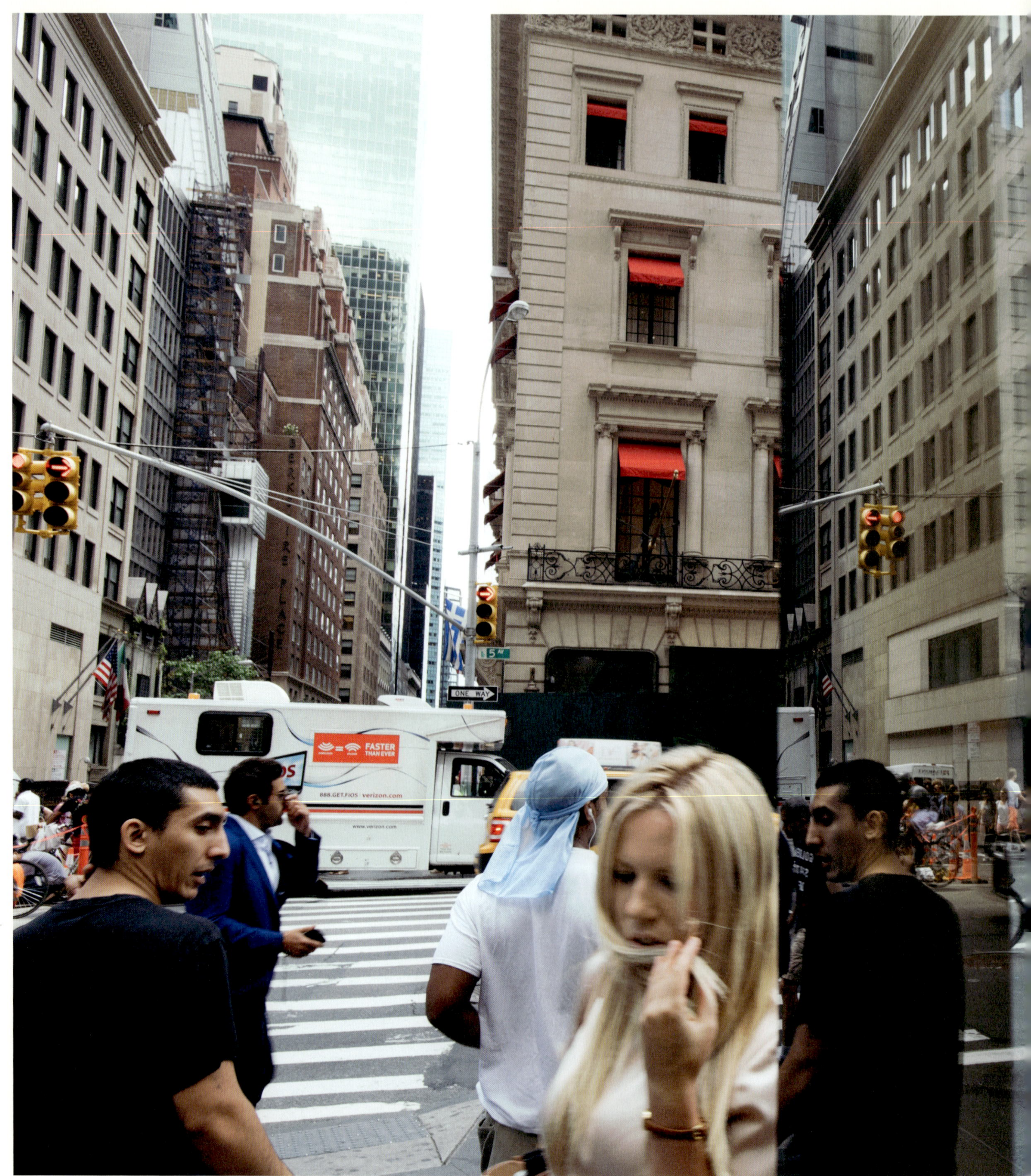
FASTER
THAN EVER
888.GET.FiOS | verizon.com
www.verizon.com
5 Av
ONE WAY

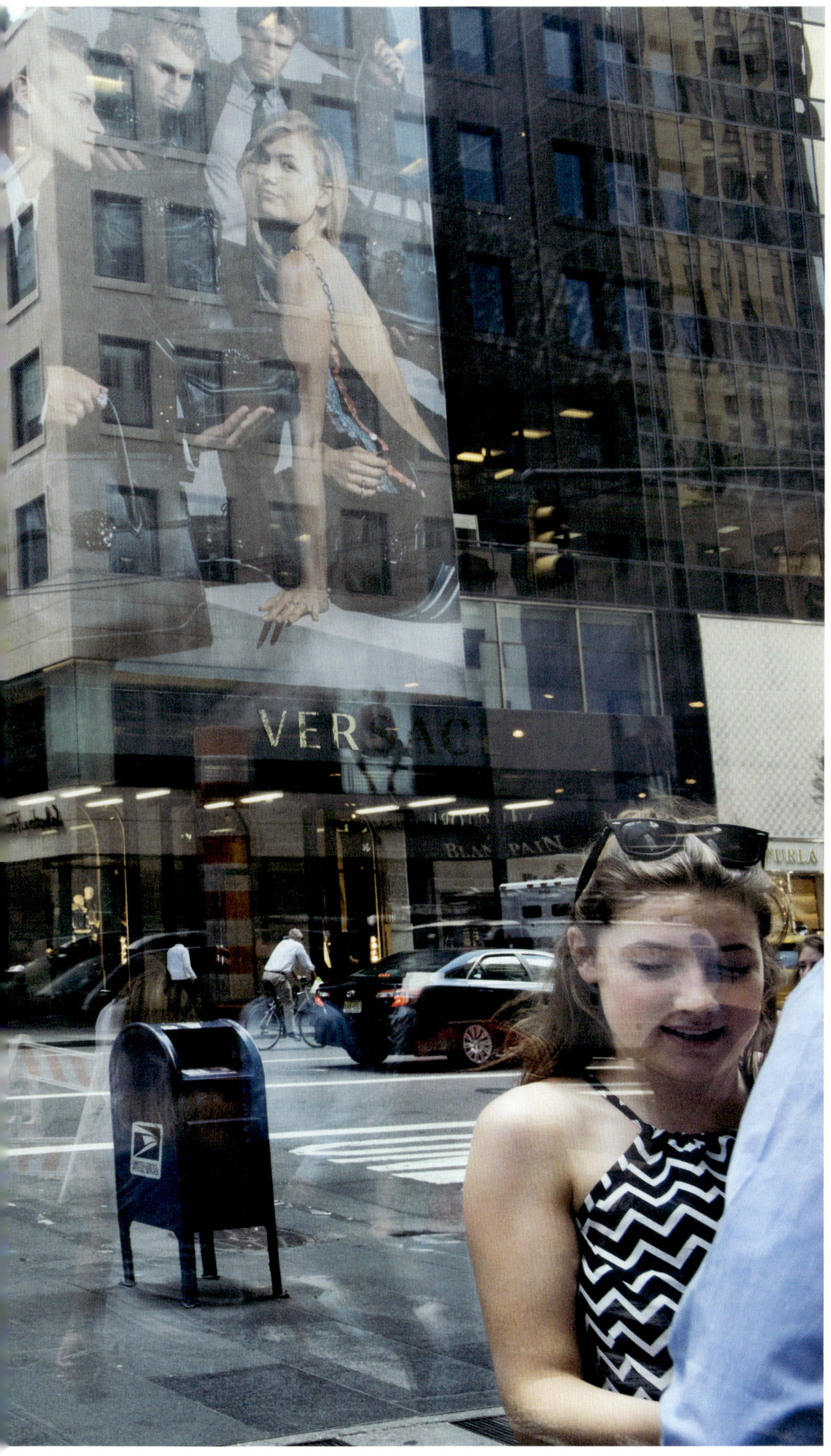

VERSACE
BLANCPAIN
FURLA

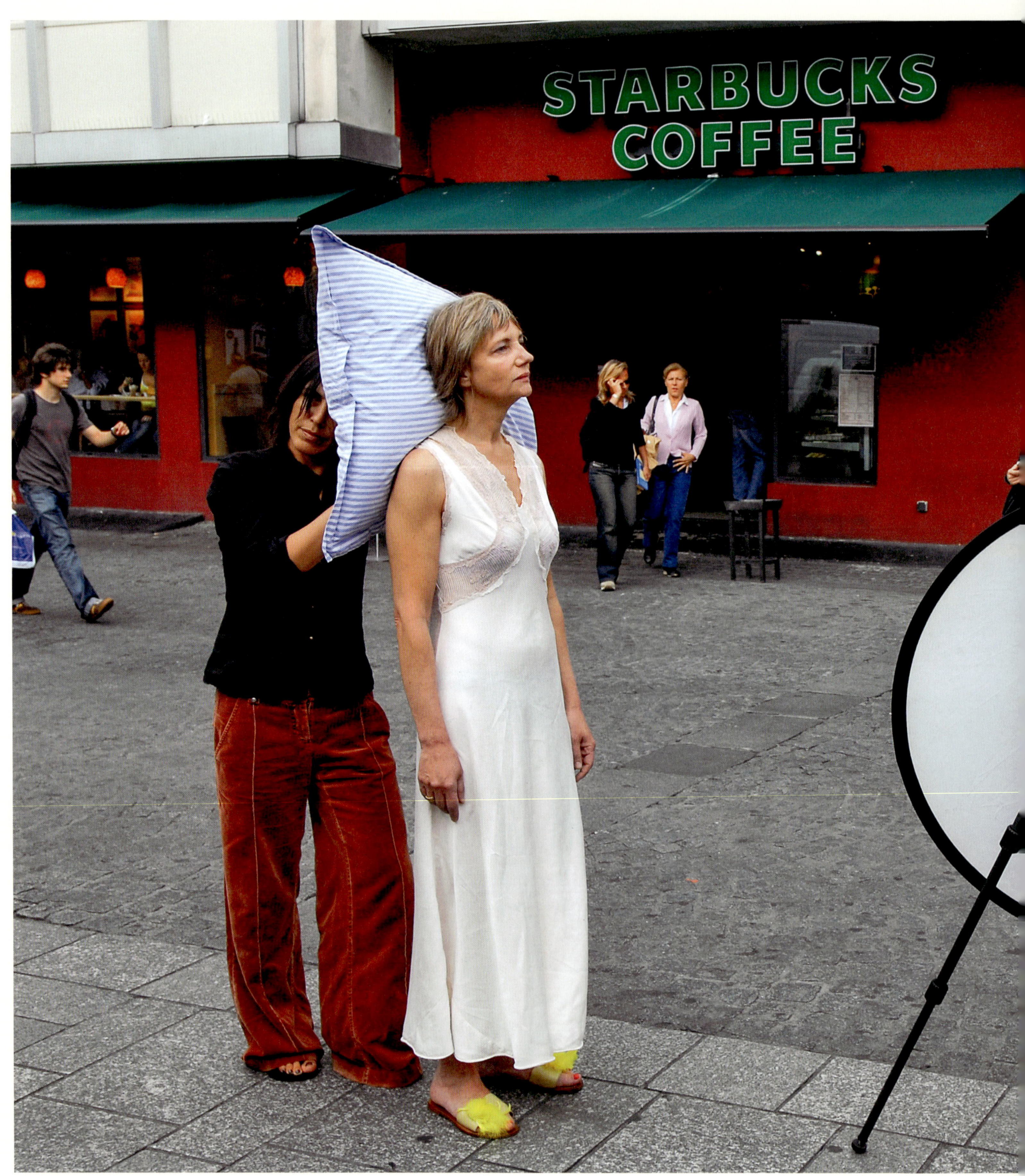

STARBUCKS
COFFEE

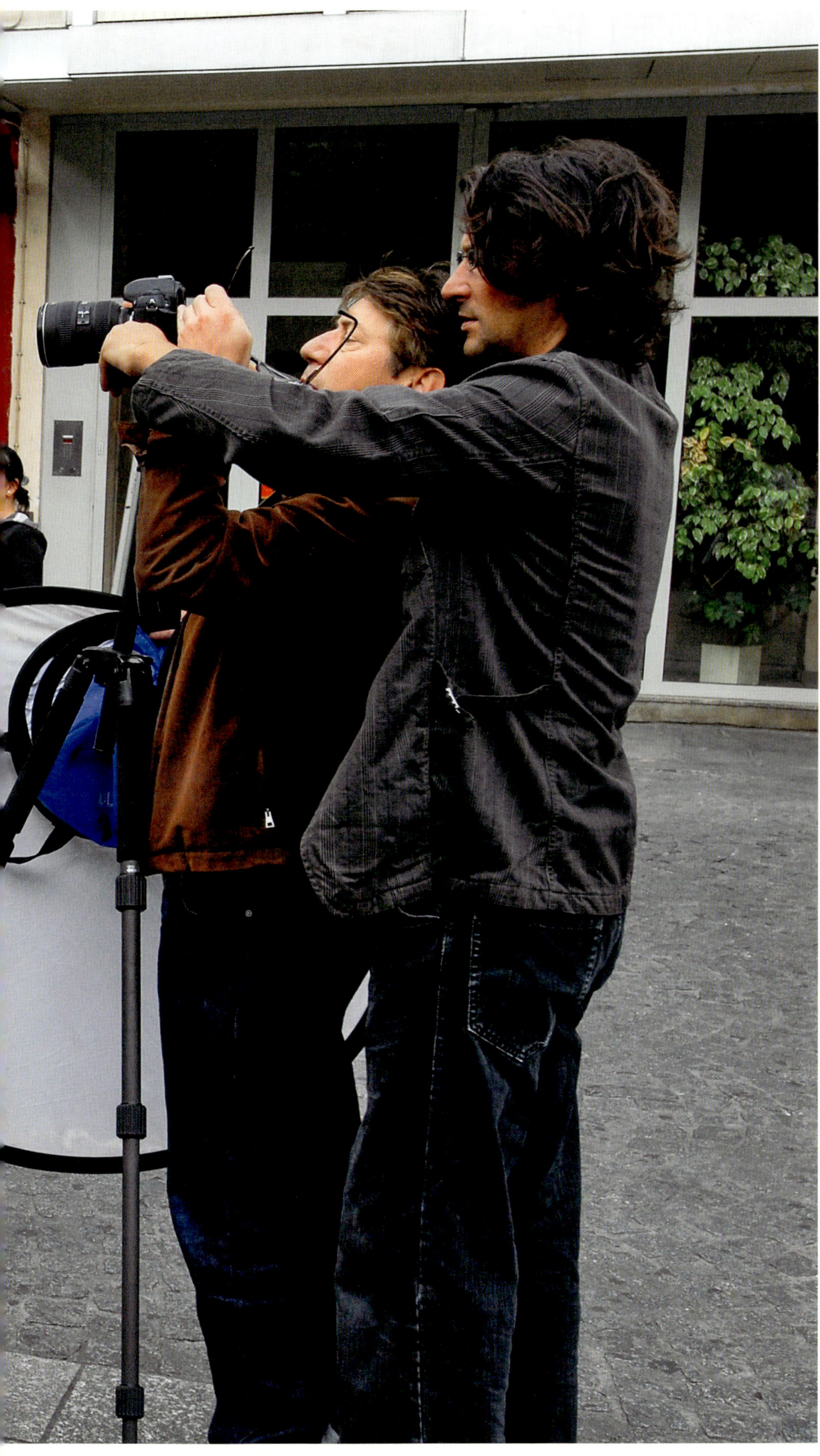

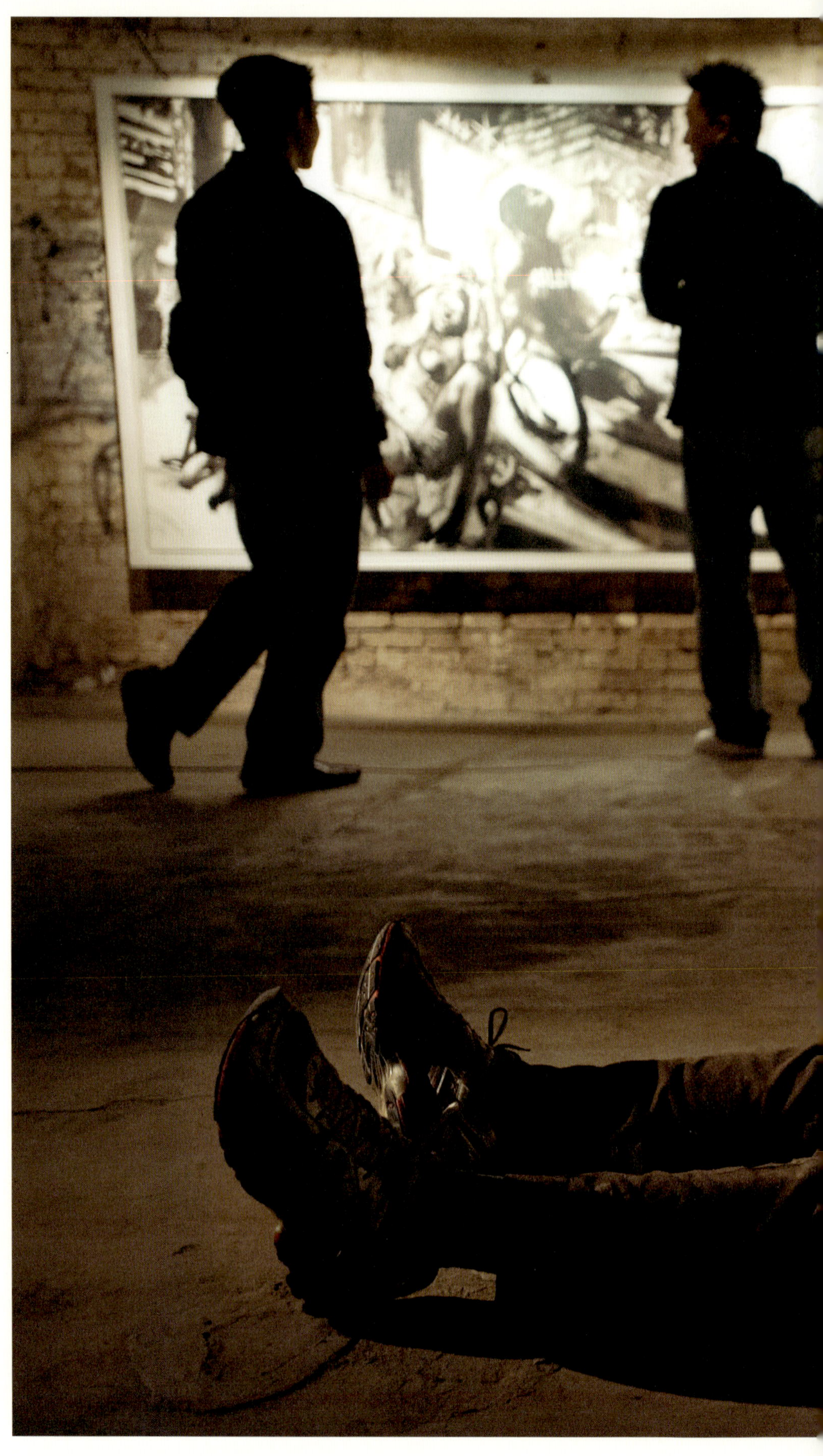

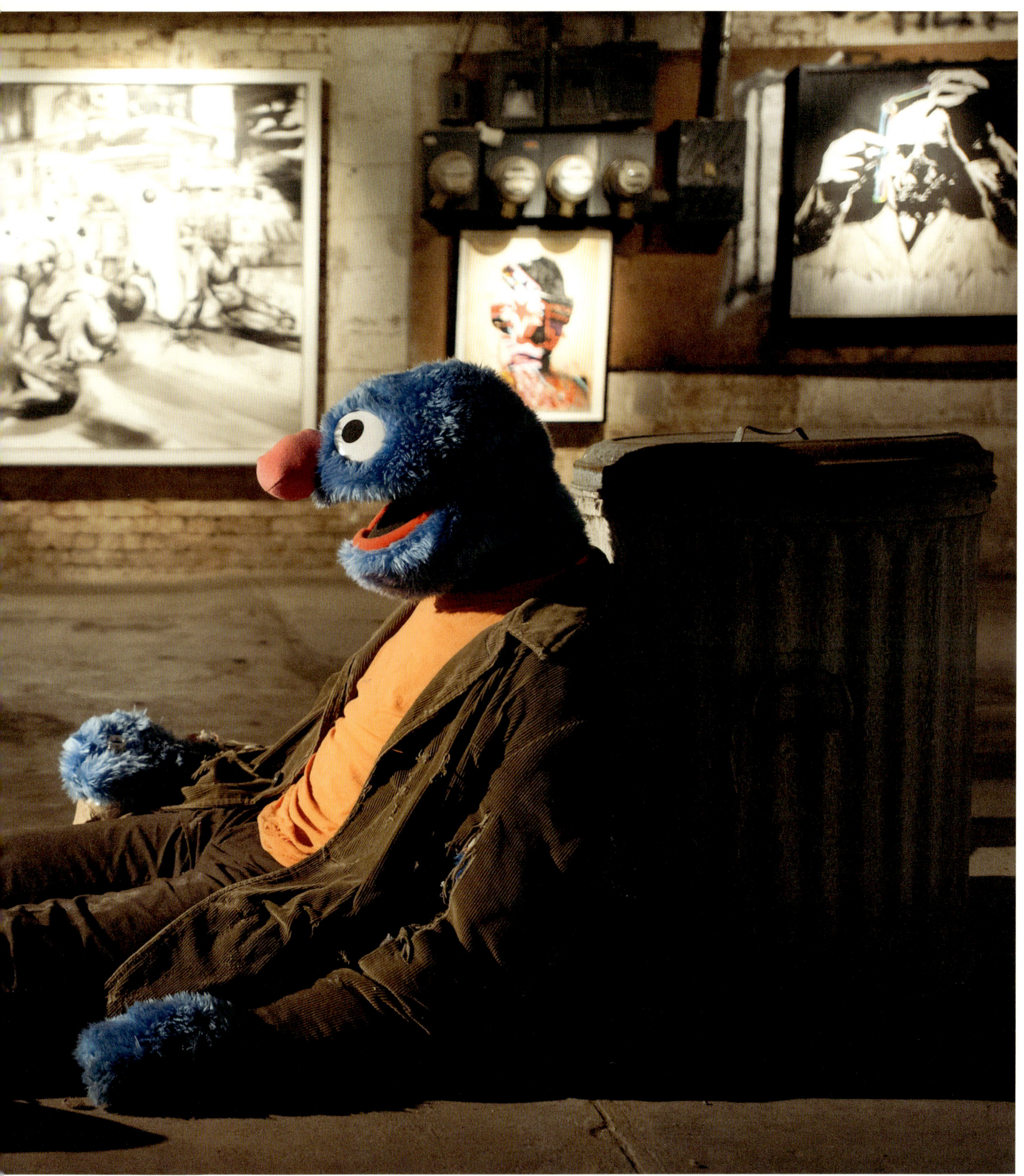

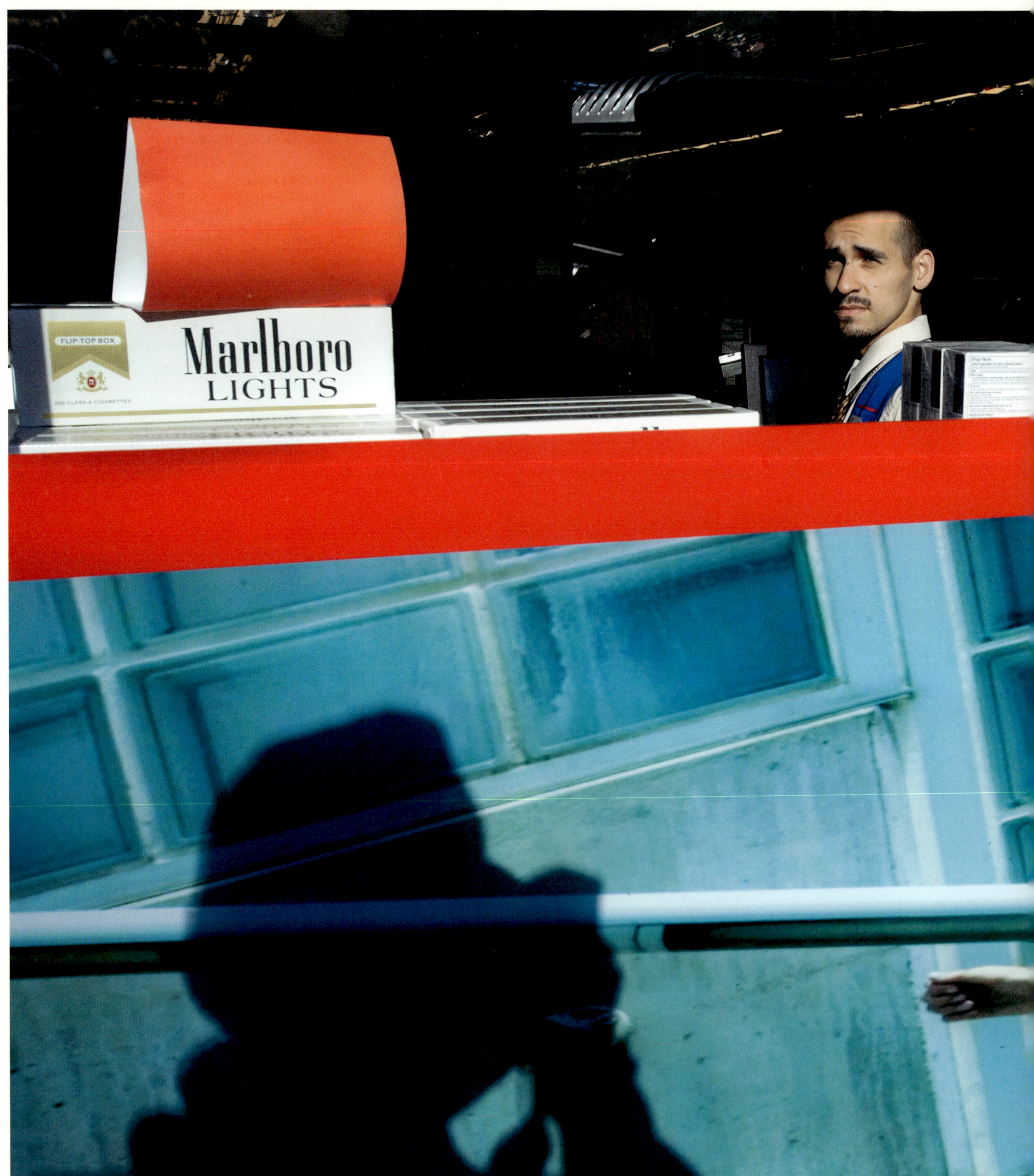

FLIP-TOP BOX
Marlboro
LIGHTS
200 CLASS A CIGARETTES

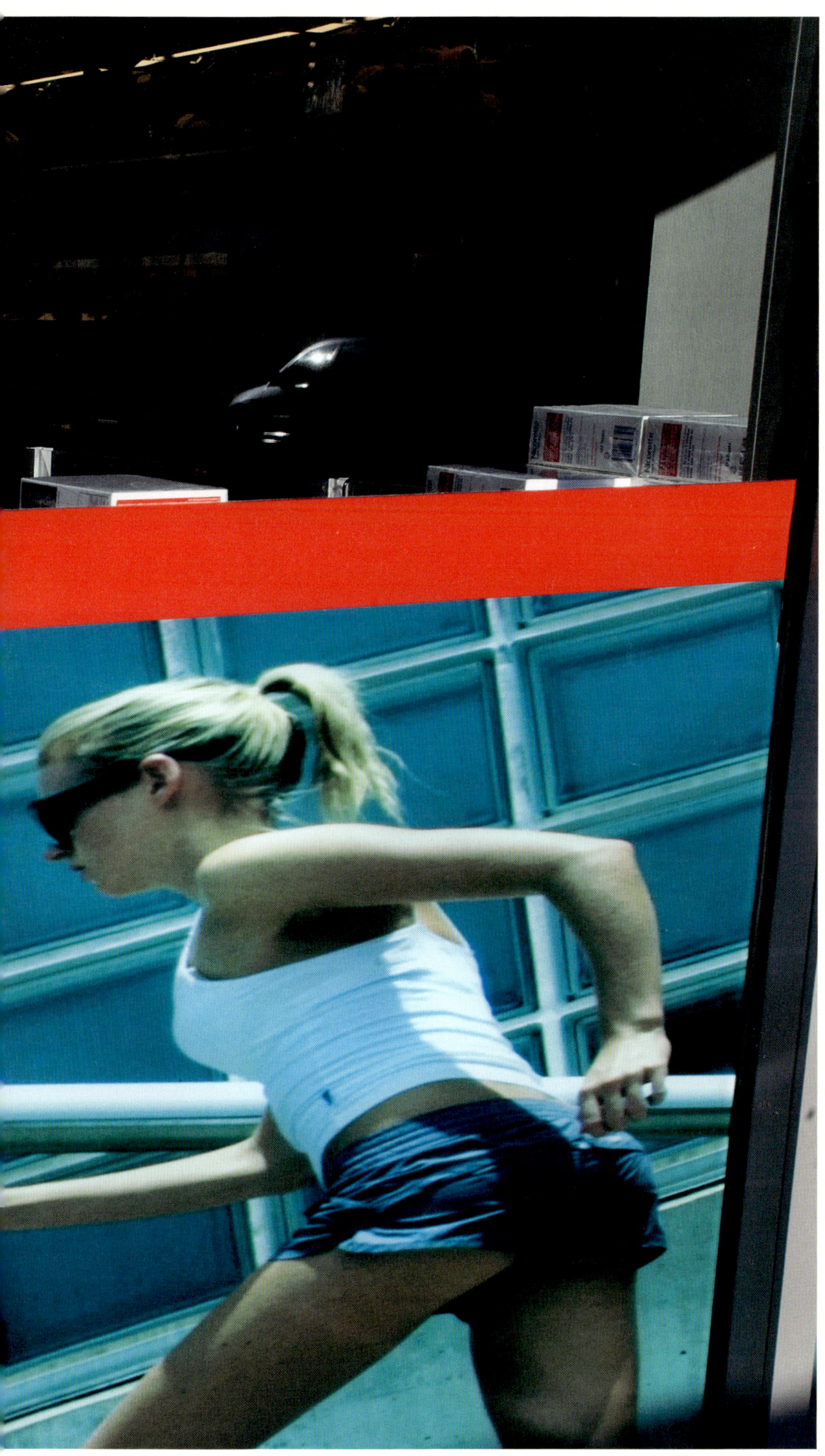

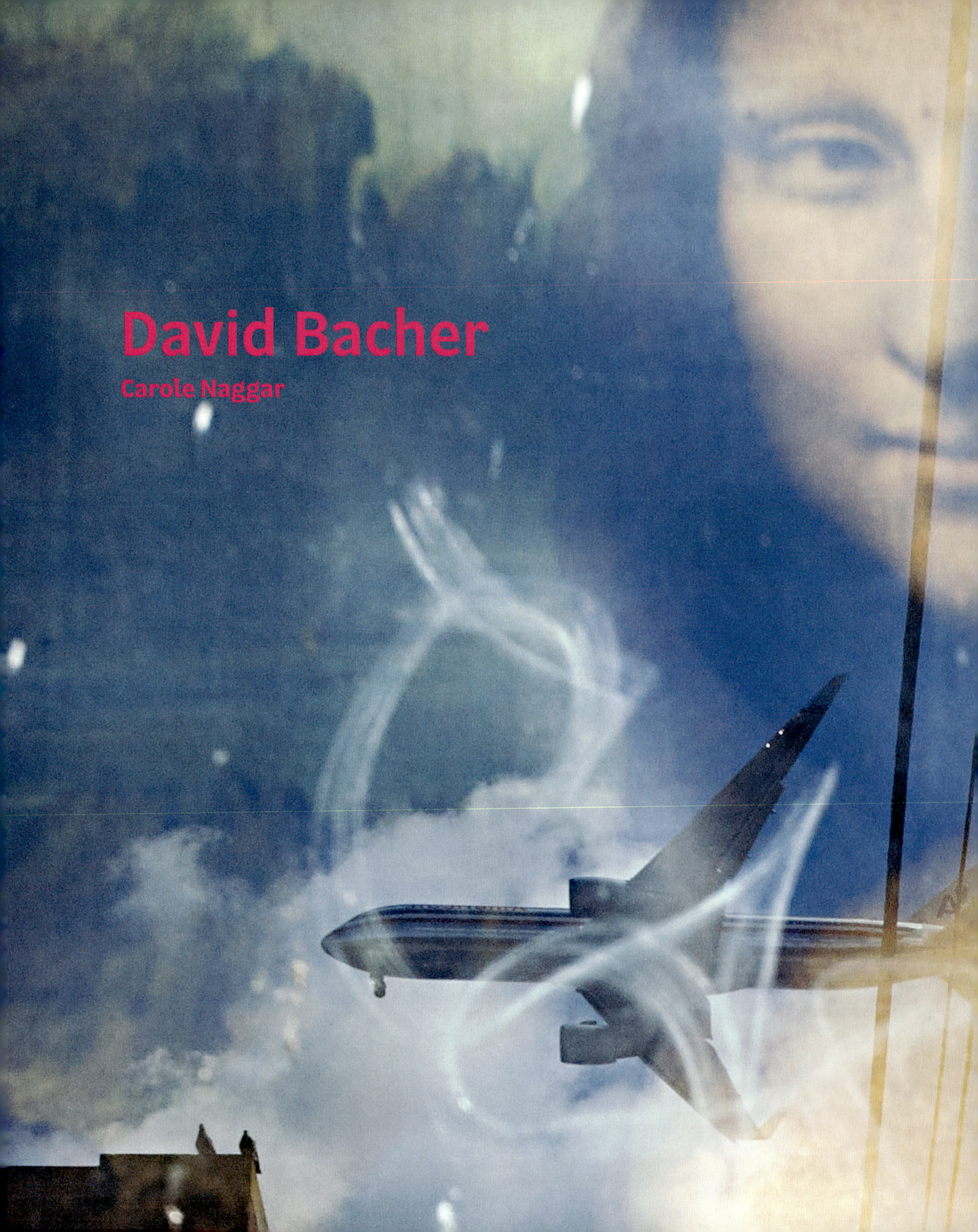

David Bacher

Carole Naggar

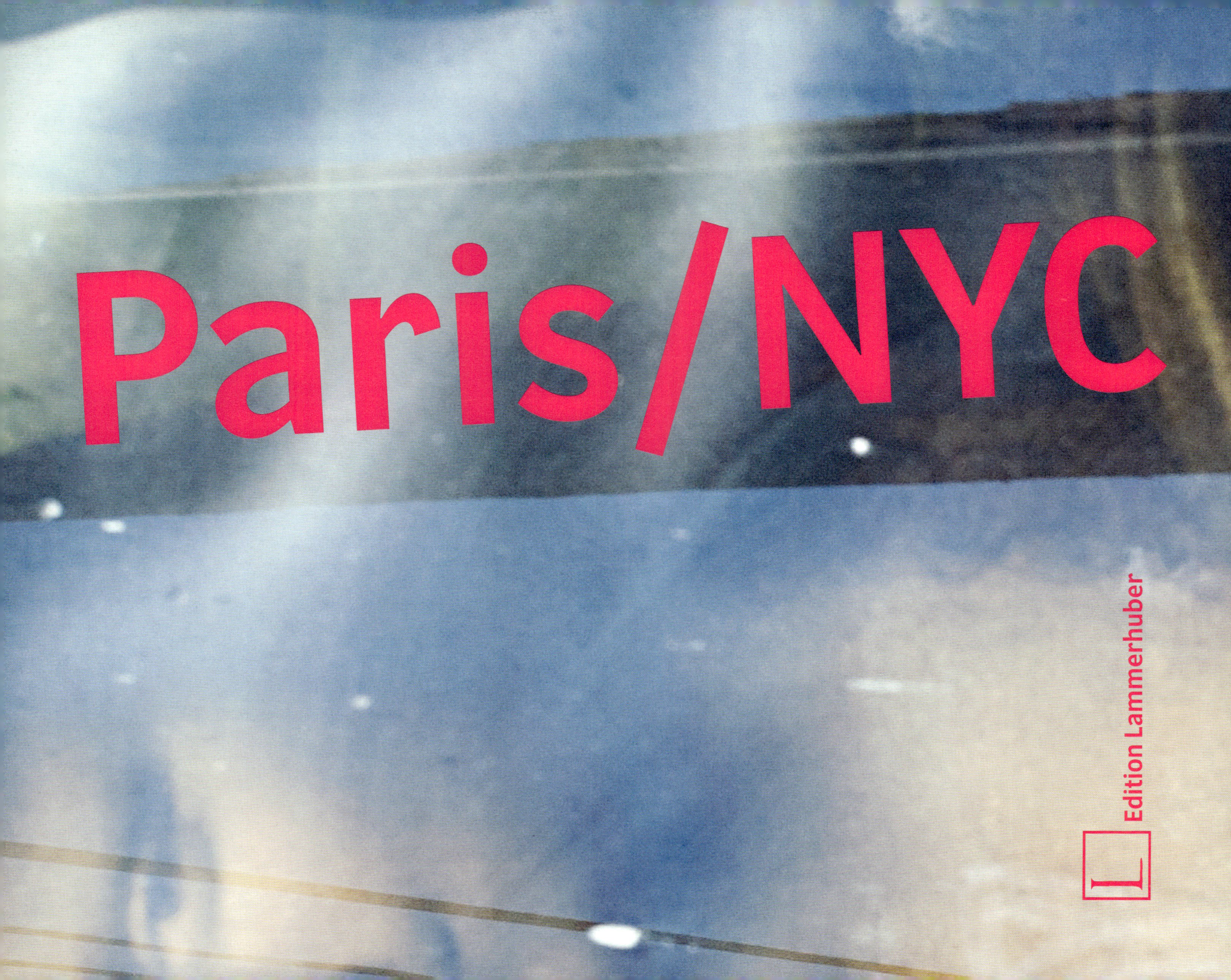

Paris/NYC
Edition Lammerhuber

CAROLE NAGGAR   **David Bacher: Un conte de deux cités**

L'histoire des mouvements des photographes entre New York et Paris remonte aux années cinquante, quand beaucoup d'artistes et d'intellectuels américains se résignent à l'exil pour fuir l'étroitesse d'esprit régnante et l'aveuglement de la répression politique pendant le Maccarthysme.

Parmi ceux qui ont travaillé le pôle de Paris et New York, on trouve Louis Stettner, avec ses images au Rolleicord pleines de douceur, d'empathie, de spiritualité. Leur composition est classique et sa sensibilité procède de l'école européenne, en particulier des photos de Brassaï, son maître qu'il a fréquenté pendant de nombreuses années. À l'opposé, William Klein nous jette ses images au visage comme d'acerbes coups de fouet. Influencé par l'esthétique du New York Daily News, il est l'un des premiers à utiliser des techniques comme le flou et s'est décrit comme « un pseudo ethnographe en quête des instantanés les plus bruts, du degré zéro de la photographie... [je voudrais] photographier un mariage comme une émeute, une manifestation comme un portrait de famille. »

L'esthétique de David Bacher, qui hérite de cette tradition, se situe quelque part entre la calme spiritualité de Stettner et la provocation post-moderniste de Klein. Son travail nous permet aussi de mesurer la distance physique et spirituelle qui sépare les années cinquante de notre présent.

Depuis quinze ans, cet Américain installé à Paris et Nantes a fait le choix de photographier Paris et New York en miroir. Ce faisant, il s'est aperçu que, pour lui, « Paris et New York sont comme deux décors de théâtre avec des milliers d'acteurs sans rôles prédéfinis ».

Contrairement à Cartier-Bresson, qui dans « America in Passing » choisissait un point de vue critique pour observer l'Amérique en crise, Bacher ne se préoccupe pas ouvertement du politique. Sa vision n'est plus celle de « l'instant décisif » : il pourrait être d'accord avec Klein, pour qui « tous les instants sont décisifs ». Son regard fluide reflète sans le mettre en scène le chaos des apparences.

Comme dans les décors du Théâtre Olympique de Palladio à Vicence, Bacher aime créer des trompe-l'œil. Il bouscule les perspectives, donnant aux reflets et aux ombres une présence aussi réelle que celle des corps et des visages qui peuplent le théâtre de ses rues. Miroirs et vitrines contribuent à brouiller la vision.

Sur les habits blancs d'une procession de religieuses, leurs ombres se projettent comme sur un écran et créent un second cortège fantomatique. Un gigantesque poupon de celluloïd semble s'échapper d'une vitrine et flotte pour survoler passants et voitures. L'ombre portée d'une dame âgée qui marche dans un cimetière se projette sur un monument de pierre qui semble vouloir la saisir. En premier plan flou, le grillage qui entoure un terrain de jeu de paume se dédouble et se projette comme un tatouage sur le visage d'un joueur qui fait une pause. Affichée sur un mur du quartier de Chinatown à Flushing, dans le Queens, une reproduction de la Joconde prend vie et se mêle au reflet des immeubles de brique, des lignes électriques et du ciel où passe un avion près d'atterrir dont son regard pensif semble suivre le trajet.

S'il n'est pas ouvertement politique, Bacher excelle toutefois dans les commentaires sociaux indirects et subtils et il saisit les incongruités et les contradictions de la vie quotidienne, en particulier les décalages interraciaux et culturels : une portraitiste de rue, par exemple, donne à son modèle, une jeune femme noire aux cheveux bouclés, une physionomie de femme blanche idéalisée aux yeux marron clair, au nez romain et à la bouche fine : elle ne voit pas celle qui lui fait face. Sur l'esplanade du Trocadéro, un homme noir, peut-être sans papiers, vend à la sauvette aux touristes une guirlande de Tours Eiffel, miniatures, avec en arrière-plan de ces simulacres la « vraie » silhouette illuminée du monument. « La douleur en moins, la légèreté en plus » promet le panneau publicitaire d'une pharmacie parisienne devant lequel une dame âgée, agrippant son cabas à roulettes, semble sur le point de trébucher.

Les images de Bacher reflètent aussi la confusion des apparences, comme si les deux capitales, glissant l'une dans l'autre, empruntaient chacune les qualités de l'autre et perdaient peu à peu leurs caractéristiques pour devenir une troisième réalité hybride qui combine en elle les signes de la modernité : accélération des rythmes de la vie quotidienne, effacement de l'histoire au profit d'une similarité de l'architecture urbaine, mélange des races et des religions (Paris devenant un « melting pot » comme New York depuis longtemps), surgissement d'une nouvelle gamme de couleurs plus stridentes et plus artificielles, modification de la gestuelle des rues devenue plus expressive et plus extrême : le joggeur devient plus commun que le flâneur.

En l'absence de légendes, il est parfois difficile d'identifier la ville où a été prise une photo, d'autant plus que Bacher, dans ses pérégrinations, évite les monuments et les lieux touristiques célèbres. Seuls quelques indices (taxis jaunes new-yorkais, langue de l'inscription sur l'auvent d'un café, bennes à ordures vertes de la Ville de Paris, typographie des plaques de rue — bleues émaillées ou blanches sur fond vert selon la ville —, drapeau américain enroulé sur sa hampe dans un parc, silhouette de l'Empire State Building en arrière-plan d'une photo) nous suggèrent le lieu. Bacher aime jouer de cette confusion et c'est un peu comme s'il demandait au spectateur de marcher sur ses traces et de s'impliquer dans un jeu de découvertes et de devinettes avec quelques symboles pour le guider.

Mais, parfois, nos questions demeurent et il est impossible de savoir où a été prise une photo : cette image, par exemple, d'une jeune fille qui peint à la bombe sur un mur un portrait aux couleurs fluo pourrait avoir été prise à Paris comme à New York ; de même celles des deux petits Fox-Terriers en pullovers tricotés marron assis aux pieds de leur maître — peut-être un hommage à Elliott Erwitt, un autre photographe américain qui a souvent photographié à Paris ?

Bacher ne porte pas de jugement. Son regard est plein d'indulgence, d'humour et de gentillesse : il photographie par exemple en plein cœur de Paris un restaurant de hot-dogs américains — quelques lettres de l'enseigne au néon sont effacées ; ou bien, sous les arbres automnaux du Jardin du Luxembourg, la version miniature coulée en bronze de la Statue de la Liberté (l'original de Bartholdi a été offert à l'Amérique par le peuple français pour symboliser l'amitié franco-américaine) et c'est un peu comme s'il faisait faire à la statue, depuis son socle de Liberty Island, un voyage de retour aux origines, un voyage parallèle au sien.

Pour moi, ce qui me retient avant tout dans les photos de David Bacher, c'est son usage de la couleur et des contrastes, qui évoque souvent les photographies d'Alex Webb au Mexique. Comme Webb, Bacher préfère presque toujours photographier en plein soleil. Des blancs éclatants aux noirs vibrants en passant par toutes les teintes naturelles ou fluo, sa gamme égrène jaunes claquants, rouges intenses, indigos purs, verts, oranges et violets ; cet usage des couleurs projette un sentiment de dynamisme, de joie de vivre et d'émerveillement sans cesse renouvelé devant ce que le quotidien des rues peut offrir à ses yeux. Les va-et-vient constants du voyageur lui permettent d'éviter que sa curiosité ne s'émousse.

Au final, les images de David Bacher me ramènent à cette question essentielle : qui suis-je, moi qui regarde et qui, comme ce photographe, transite régulièrement entre Paris et New York ? Est-ce que je ne perçois des différences entre mes deux villes que parce que mon regard est brouillé par les filtres contraires de l'espoir et de la nostalgie ?

Et si, dans ce va-et-vient de ville en ville, j'avais perdu mon identité sans en acquérir une nouvelle ? Et si j'étais devenue comme la bille de métal d'un flipper, roulant sans fin d'un côté à l'autre de l'océan ? Et si Paris et New York étaient toutes deux devenues des villes mondiales, avec peu de choses pour les différencier ? Et si le temps avait effacé leurs différences et que les deux villes ne possédaient plus d'essence distincte ? Et si voyager n'avait plus de sens ? Et si les couleurs et le chaos de la modernité avaient tout envahi ? Et si passé et histoire étaient désormais submergés dans ce flux indistinct que nous appelons présent ?

Ces questions, parmi beaucoup d'autres, David Bacher sait les poser et les laisser ouvertes.

CAROLE NAGGAR   **David Bacher: A Tale of Two Cities**

The history of photographers' movements between New York and Paris dates back to the 1950s, when many American artists and intellectuals resigned themselves to exile to flee the prevailing narrow-mindedness, and the blindness of political repression during McCarthysm.

Among those who worked in Paris and New York, there is Louis Stettner, with his Rolleicord images full of tenderness, empathy and spirituality. Their composition is classic and their sensitivity comes from the European school, especially from Brassaï's photos, his mentor with whom he spent much time over the years. In contrast, William Klein throws his images in our faces like sharp lashes. Influenced by the aesthetics of the New York Daily News, he is one of the first to use techniques such as 'out of focus' and described himself as "a pseudo ethnographer in search of the most raw snapshots, the zero degree of photography ... [I would like] to photograph a wedding like a riot, a demonstration like a family portrait".

David Bacher's aesthetics, inheriting this tradition, lie somewhere between Stettner's calm spirituality and Klein's post-modernist provocation. His work also allows us to measure the physical and spiritual distance that separates the fifties from our present time.

Fifteen years ago, this American living in Paris and in Nantes decided to take mirror images of New York and Paris. In doing so, he realized that for him "Paris and New York are like two theater sets with thousands of actors without predefined roles".

Unlike Cartier-Bresson, who in 'America in Passing' chose a critical point of view to observe America in crisis, Bacher does not openly worry about politics. His vision is no longer that of "the decisive moment": he could agree with Klein, for whom "every moment is decisive". His fluid gaze reflects the chaos of appearances without staging it. As in the set of Palladio's Teatro Olimpico in Vicenza, Bacher likes to create optical illusions. He jostles perspectives, giving reflections and shadows a presence as real as that of the bodies and faces which inhabit the theater of his work, the streets. Mirrors and store windows help to blur the view.

On the white habits of nuns in a procession, their shadows are projected as onto a screen, and create a second ghostly procession. A gigantic baby doll seems to escape from a window and float, flying by cars and pedestrians. The shadow of an elderly lady walking in a cemetery is cast onto a stone monument that seems to want to seize it. In the fuzzy foreground, the fence around a handball court doubles up and is projected like a tattoo on the face of a player taking a break. Displayed on a wall in the Chinatown neighborhood of Flushing, Queens, a reproduction of the Mona Lisa comes to life and mingles with the reflection of brick buildings, power lines, and the sky. A passing plane is about to land and her thoughtful gaze seems to follow its path.

While not openly political, Bacher excels in indirect and subtle social commentary, and captures the incongruities and contradictions of everyday life, especially interracial and cultural differences: a street portraitist, for example, gives her model, a young black woman with curly hair, the appearance of an idealized white woman with light brown eyes, a Roman nose and a thin mouth: she does not see the one facing her. On the Trocadero esplanade, a black man, perhaps an undocumented immigrant, sells a garland of miniature Eiffel Towers to tourists. In the background of these trinkets stands the 'real' illuminated silhouette of the monument. "Less pain, more lightness" promises the billboard of a Parisian pharmacy in front of which an elderly lady, clutching her shopping trolley, seems on the verge of stumbling.

Bacher's images also reflect the confusion of appearances, as if the two capitals were slipping into each other, each borrowing the qualities of the other and gradually losing their characteristics to become a third hybrid reality combining signs of modernity: the acceleration of the pace of everyday life, the erasing of history in favor of a similar urban architecture, a mixture of races and religions (Paris becoming a 'melting pot' like New York has been for a long time), the emergence of a new range of strident and more artificial colors, the change of gestures on the streets which have become more expressive and more extreme: Jogging is now more common than strolling.

In the absence of captions, it is sometimes difficult to identify the city where a photo was taken, especially since Bacher, in his peregrinations, avoids monuments and famous tourist places. Only a few indications (New York's yellow taxis, the writing on the awning of a café, green garbage dumpsters in the city of Paris, the typography of street signs, blue enameled or white on a green background depending on the city, an American flag wrapped around its pole in a park, the silhouette of the Empire State Building) in the background of a photo are hinting at the place. Bacher likes to play with this confusion and it's a bit like asking the viewer to follow his tracks and get involved in a game of discoveries and riddles with some symbols to guide him or her.

But sometimes our questions remain, and it is impossible to know where a photo was taken: this image, for example, of a young girl who is spray painting a portrait in neon colors on a wall could have been taken in Paris or in New York; likewise those of the two small fox terriers in brown knitwear sitting at the feet of their master — perhaps a tribute to Elliott Erwitt, another American photographer who often photographed in Paris?

Bacher is not judgmental. His gaze is full of indulgence, humor and kindness: for example in the heart of Paris he photographs an American hot dog restaurant — some letters of the neon sign are erased. Under the fall foliage of the Luxembourg Gardens, he captures the cast bronze miniature version of the Statue of Liberty (Bartholdi's original was offered to America by the French people to symbolize Franco-American friendship) and it's a bit like taking the statue, from its pedestal on Liberty Island, on a journey back to its origins, a journey parallel to his.

What strikes me most about David Bacher's photos is his use of color and contrasts, which often evokes Alex Webb's photographs in Mexico. Like Webb, Bacher almost always prefers to photograph in full sun. From sparkling whites to vibrant blacks through all natural or neon hues, its range includes bright yellows, intense reds, pure indigos, greens, oranges and purples; this use of colors projects a sense of dynamics, joy of life and a constantly renewed wonder at what daily life in the streets can offer to his eyes. The constant comings and goings of the traveler allow him to keep his curiosity alive.

In the end, David Bacher's images bring me back to this essential question: Who am I, me who is looking, and who, like this photographer, travels regularly between Paris and New York? Do I perceive differences between my two cities only because my eyes are blurred by the contrary filters of hope and nostalgia?

And what if, in this back and forth between the two cities, I had lost my identity without acquiring a new one? What if I had become like the metal sphere of a pinball machine, rolling endlessly back and forth across the ocean? And what if Paris and New York had both become world cities, with little to differentiate them? And what if time had erased their differences and the two cities no longer had a distinct essence? And what if traveling did not make sense anymore? And what if the colors and chaos of modernity had invaded everything? What if past and history were now submerged in this indistinct flow we call present?

David Bacher knows how to ask these questions, among many others, and how to leave them open.

Die Geschichte des fotografischen Austausches zwischen New York und Paris reicht bis in die 1950er-Jahre zurück, als zahlreiche amerikanische Künstler und Intellektuelle ins Exil gingen, um der herrschenden Engstirnigkeit und den blindwütigen Repressalien der Politik der McCarthy-Ära zu entfliehen.

Einer der Wanderer auf der Achse New York — Paris war Louis Stettner, der mit seiner Rolleicord Aufnahmen voller Sanftheit, Empathie und Spiritualität geschaffen hat. Aus seinen Fotos, die stets einem klassischen Bildaufbau folgen, spricht ein Feingefühl europäischer Prägung, wie wir es insbesondere von Brassaï kennen, der über Jahre hinweg Stettners Lehrmeister war. William Klein dagegen schleudert uns seine Bilder geradezu wie harte Peitschenschläge ins Gesicht. Beeinflusst von der Ästhetik der *New York Daily News,* verwendete er als einer der ersten Fotografen neue gestalterische Elemente wie etwa die Weichzeichnung. Klein nannte sich selbst einen „Pseudo-Ethnograph[en] auf der Suche nach dem schonungslosen Schnappschuss, dem Nullpunkt der Fotografie … [Ich möchte] eine Hochzeit wie Straßenkrawalle fotografieren, eine Demonstration wie eine traute Familie."

Die fotografische Ästhetik von David Bacher, der sich in diese Tradition einreiht, oszilliert zwischen Stettners ruhiger Spiritualität und Kleins postmoderner Provokation. Seine Arbeit lässt erkennen, wie lange die 1950er-Jahre zurückliegen und wie sehr sich ihre geistige Prägung von der unserer Gegenwart unterscheidet.

Vor fünfzehn Jahren hat der Amerikaner Bacher, der in Paris und Nantes lebt, damit begonnen, die Städte Paris und New York zu fotografieren. Die beiden Metropolen, die in seinen Bildern einander spiegeln, sind für ihn „wie zwei Theaterkulissen, die von Tausenden Akteuren ohne festgelegte Rollen bevölkert werden".

Anders als Cartier-Bresson, der in seinem Buch *America in Passing* einen kritischen Blick auf ein krisengeschütteltes Amerika warf, hat Bacher nicht in erster Linie ein politisches Anliegen. Er sucht nicht nach dem „entscheidenden Augenblick". Vermutlich würde er Klein zustimmen, für den „jeder Augenblick entscheidend ist". Mit seinem Blick fängt er die sichtbare Welt in all ihrer Unordnung ein, ohne sie zu inszenieren.

David Bacher arbeitet in seinen Fotografien oftmals mit dem Trompe-l'Œil-Effekt, wie er uns etwa auch in den Kulissen von Palladios Teatro Olimpico in Vicenza begegnet. Er wirbelt die Perspektiven durcheinander, und Lichtreflexe und Schatten sind in seinen Bildern nicht weniger wirklich als die Körper und Gesichter, die die Straßen bevölkern und so zur Bühne werden lassen. Spiegel und Schaufensterscheiben steigern das visuelle Verwirrspiel.

In einer Prozession von Ordensfrauen fangen sich die Schatten auf den weißen Gewändern wie auf Leinwänden und bilden einen zweiten, geisterhaften Zug. Eine riesenhaft wirkende Puppe aus Zelluloid scheint ein Schaufenster zu durchbrechen und über Passanten und Autos zu schweben. Auf einem Friedhof fällt der Schatten einer älteren Dame auf ein steinernes Grabmal, das nach ihr zu greifen scheint. Ein Gitterzaun, der ein Jeu-de-Paume-Feld umschließt und im Vordergrund des Bildes verschwommen zu sehen ist, wirft seinen Schatten wie ein Tattoo über das Gesicht eines Spielers, der eine Pause macht. In der Chinatown von Flushing im New Yorker Stadtteil Queens erwacht die Darstellung der Mona Lisa an einer Hauswand zum Leben und verschwimmt mit dem Spiegelbild der Backsteingebäude, der Stromkabel und des Himmels, durch den ein Flugzeug im Landeanflug sinkt, das sie mit ihrem nachdenklichen Blick zu verfolgen scheint.

Bachers Fotografie ist zwar nicht ausdrücklich politisch, illustriert jedoch häufig auf indirekte und subtile Art gesellschaftliche Themen und deckt Ungereimtheiten und Widersprüche des Alltags auf, insbesondere Bruchlinien auf ethnischem und kulturellem Gebiet. Eine Straßenkünstlerin verleiht ihrem Modell, einer jungen schwarzen Frau mit lockigen Haaren, das idealisierte Aussehen einer Weißen, mit hellbraunen Augen, römischer Nase und schmalen Lippen — ohne Blick für ihr Gegenüber. Ein Dunkelhäutiger, vielleicht ein illegaler Einwanderer, verkauft auf der Esplanade du Trocadéro unter der Hand Miniatur-Eiffeltürme an Touristen, während im Hintergrund die Silhouette des hell erleuchteten Originals aufragt. Ein Werbeplakat in einer Pariser Apotheke verspricht „Weniger Schmerzen, mehr Leichtigkeit", davor eine ältere Dame, die sich auf ihren Einkaufstrolley stützt und zu straucheln scheint.

In Bachers Bildern verschmelzen die Erscheinungsformen miteinander, als würden sich die Metropolen über-
lagern, die Eigenschaften der jeweils anderen annehmen, nach und nach ihre Besonderheiten verlieren und
eine dritte Stadt bilden, die in einer hybriden Wirklichkeit angesiedelt ist und alle Charakteristika der Moderne
in sich vereint: ein immer hastigerer Alltag, eine geschichtsvergessene, gleichförmige urbane Architektur, eine
multiethnische und multireligiöse Bewohnerschaft (wie New York ist auch Paris schon seit Langem ein *melting
pot*), das Vordringen eines immer grelleren und unnatürlicheren Farbspektrums, ein öffentliches Gebaren,
das immer extrovertierter und extremer wird — der Jogger hat den Flaneur abgelöst.

Da den Fotografien keine Bildunterschriften beigefügt sind, ist bei manchen Aufnahmen nur schwer zu erkennen,
in welcher der beiden Städte sie entstanden sind, zumal Bacher auf seinen Streifzügen Sehenswürdigkeiten
und Touristenmagnete links liegen lässt. Dann geben nur Details einen Hinweis darauf, wo wir uns befinden:
gelbe New Yorker Taxis, die Sprache auf der Markise eines Cafés, die grünen Mülltonnen von Paris, das Design
der Straßenschilder (blau emailliert oder weiß auf grünem Grund), eine amerikanische Flagge, die schlaff an
einem Mast in einem Park hängt, das Empire State Building im Hintergrund. Bacher spielt mit dieser Unein-
deutigkeit, als wolle er den Betrachter einladen, ihm zu folgen und sich auf ein Spiel voller Entdeckungen
und Rätsel einzulassen, das als Anhaltspunkte nur einige Symbole bietet.

Bisweilen bleiben jedoch Fragen offen und der Betrachter im Ungewissen darüber, wo das Foto gemacht
wurde. Das Bild der jungen Frau etwa, die in leuchtenden Farben ein Porträt auf eine Mauer sprüht, könnte
sowohl in Paris als auch in New York aufgenommen worden sein. Ebenso das Foto mit den beiden Foxterriern
in gestrickten dunkelbraunen Leibchen, die zu Füßen ihres Herrchens sitzen — vielleicht eine Hommage an
Elliot Erwitt, gleichfalls ein amerikanischer Fotograf, der häufig in Paris gearbeitet hat?

Bacher urteilt nicht, sondern blickt voll Nachsicht, Humor und Sanftmut auf die Welt. So zeigt er etwa ein
Restaurant, das mitten in Paris amerikanische Hotdogs serviert und in dessen Neonreklame einige Buchstaben
defekt sind, oder, inmitten der herbstlich gefärbten Bäume des Jardin du Luxembourg, die in Bronze gegossene
Miniaturversion der Freiheitsstatue (das Original von Bartholdi war ein Geschenk des französischen Volkes
an Amerika, zum Zeichen der französisch-amerikanischen Freundschaft). Dabei scheint es fast, als hätte er
sie von Liberty Island zurück zu ihren Ursprüngen geholt — eine Reise, wie auch er selbst sie gemacht hat.

Mich persönlich fesselt an David Bachers Fotografien vor allem die Art, wie er mit Farben und Kontrasten umgeht.
Häufig erinnern seine Arbeiten an die Bilder, die Alex Webb in Mexiko gemacht hat. Wie Webb fotografiert
Bacher fast ausschließlich bei hellem Sonnenlicht. Die Farbpalette seiner Aufnahmen reicht von gleißendem
Weiß über sämtliche natürliche Schattierungen und Neontöne bis zu dröhnendem Schwarz und enthält die
unterschiedlichsten Nuancen von Knallgelb, intensivem Rot, reinem Indigo, Grün, Orange und Violett. Dieser
Farbenreichtum vermittelt Tatkraft und Lebensfreude sowie die Begeisterung, die der Alltag auf den Straßen
bei Bacher immer wieder hervorzurufen vermag. Und dass er als Reisender fortwährend unterwegs ist, ver-
hindert, dass seine Neugierde jemals abflaut.

Schließlich führen mich die Bilder von Bacher zu einer fundamentalen Frage: Wer bin ich selbst, eine Betrachte-
rin, die wie Bacher regelmäßig zwischen Paris und New York pendelt? Entgehen mir die Unterschiede zwischen
meinen beiden Städten, nur weil Hoffnung und Nostalgie — zwei widersprüchliche Kräfte — meinen Blick trüben?

Habe ich durch das Hin und Her zwischen zwei Städten meine Identität verloren und noch keine neue gefunden?
Bin ich eine Flipperkugel geworden, die unentwegt von einer Küste des Ozeans zur anderen rollt? Unterschei-
den sich die Weltstädte Paris und New York überhaupt noch in irgendetwas? Hat die Zeit die Unterschiede
verwischt und haben die Städte ihren Wesenskern verloren? Hat Reisen überhaupt noch einen Sinn? Haben
die Farben und das Chaos der modernen Welt schon alles überschwemmt? Sind Vergangenheit und Geschichte
nicht schon längst in der opaken Flut untergegangen, die wir Gegenwart nennen?

Diese und viele weitere Fragen berührt David Bacher in seinen Bildern. Er stellt sie — und lässt sie offen.

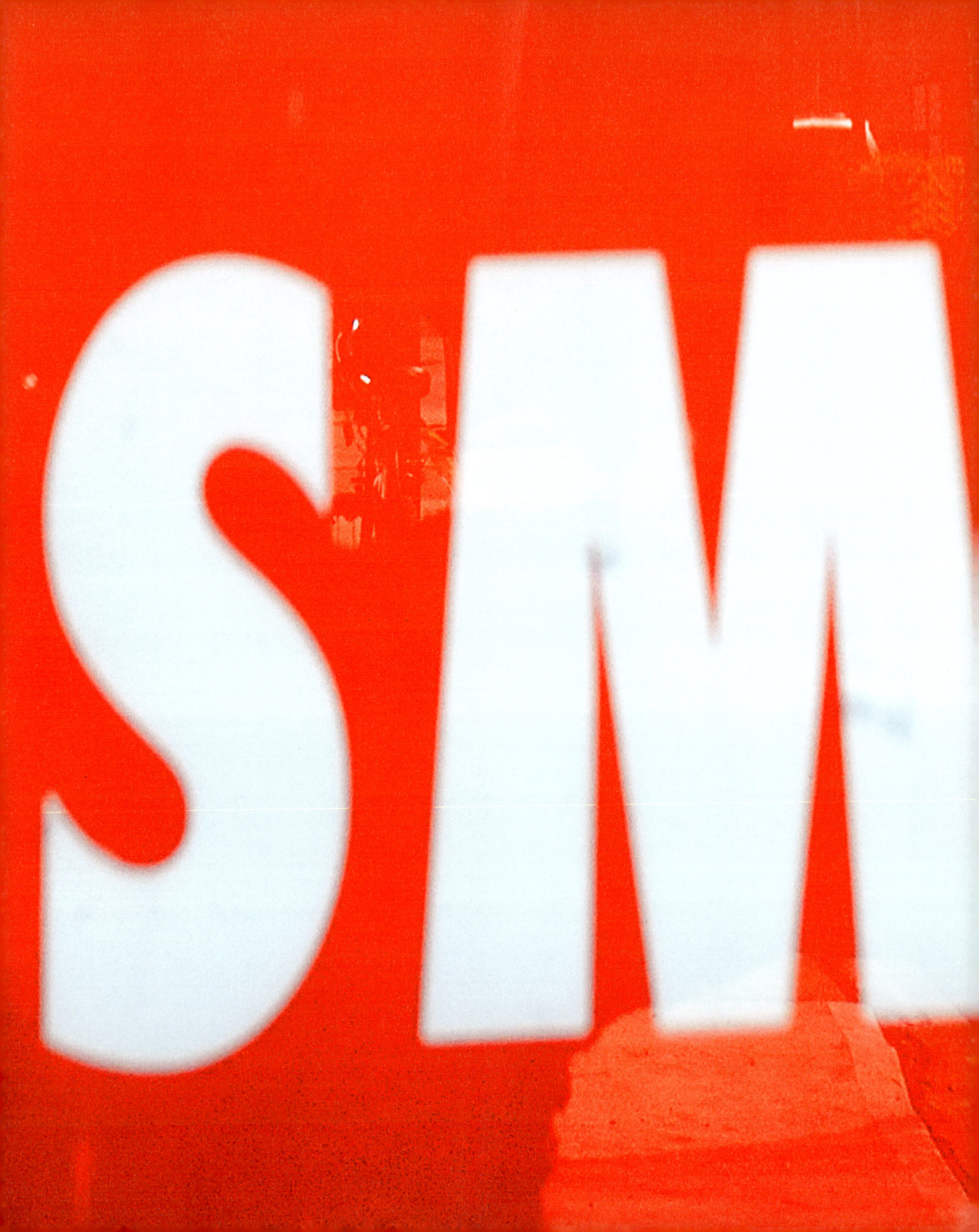
SM

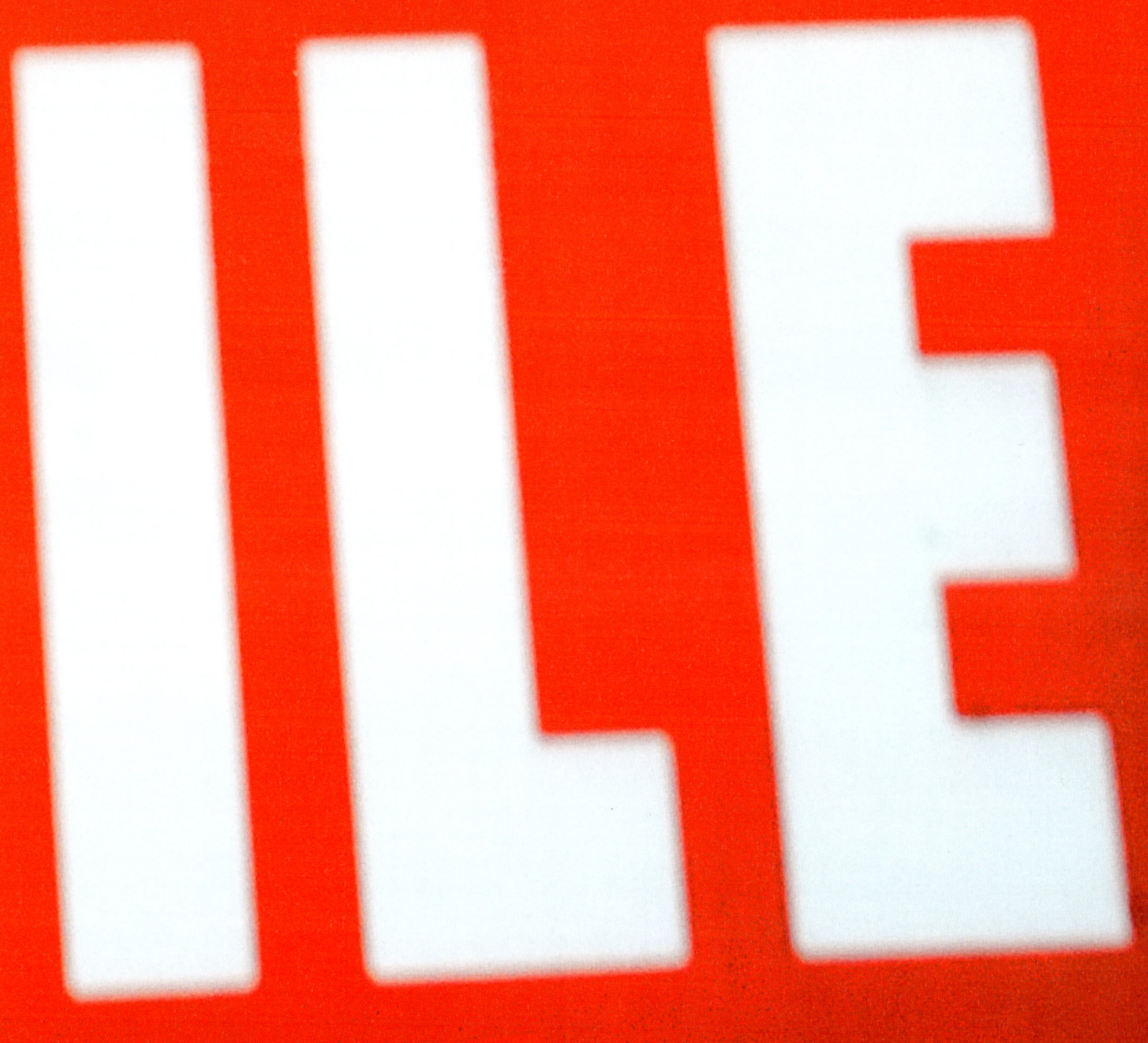

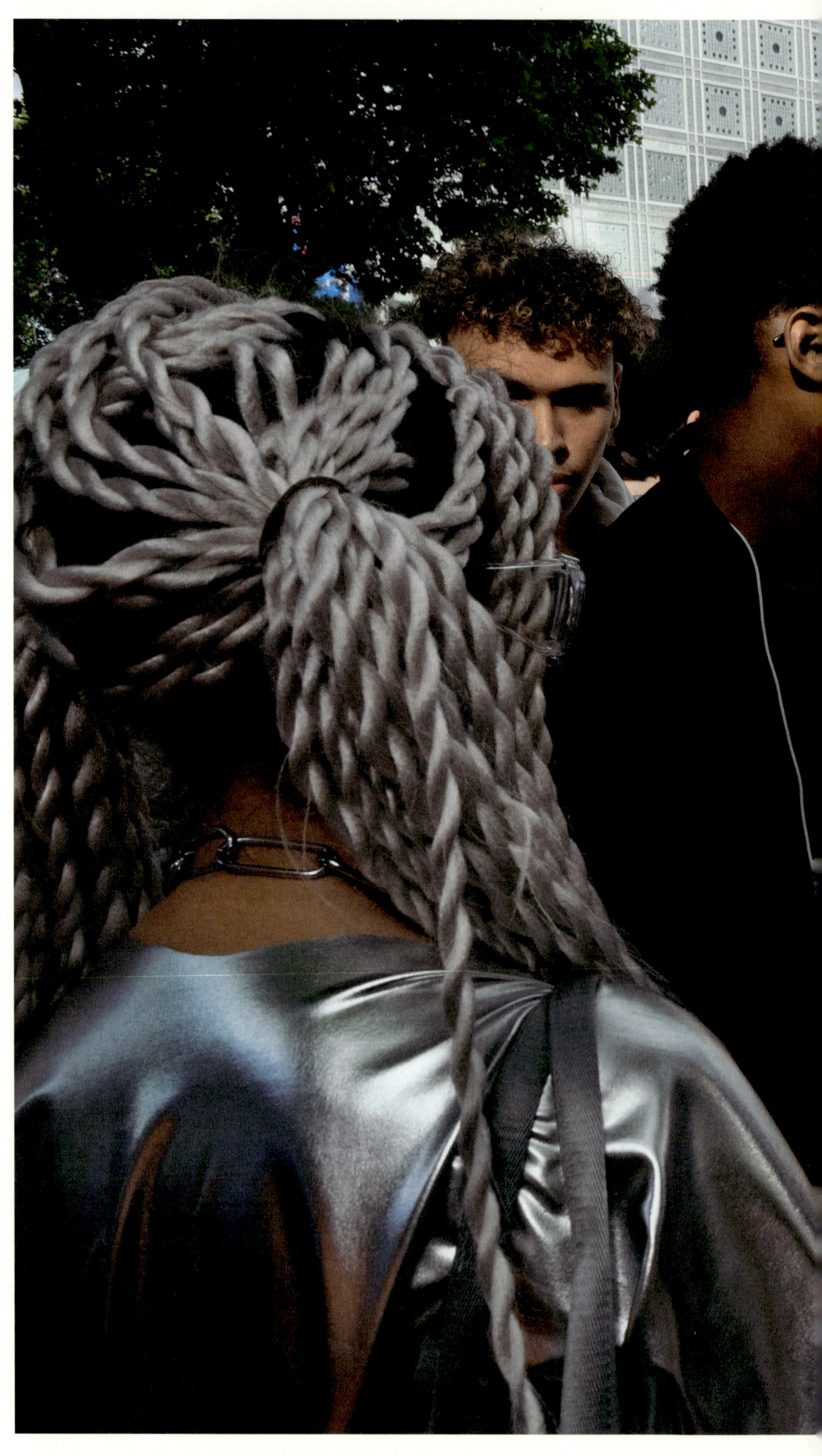

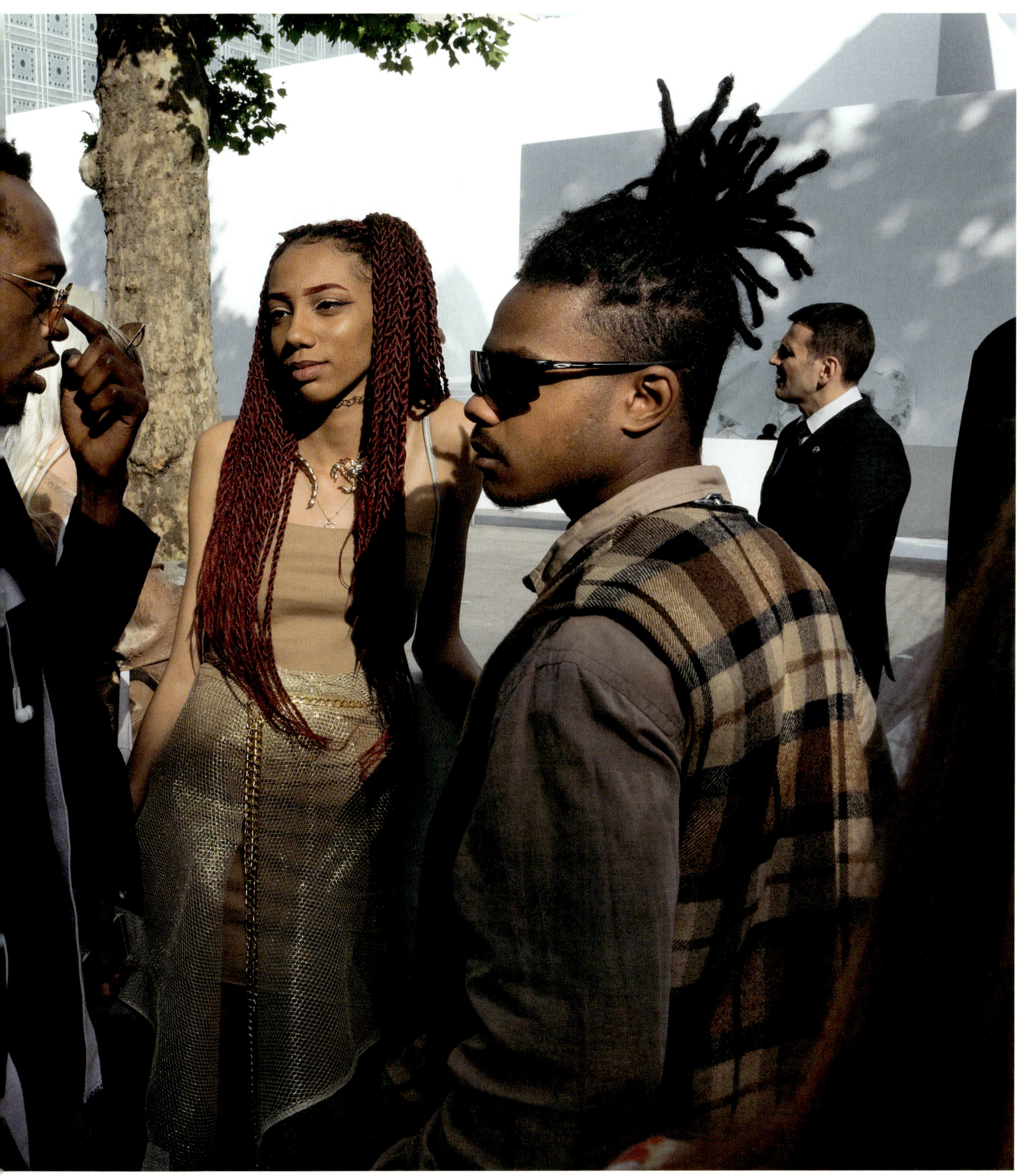

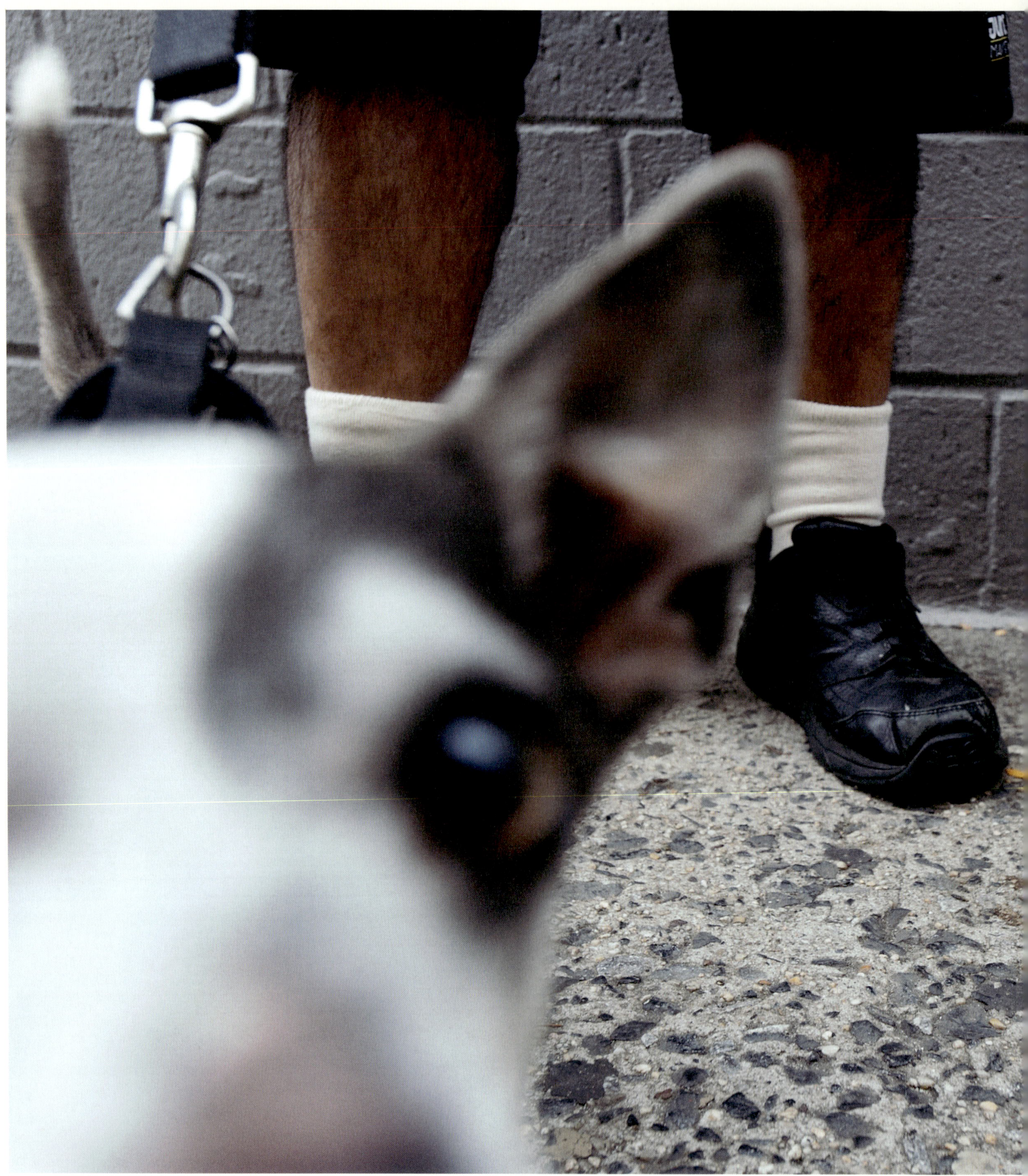

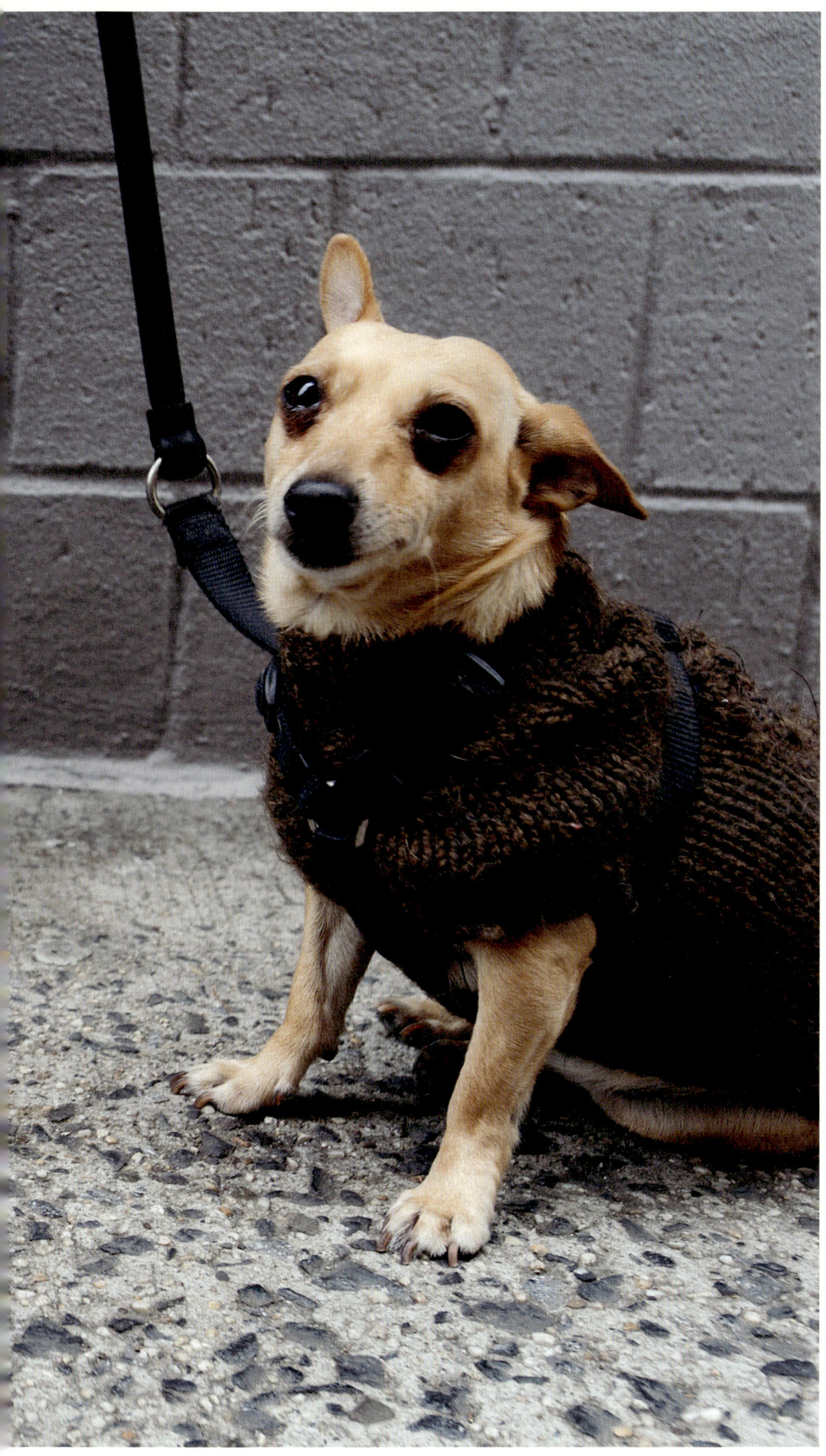

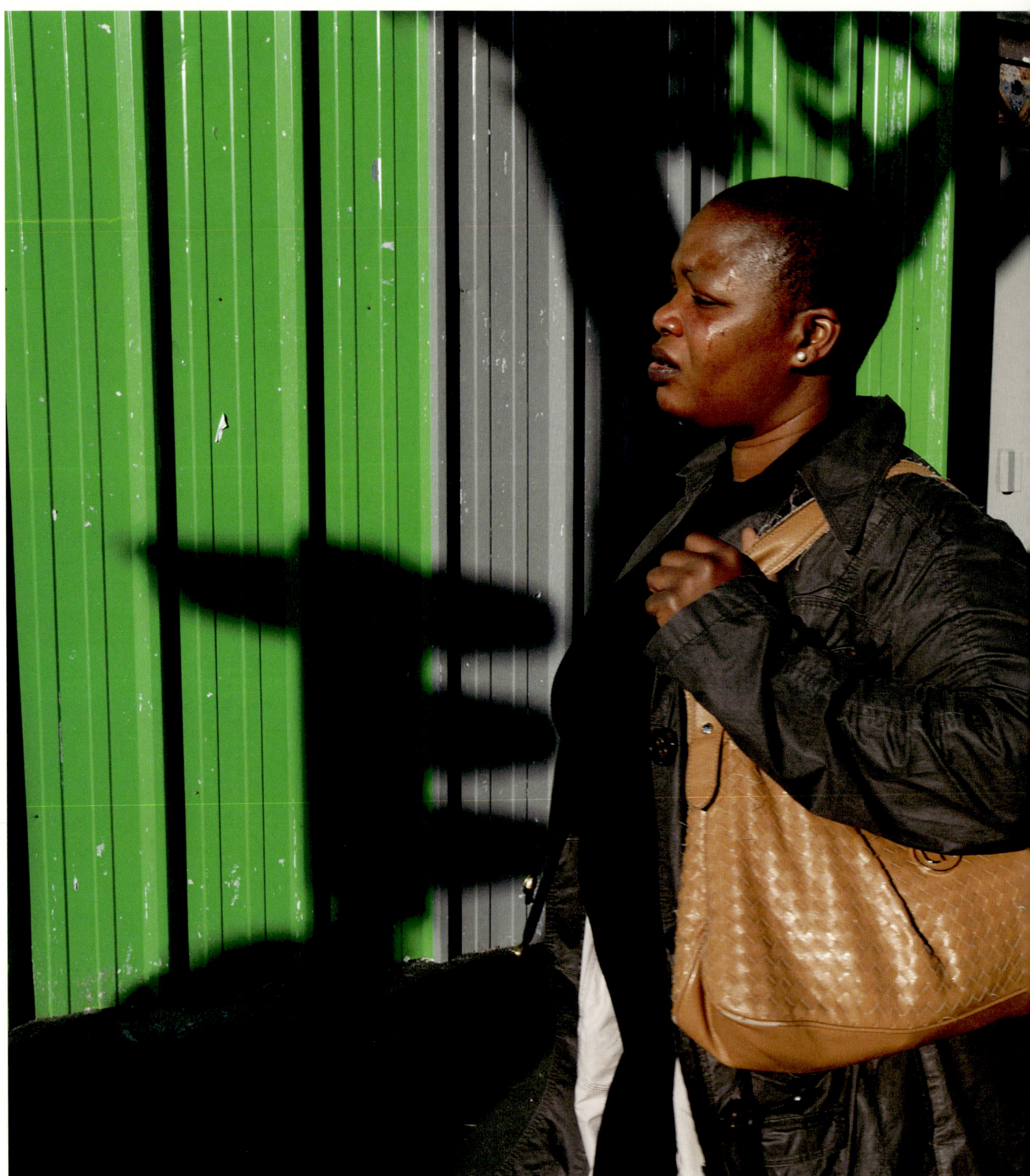

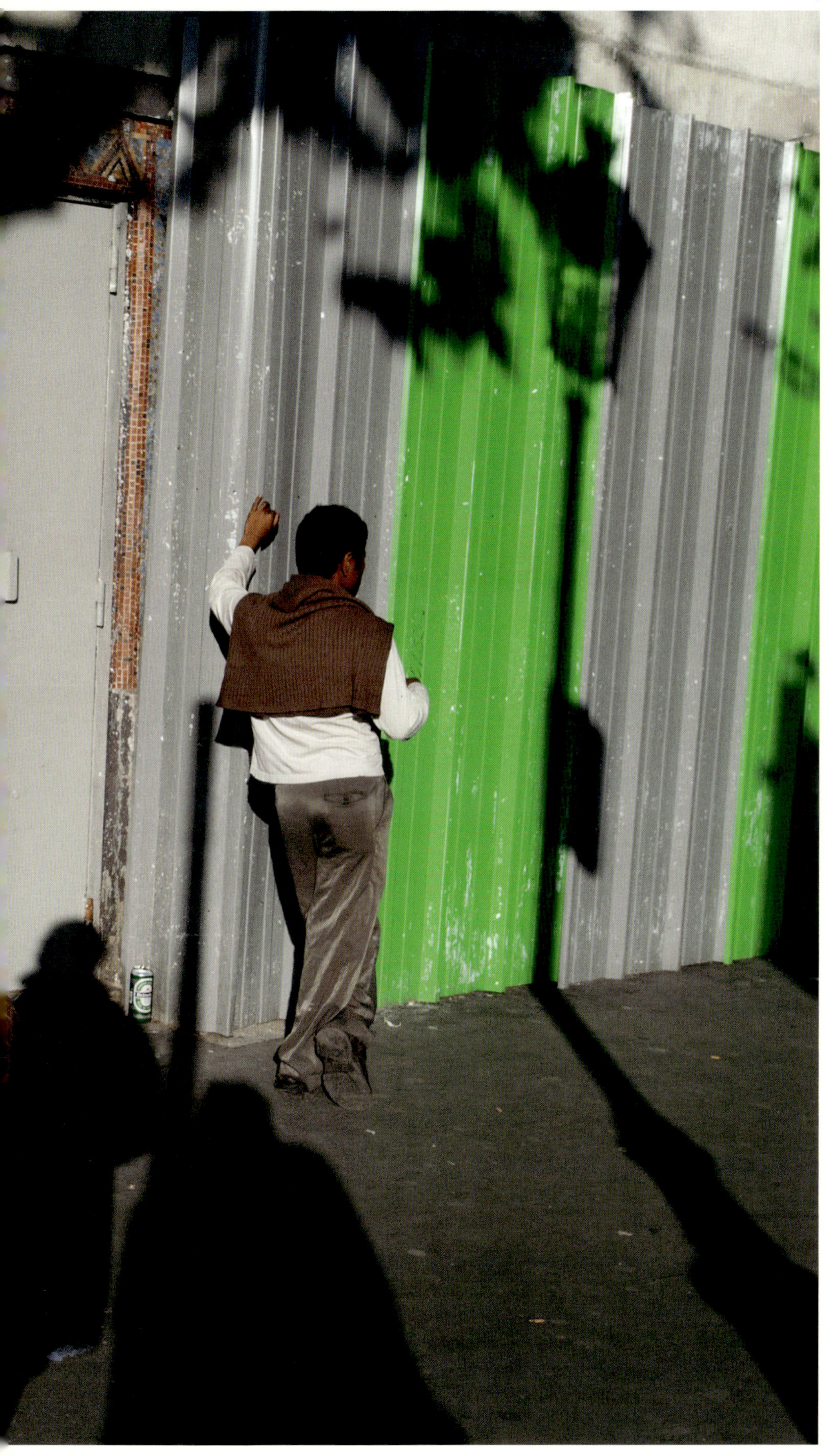

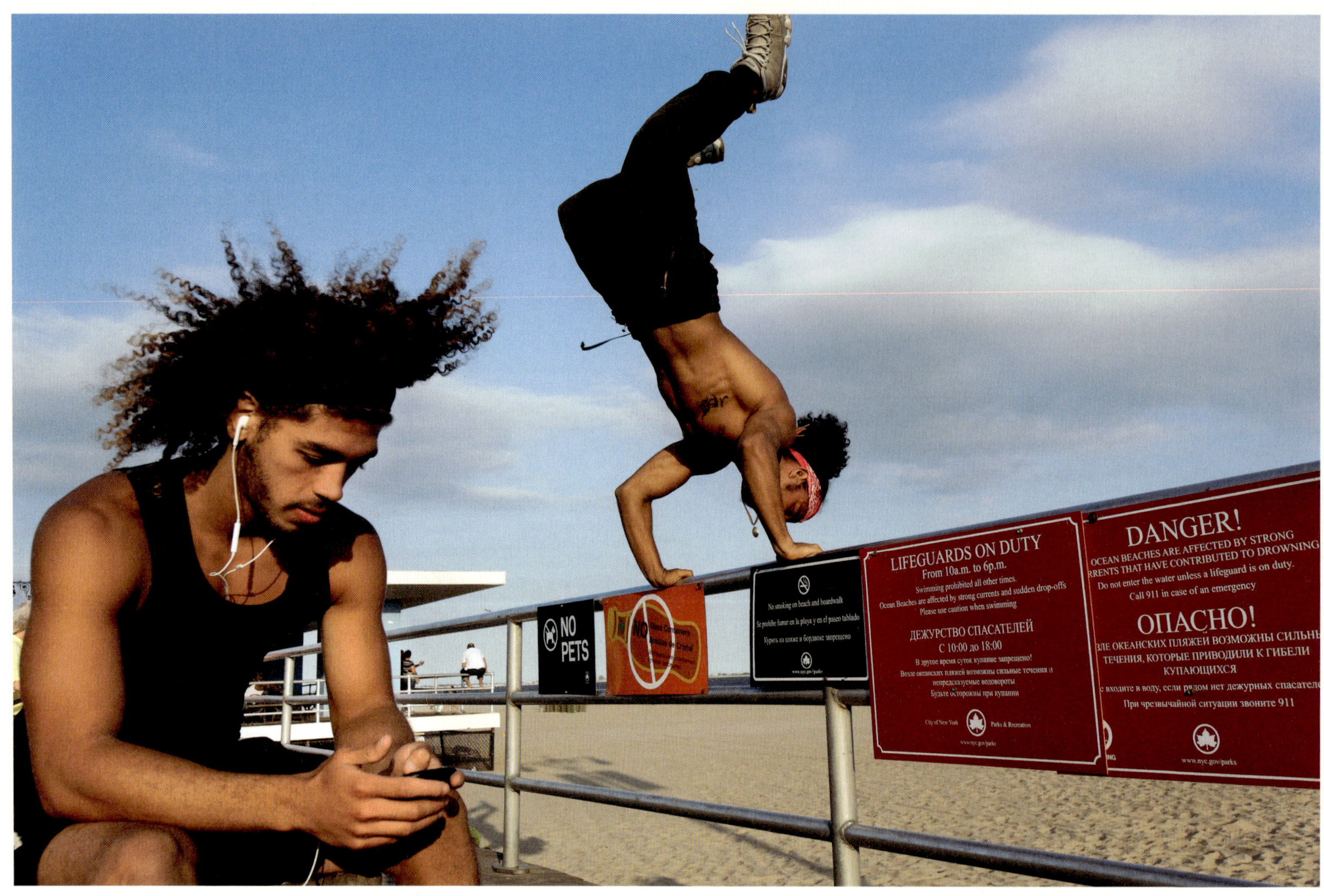
NO
PETS
NO
No smoking on beach and boardwalk
Se prohíbe fumar en la playa y en el paseo tablado
Курить на пляже и бордюре запрещено
LIFEGUARDS ON DUTY
From 10a.m. to 6p.m.
Swimming prohibited all other times.
Ocean Beaches are affected by strong currents and sudden drop-offs
Please use caution when swimming
ДЕЖУРСТВО СПАСАТЕЛЕЙ
С 10:00 до 18:00
В другое время суток купание запрещено!
Везде океанских пляжей возможны сильные течения и
непредсказуемые водовороты
Будьте осторожны при купании
City of New York   Parks & Recreation
www.nyc.gov/parks
DANGER!
OCEAN BEACHES ARE AFFECTED BY STRONG
CURRENTS THAT HAVE CONTRIBUTED TO DROWNING
Do not enter the water unless a lifeguard is on duty.
Call 911 in case of an emergency
ОПАСНО!
ВОЗЛЕ ОКЕАНСКИХ ПЛЯЖЕЙ ВОЗМОЖНЫ СИЛЬНЫ
ТЕЧЕНИЯ, КОТОРЫЕ ПРИВОДИЛИ К ГИБЕЛИ
КУПАЮЩИХСЯ
Не входите в воду, если рядом нет дежурных спасателе
При чрезвычайной ситуации звоните 911
www.nyc.gov/parks

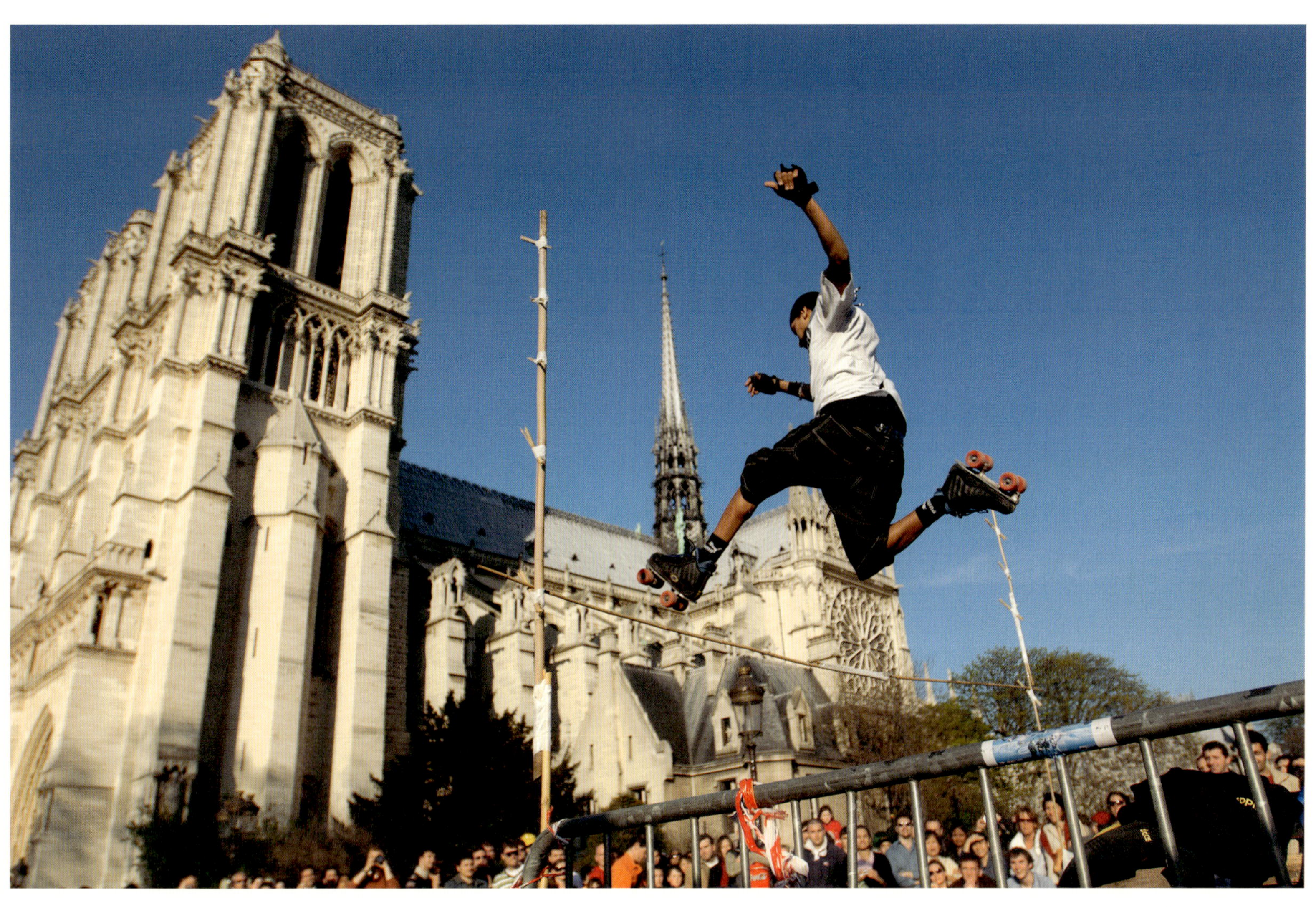

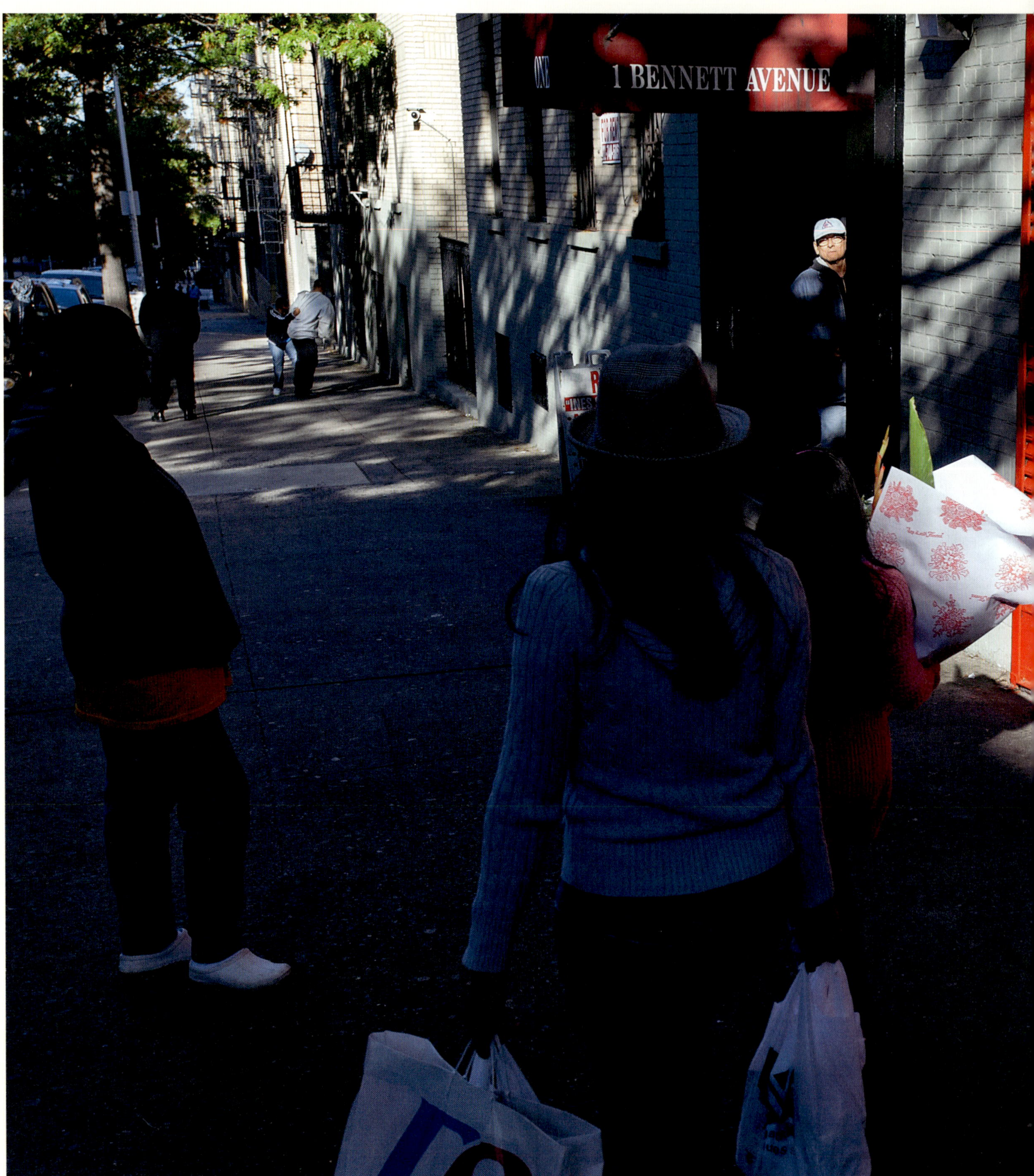

ONE
1 BENNETT AVENUE

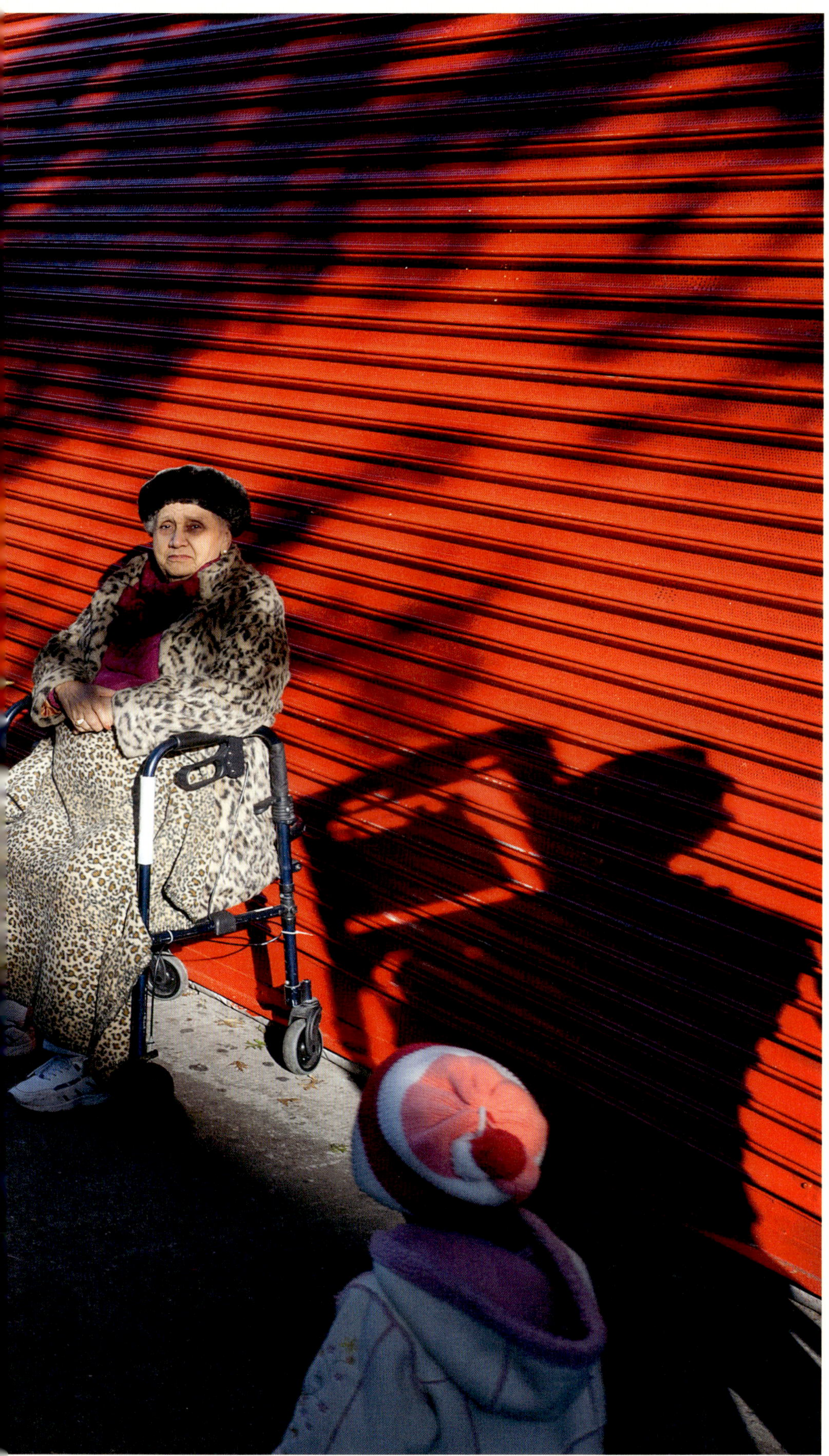

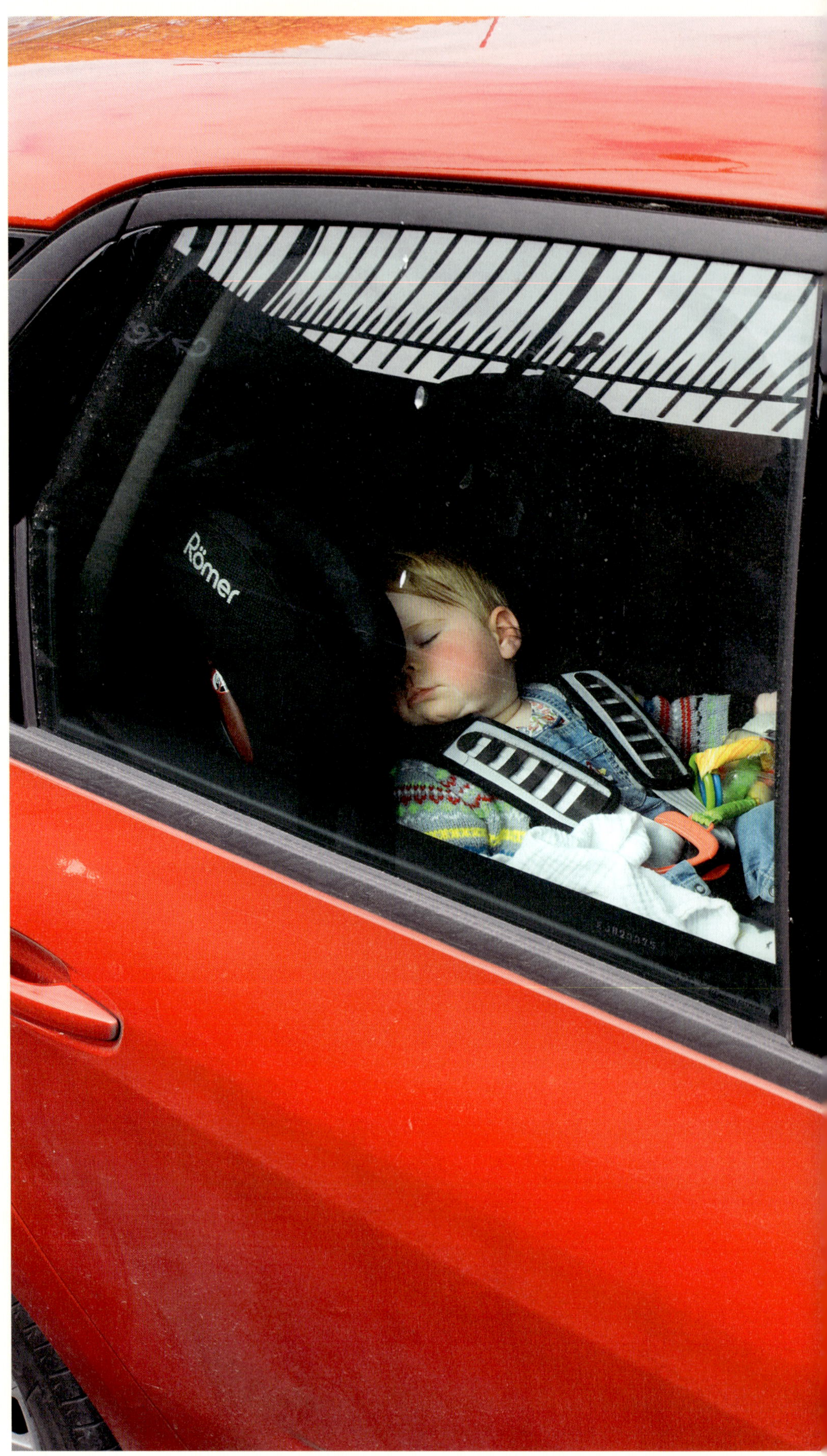

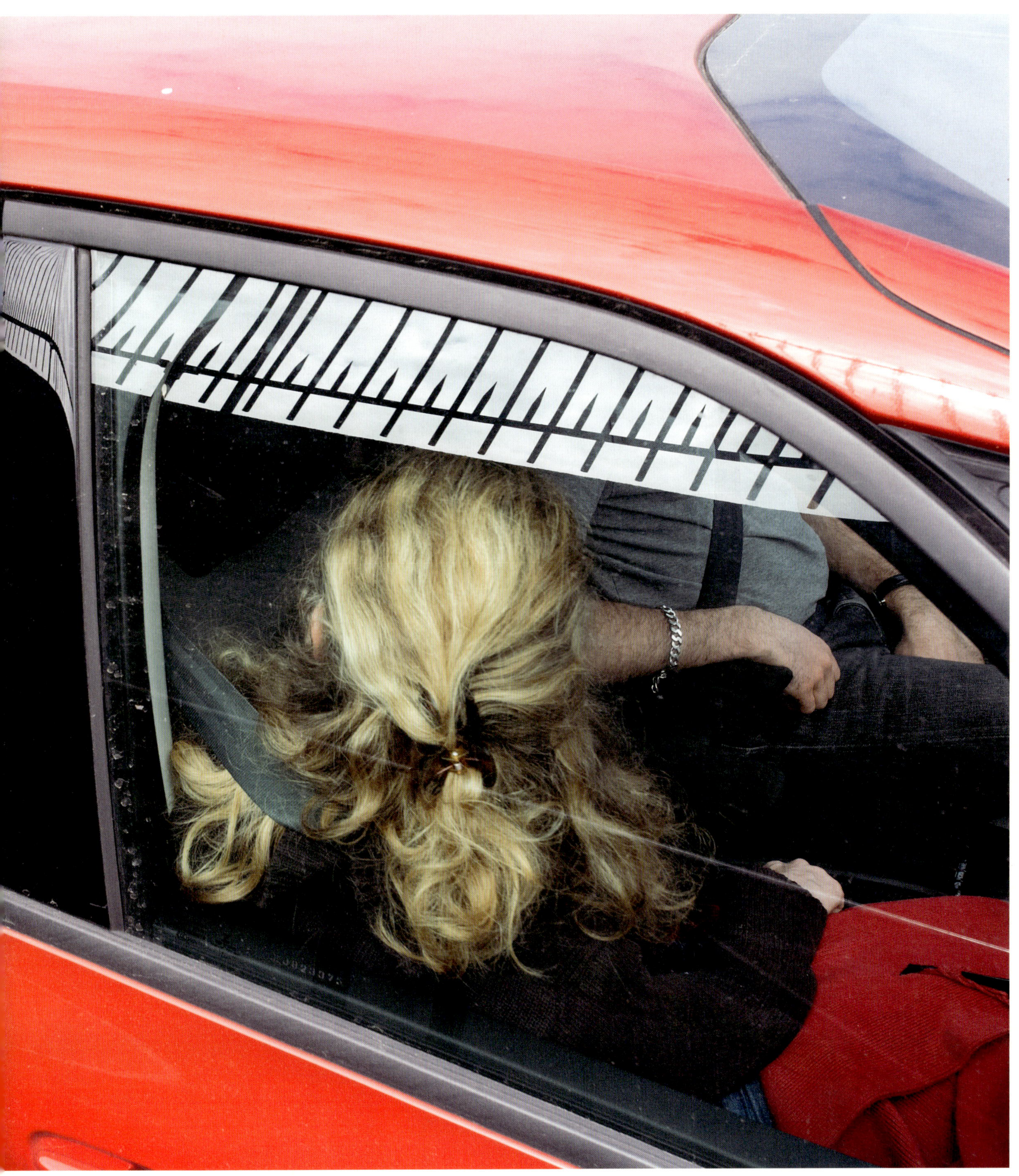

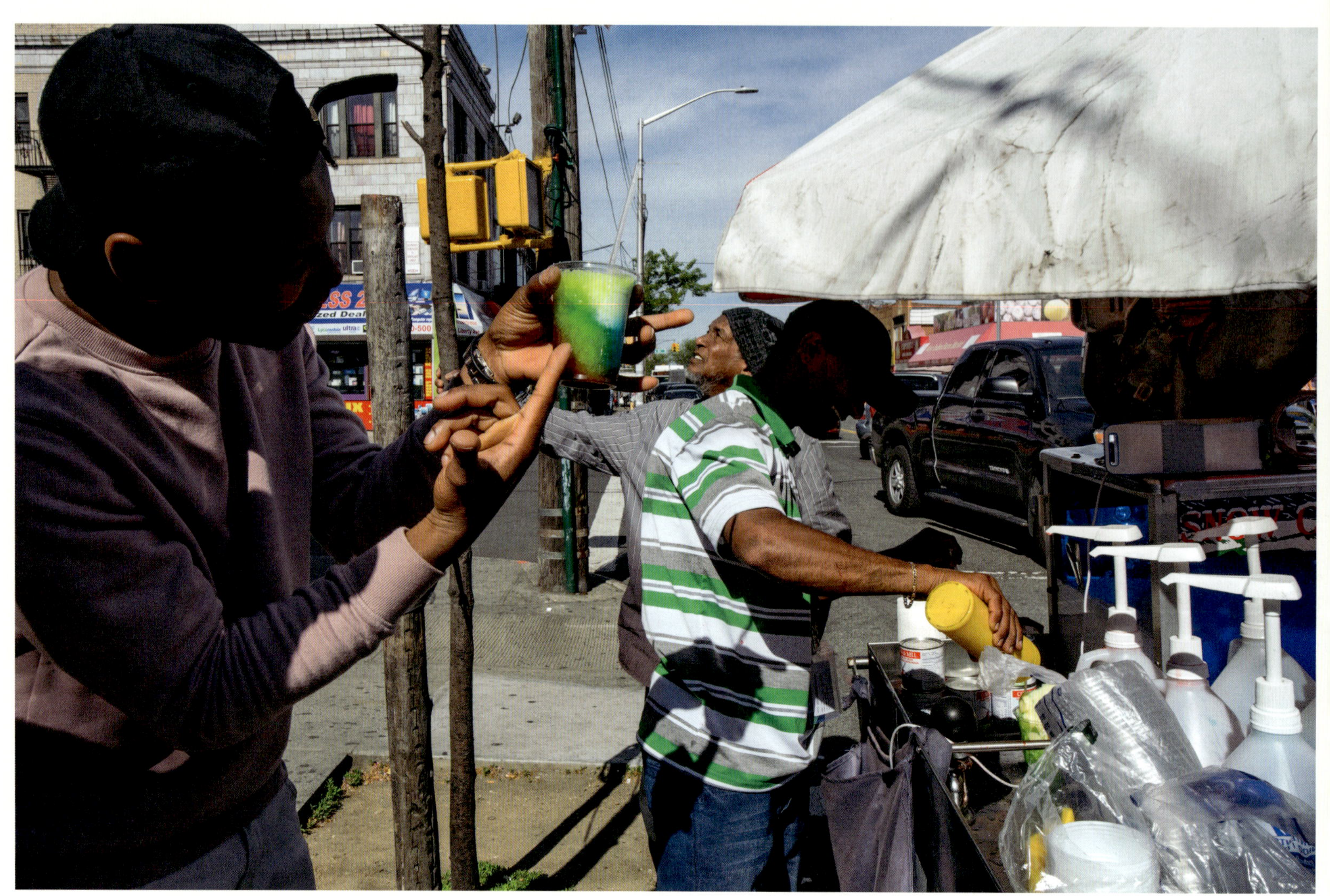

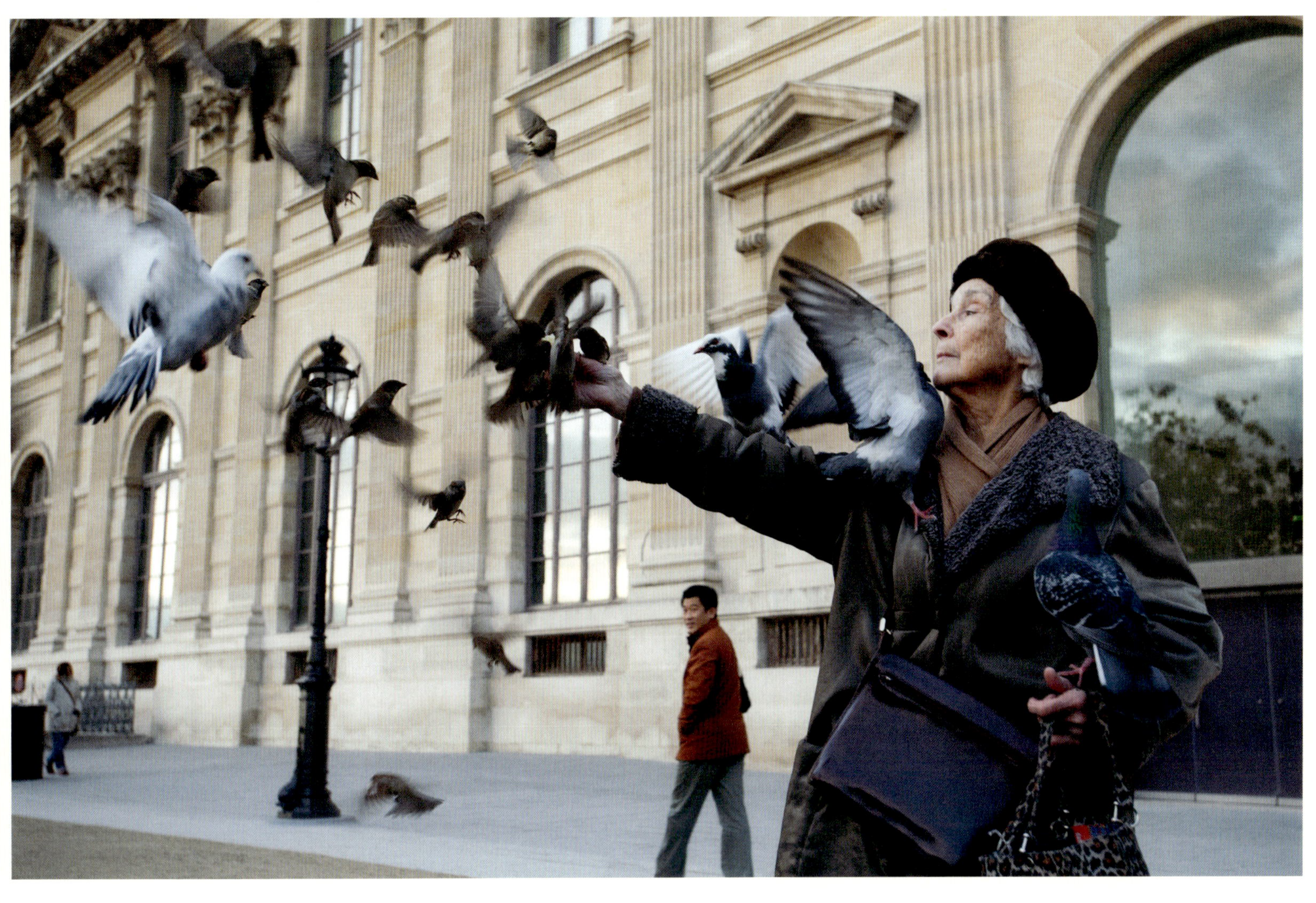

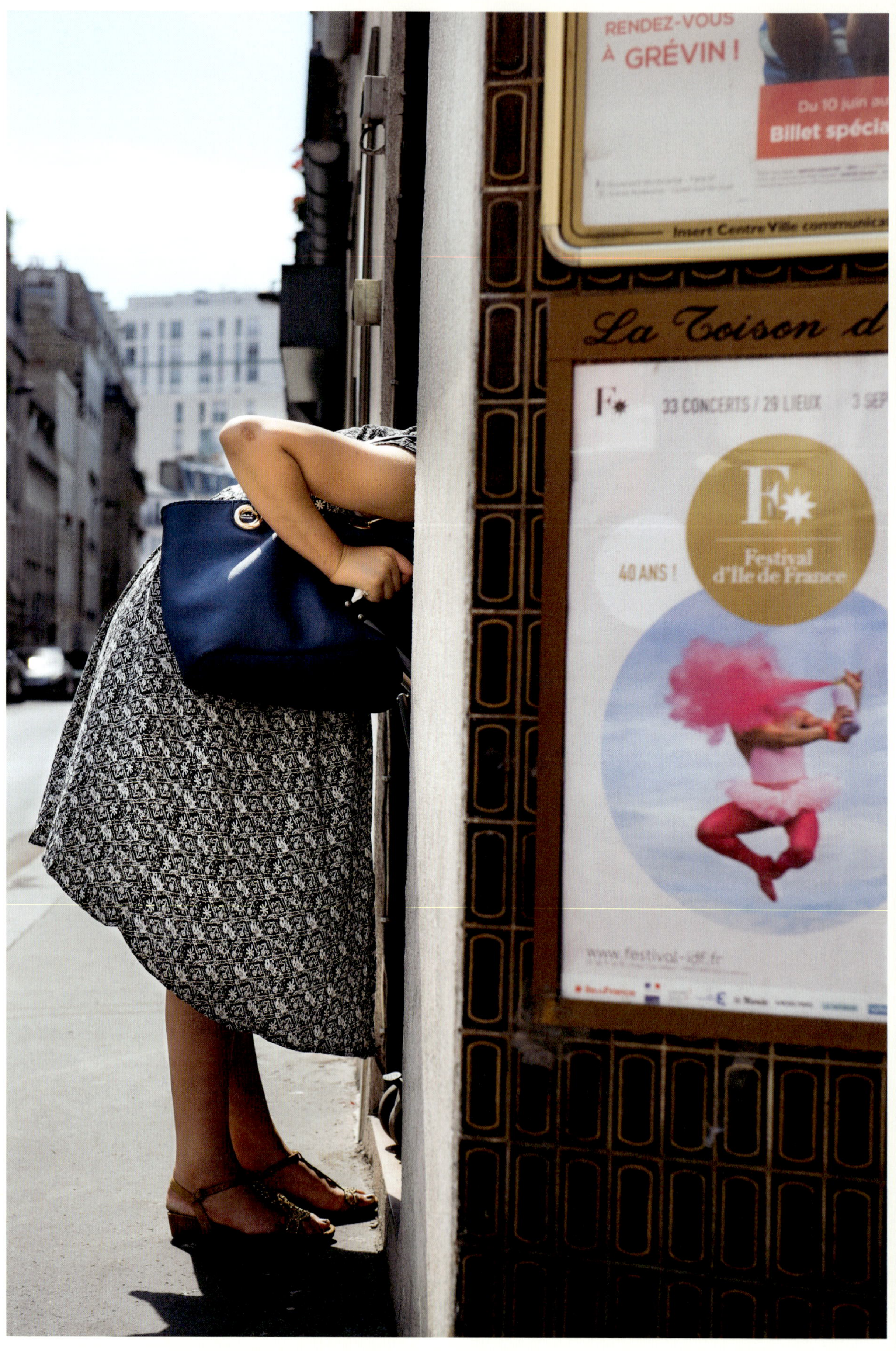

RENDEZ-VOUS
À GRÉVIN !
Du 10 juin au
Billet spécia
Insert Centre Ville communica
La Toison d
33 CONCERTS / 29 LIEUX   3 SEP
40 ANS !
Festival
d'Île de France
www.festival-idf.fr

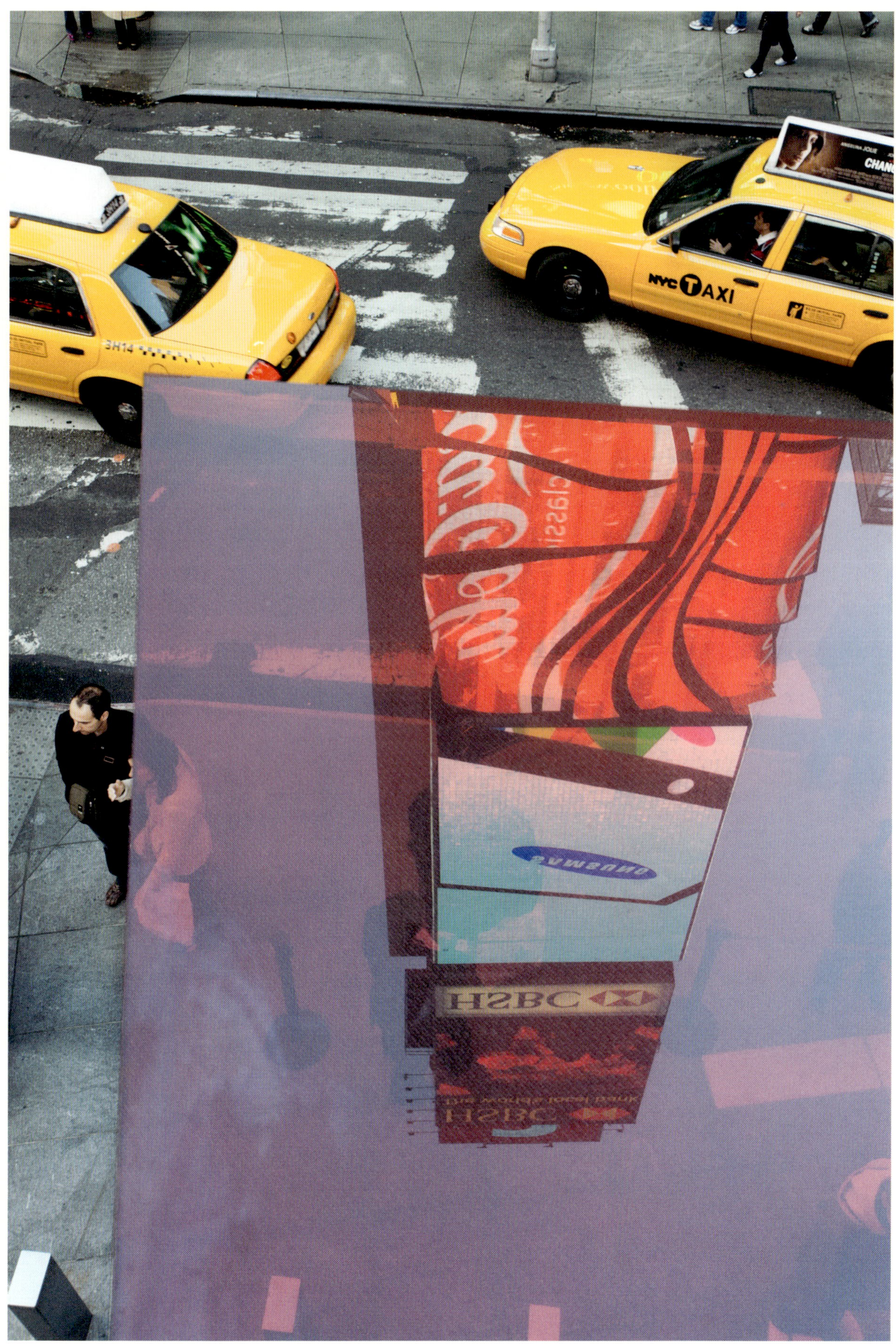

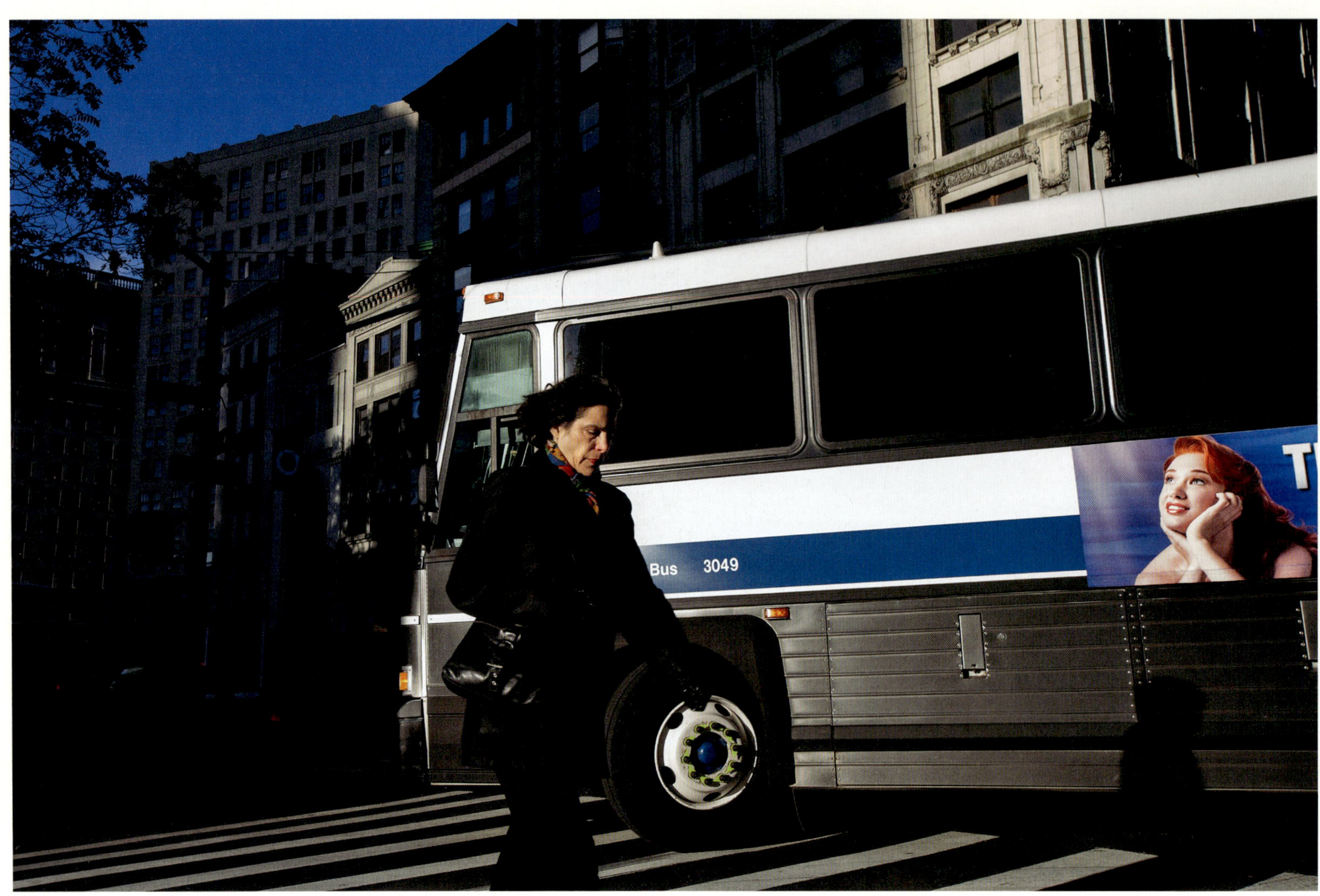
Bus   3049

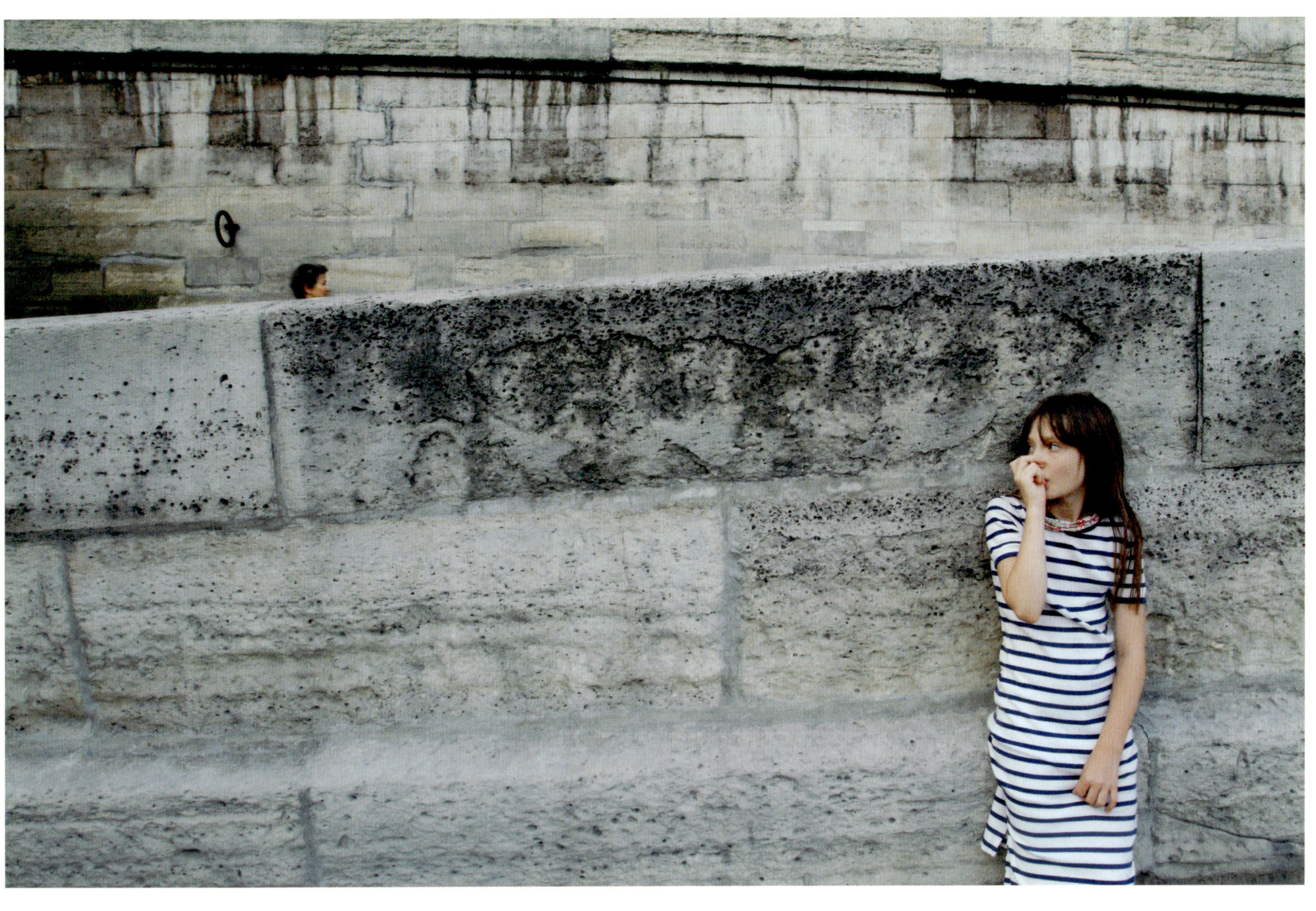

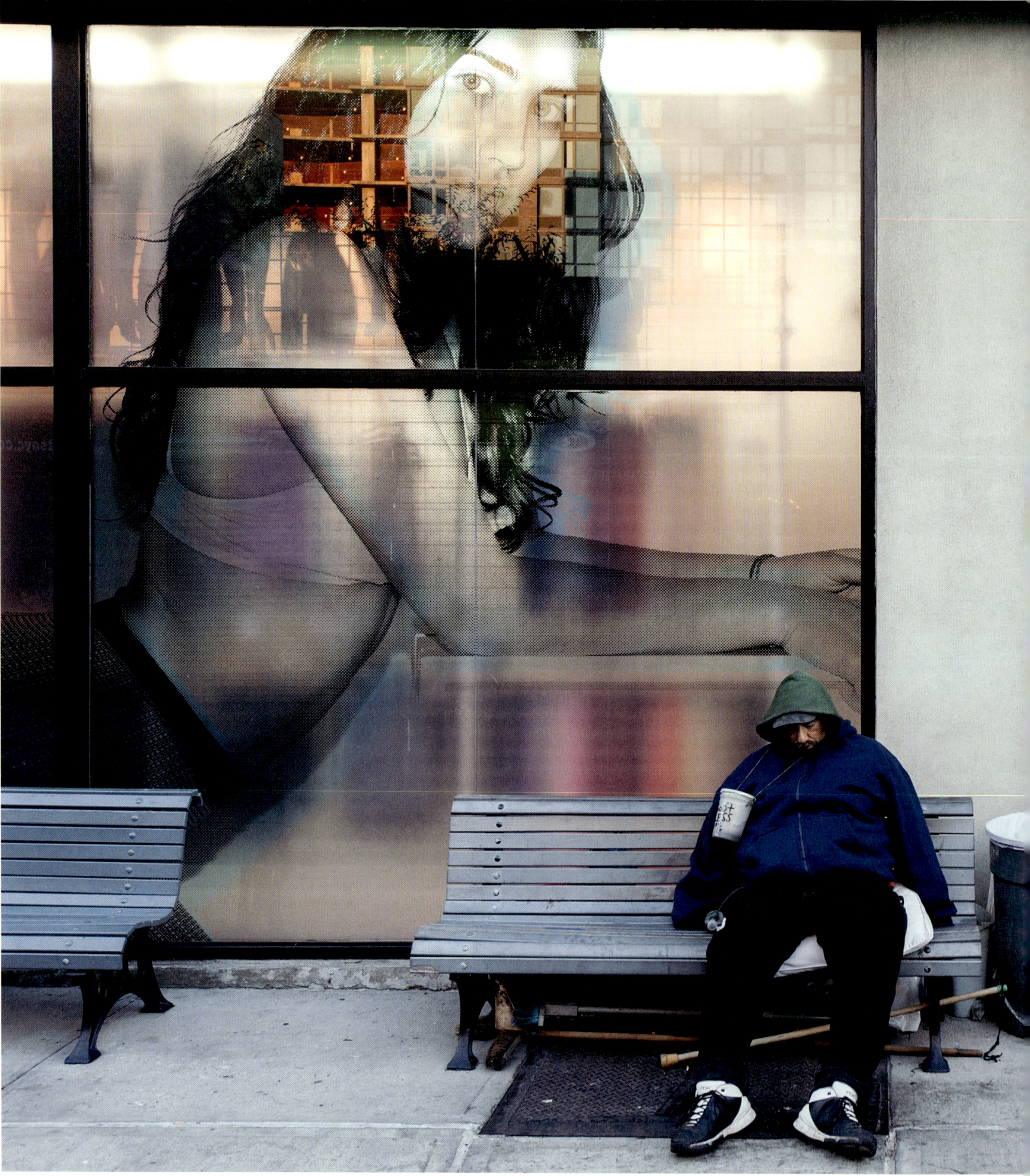

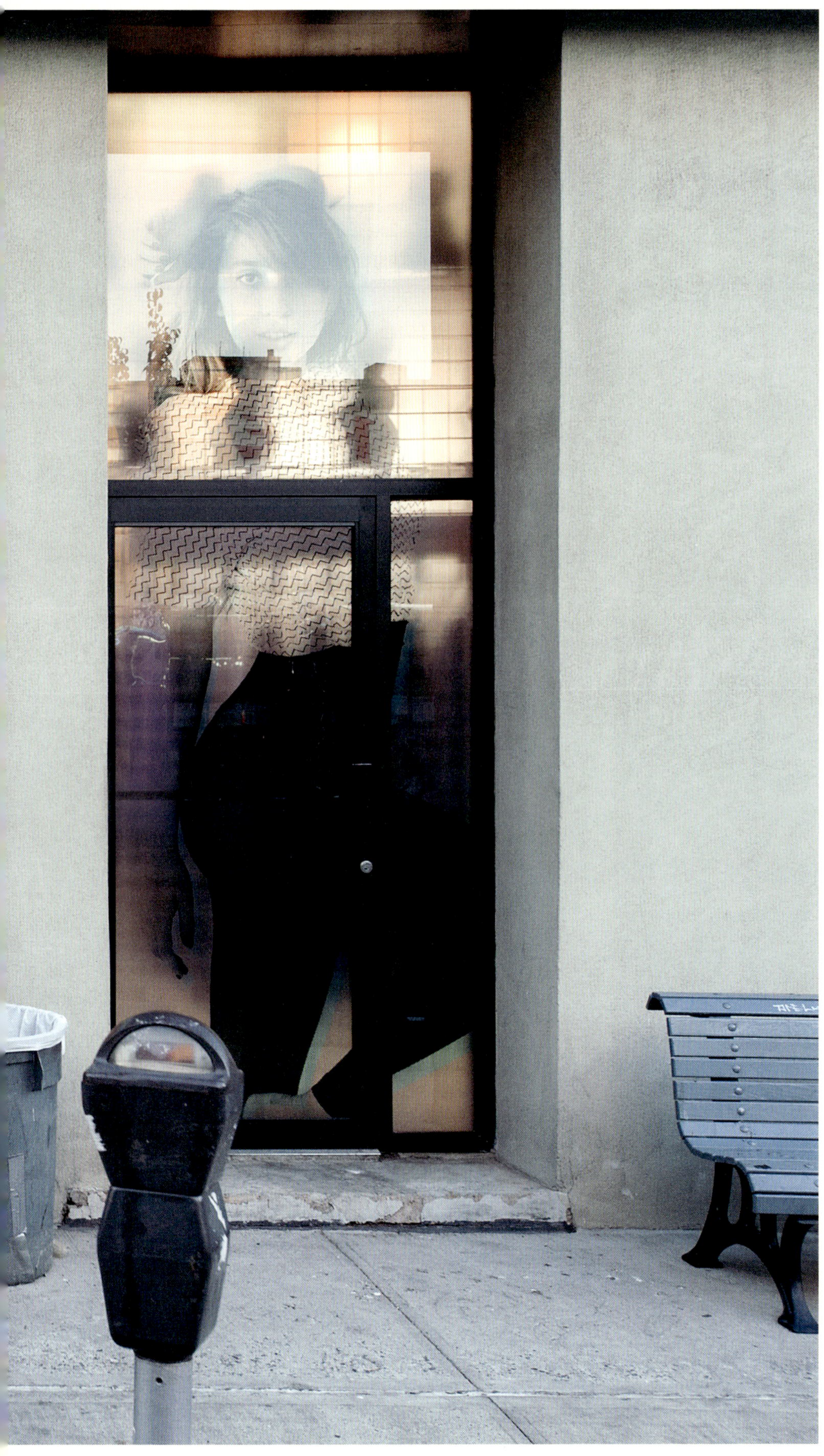

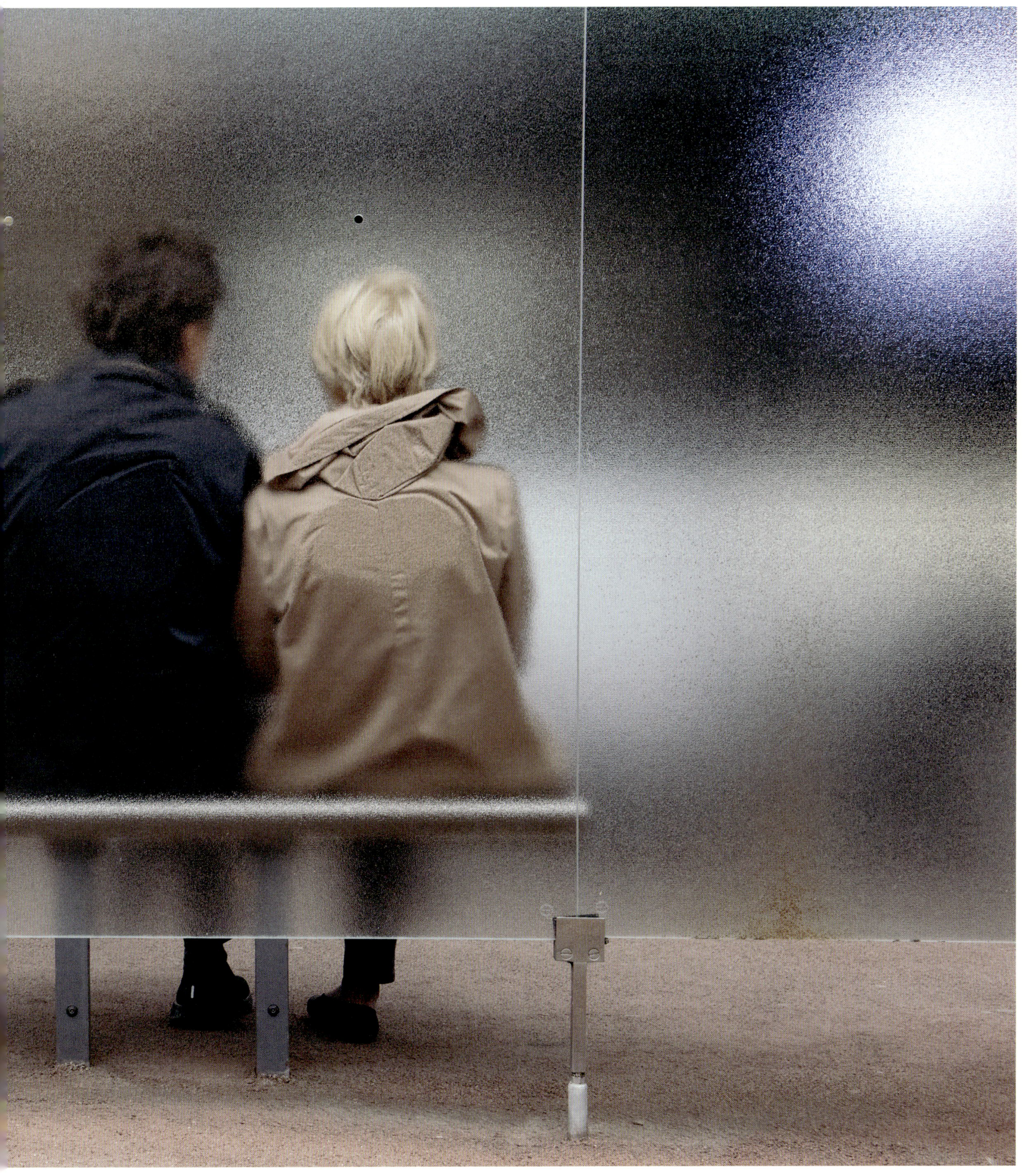

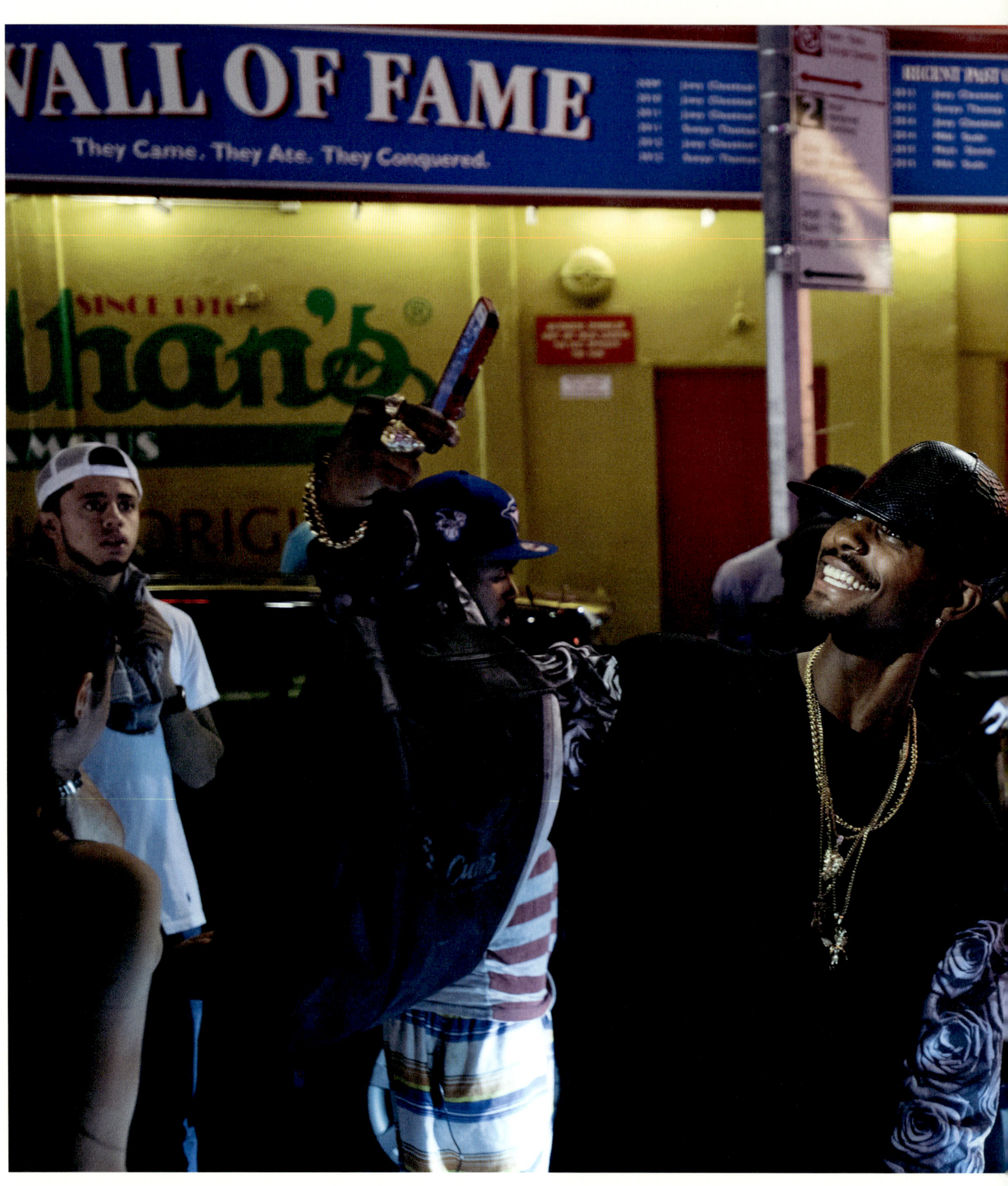
WALL OF FAME
They Came. They Ate. They Conquered.
SINCE 1916
nathan's
FAMOUS
ORIGIN

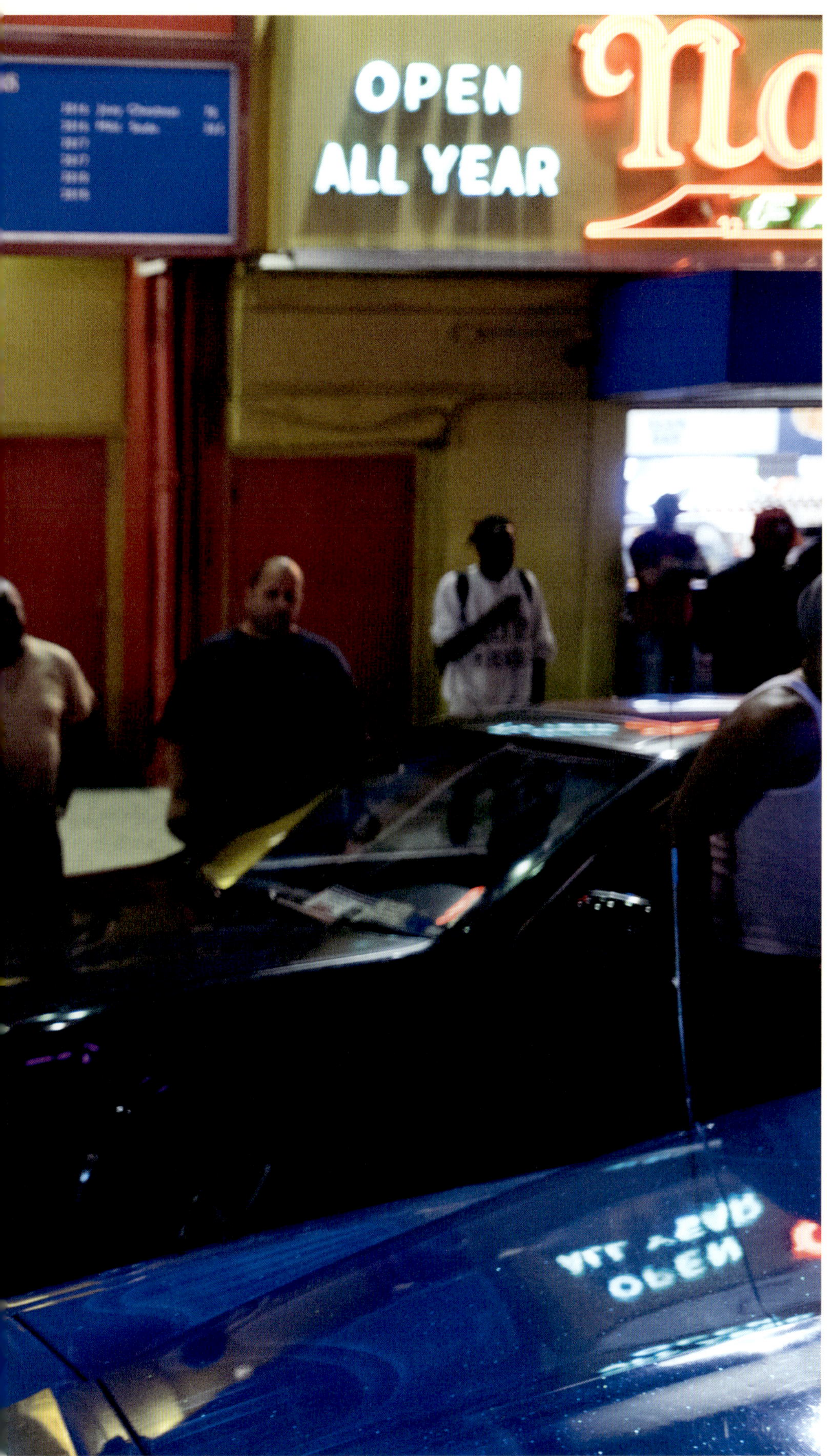

OPEN
ALL YEAR

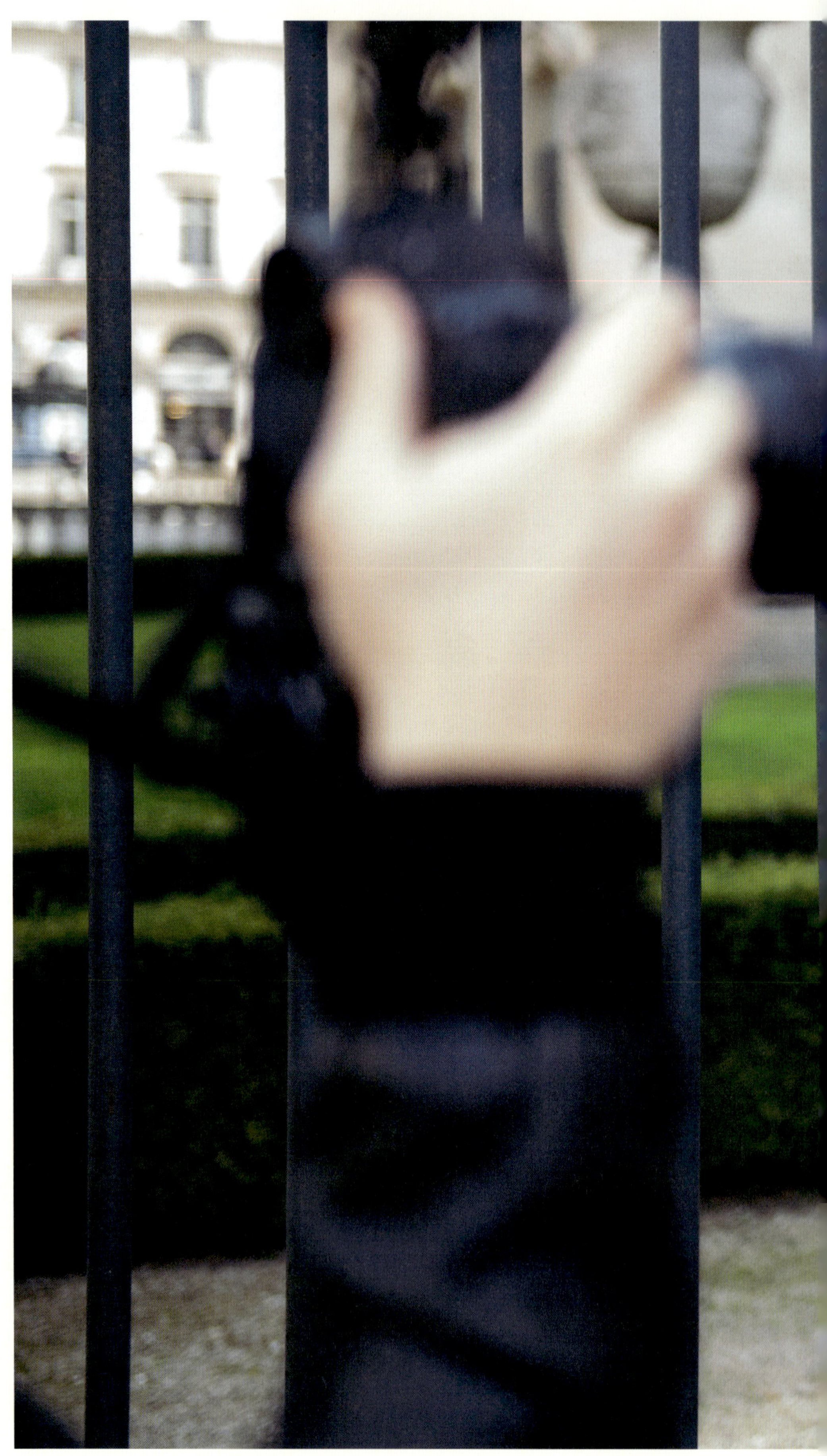

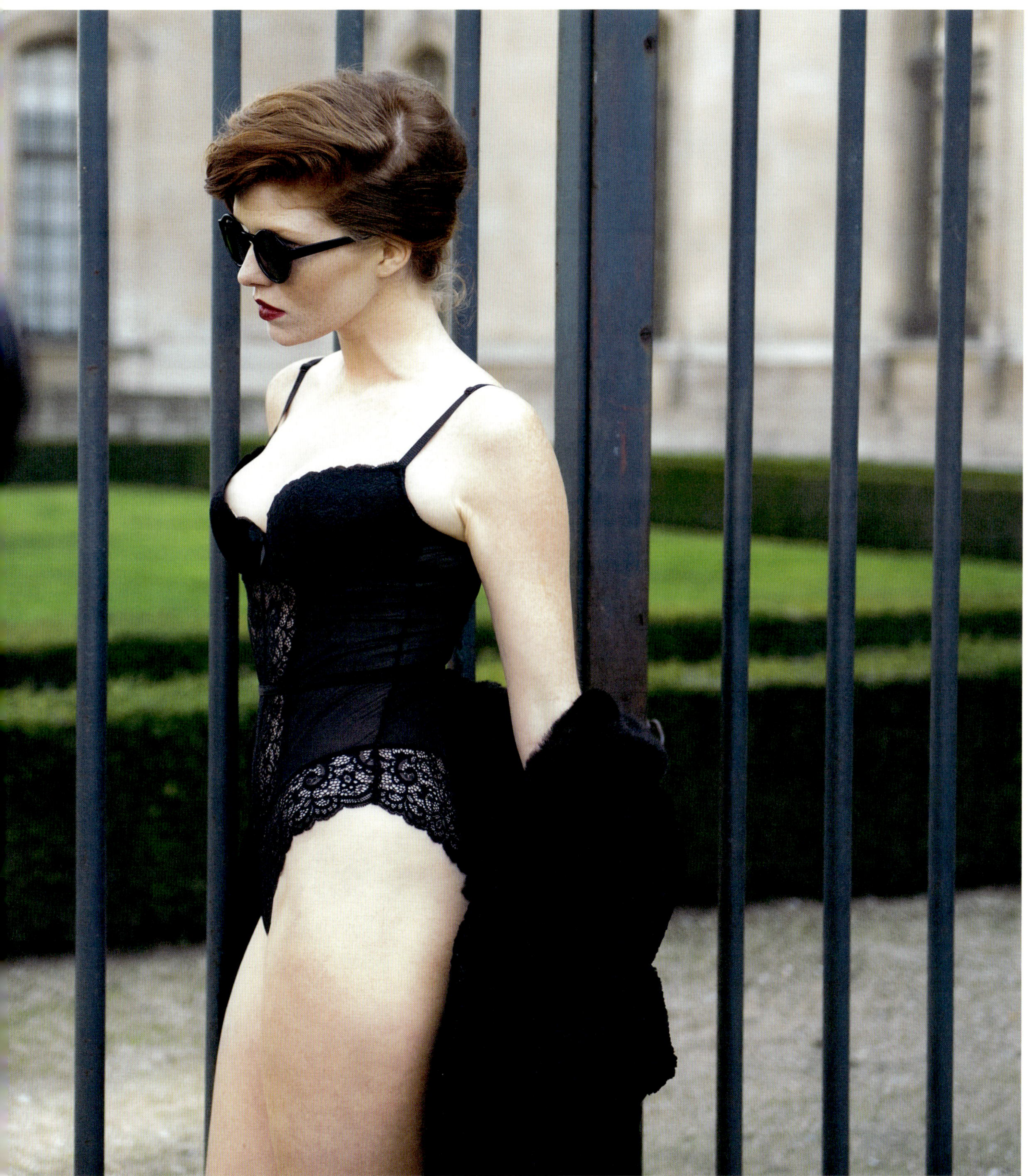

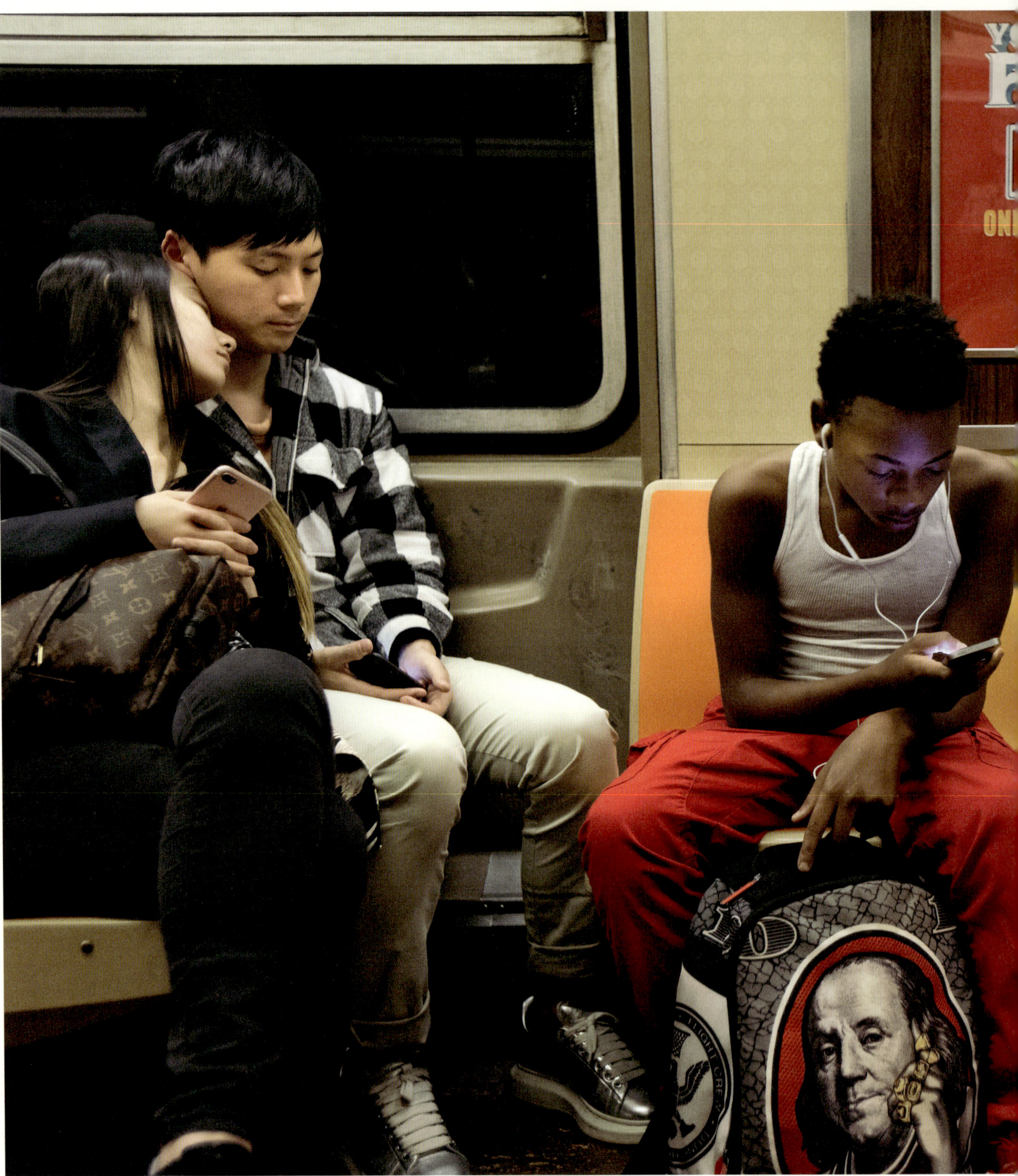

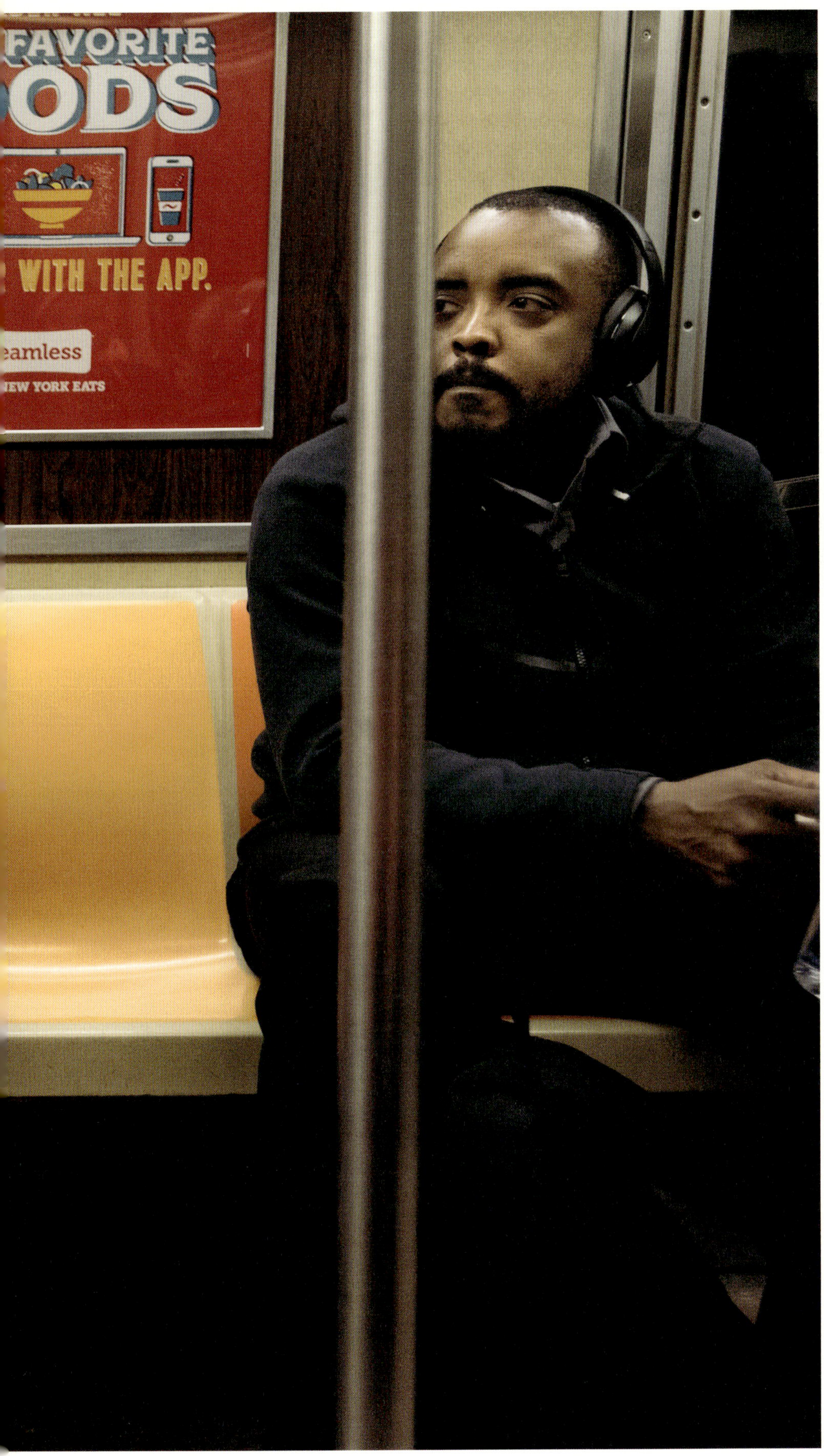
FAVORITE
ODS
WITH THE APP.
eamless
NEW YORK EATS

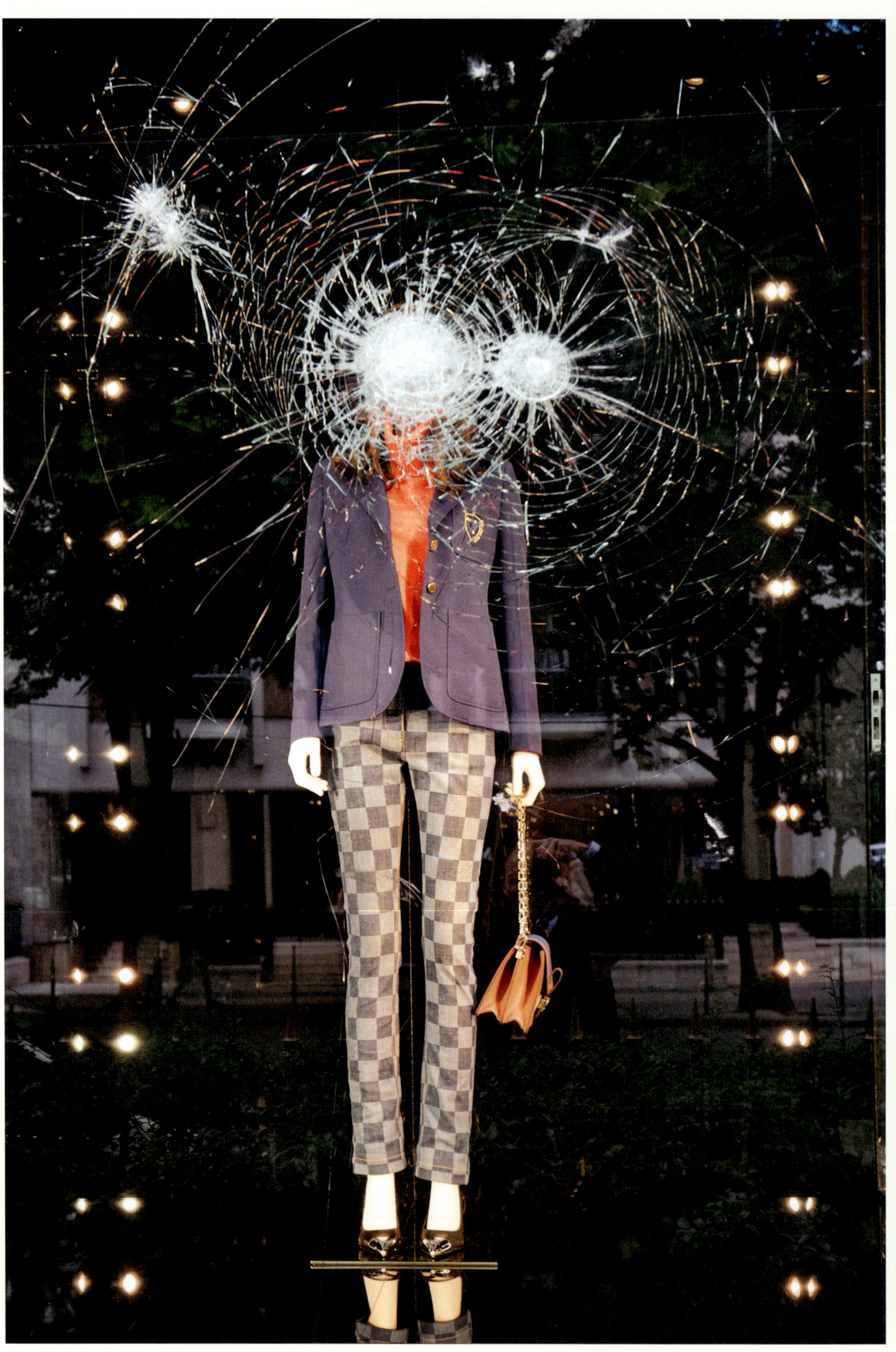

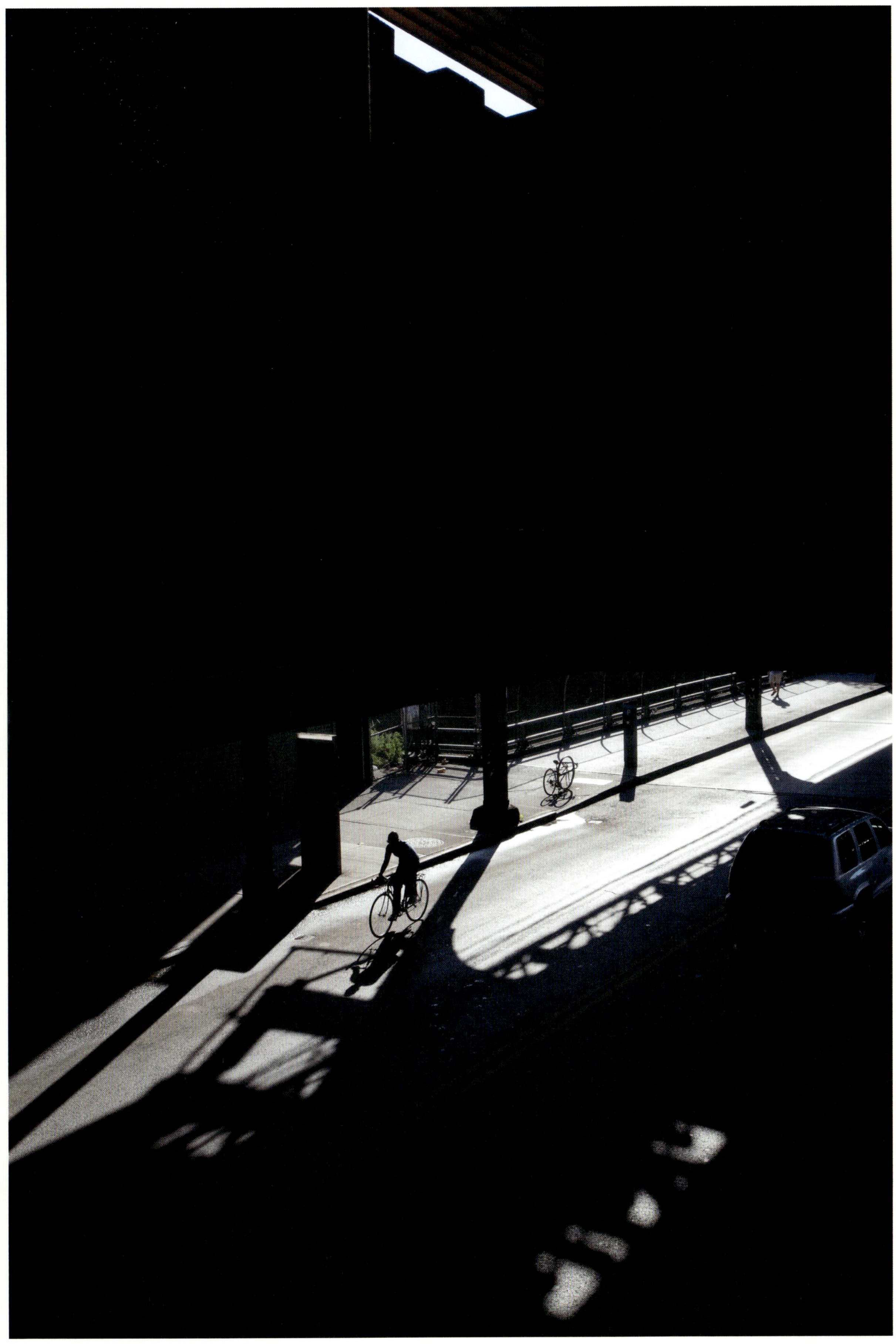

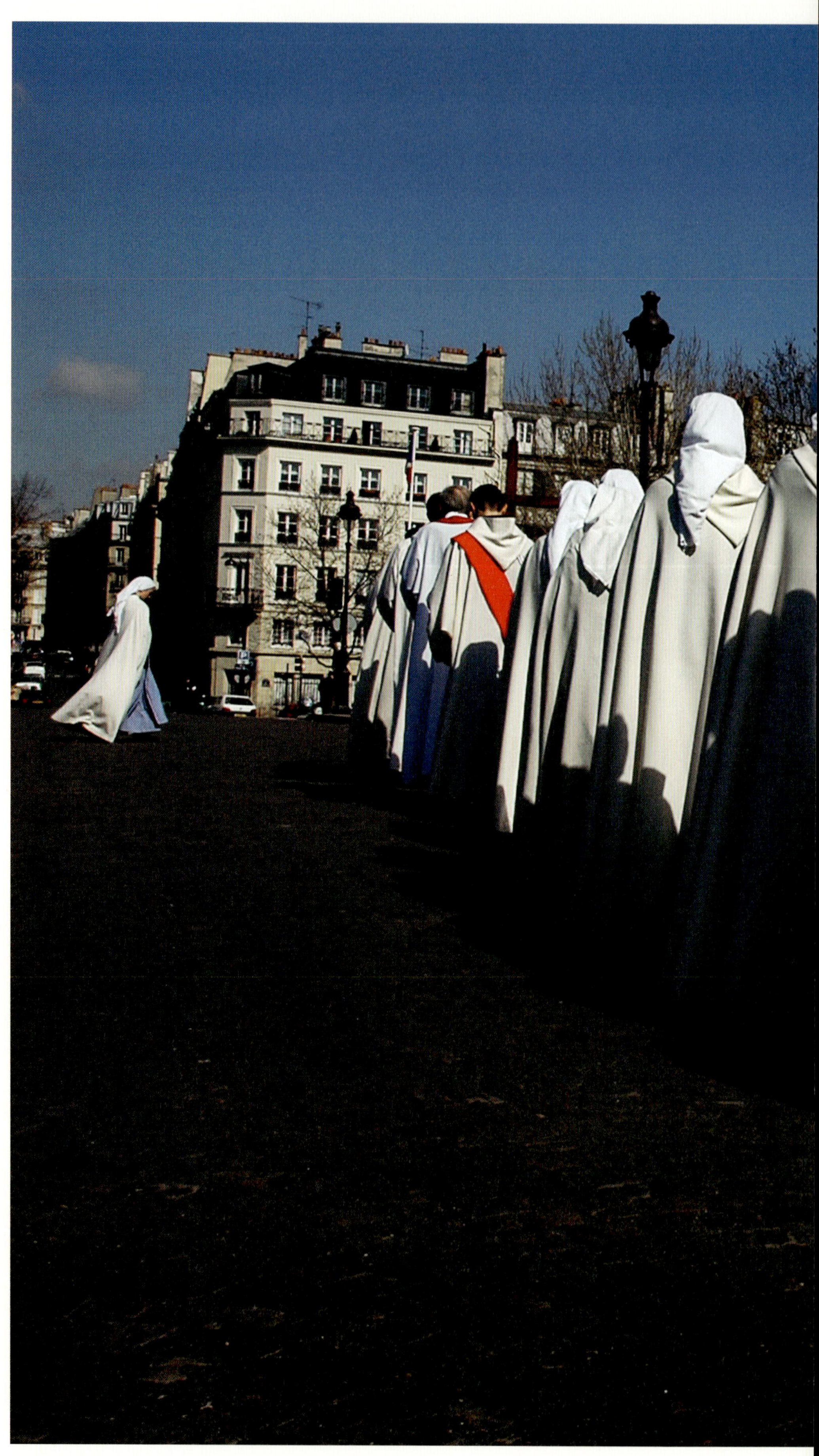

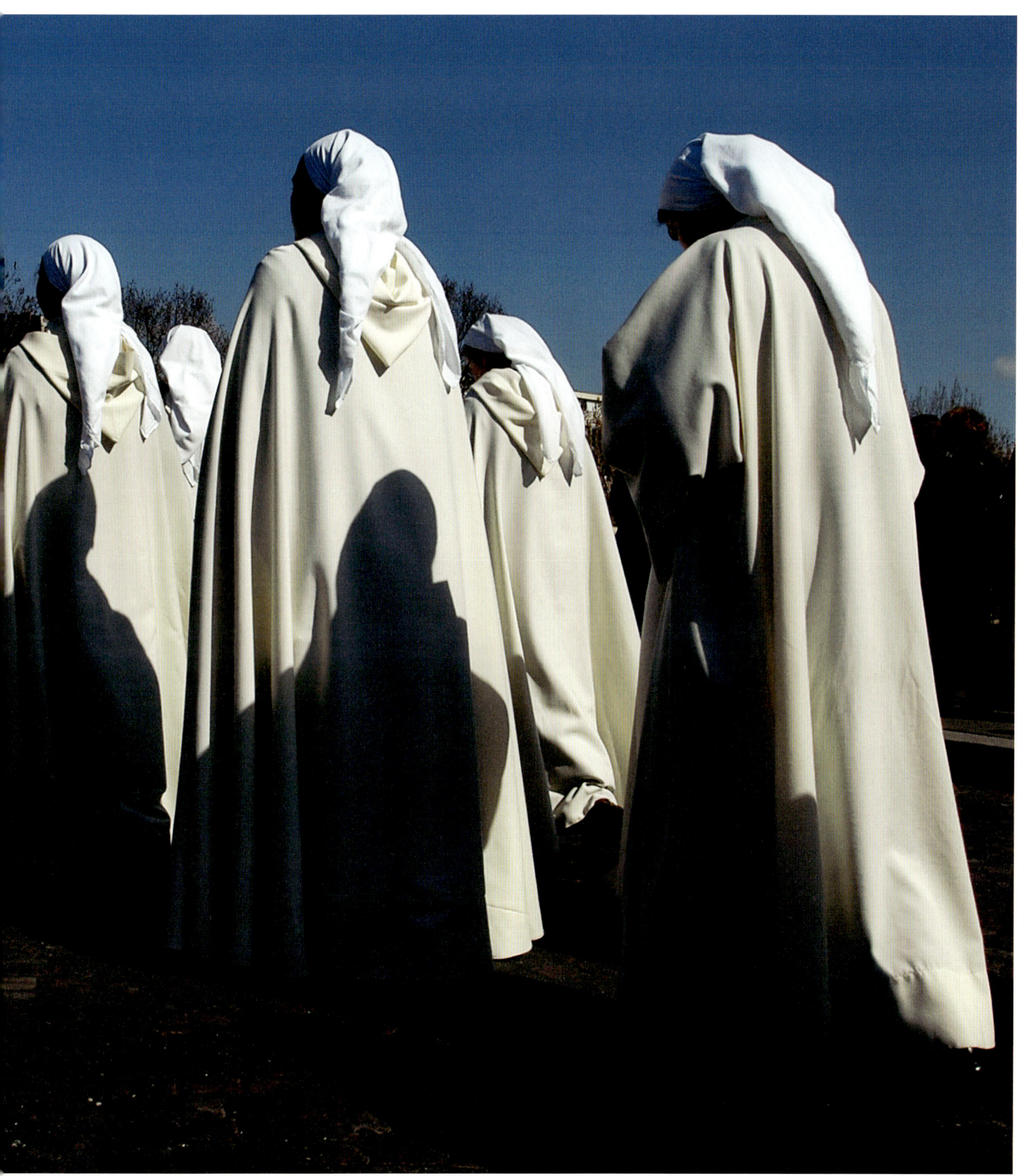

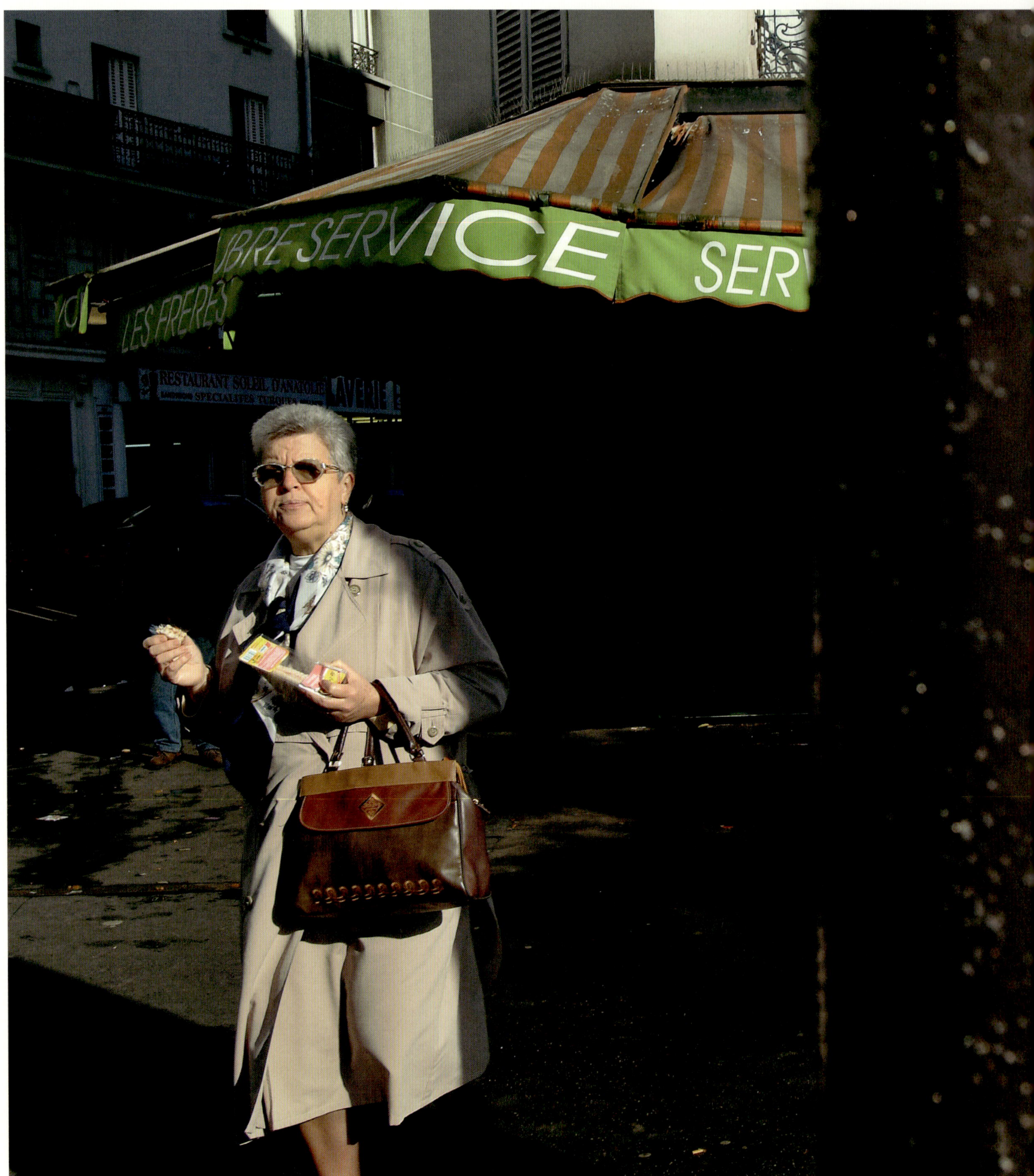
LIBRE SERVICE
LES FRÈRES
RESTAURANT SOLEIL D'ANATOLIE
SPÉCIALITÉS TURQUES
L'AVENUE

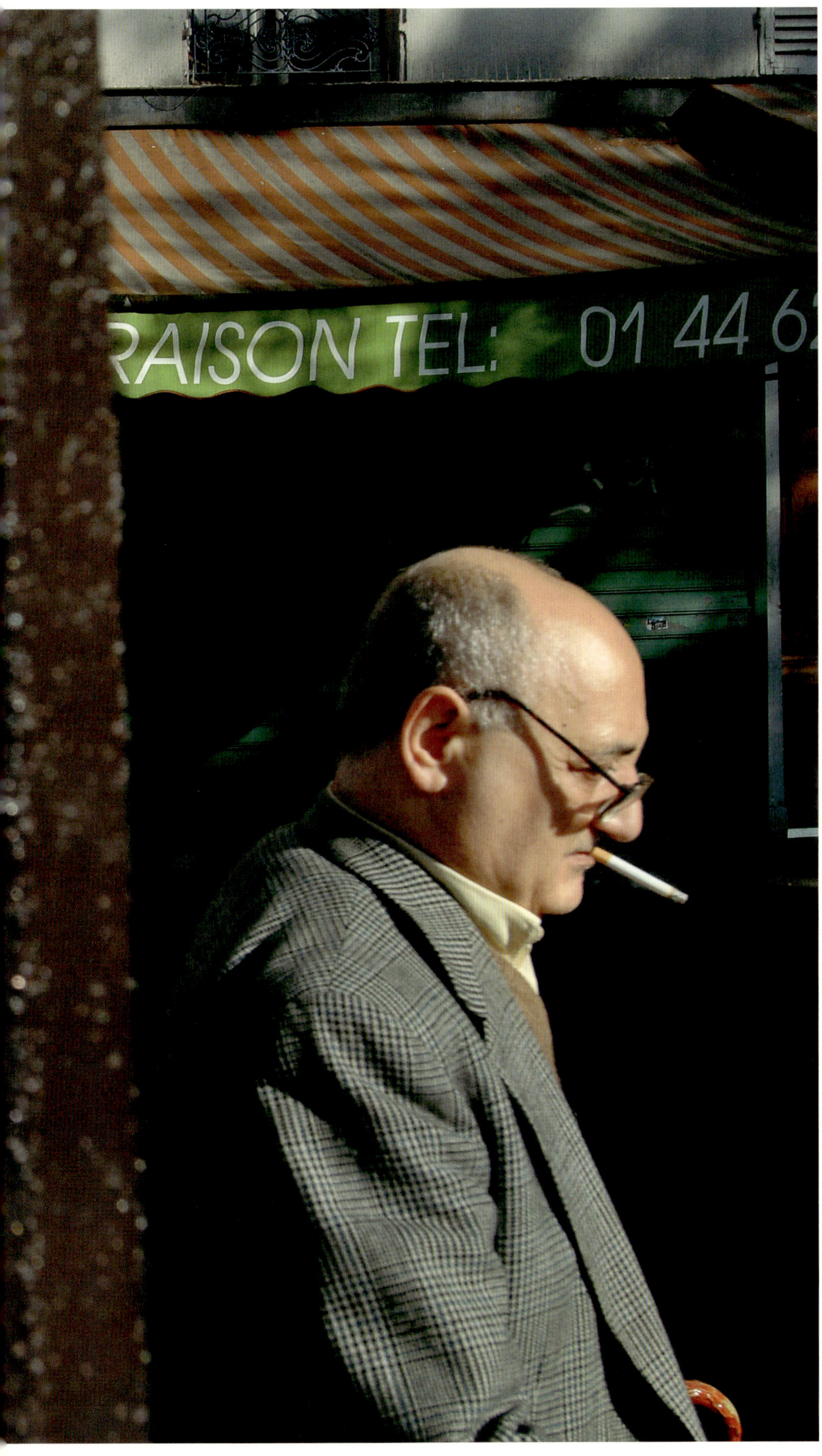
RAISON TEL: 01 44 6

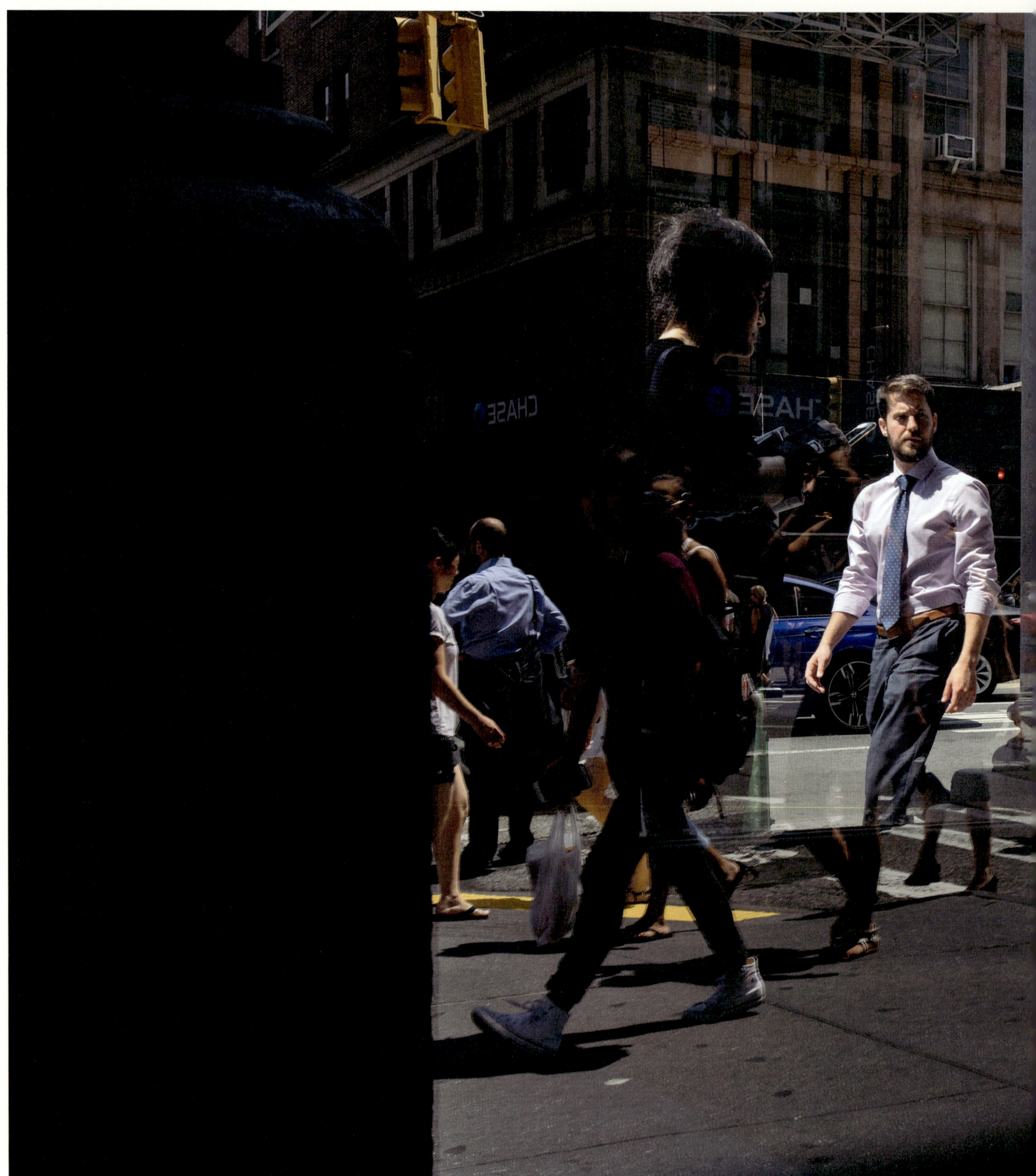

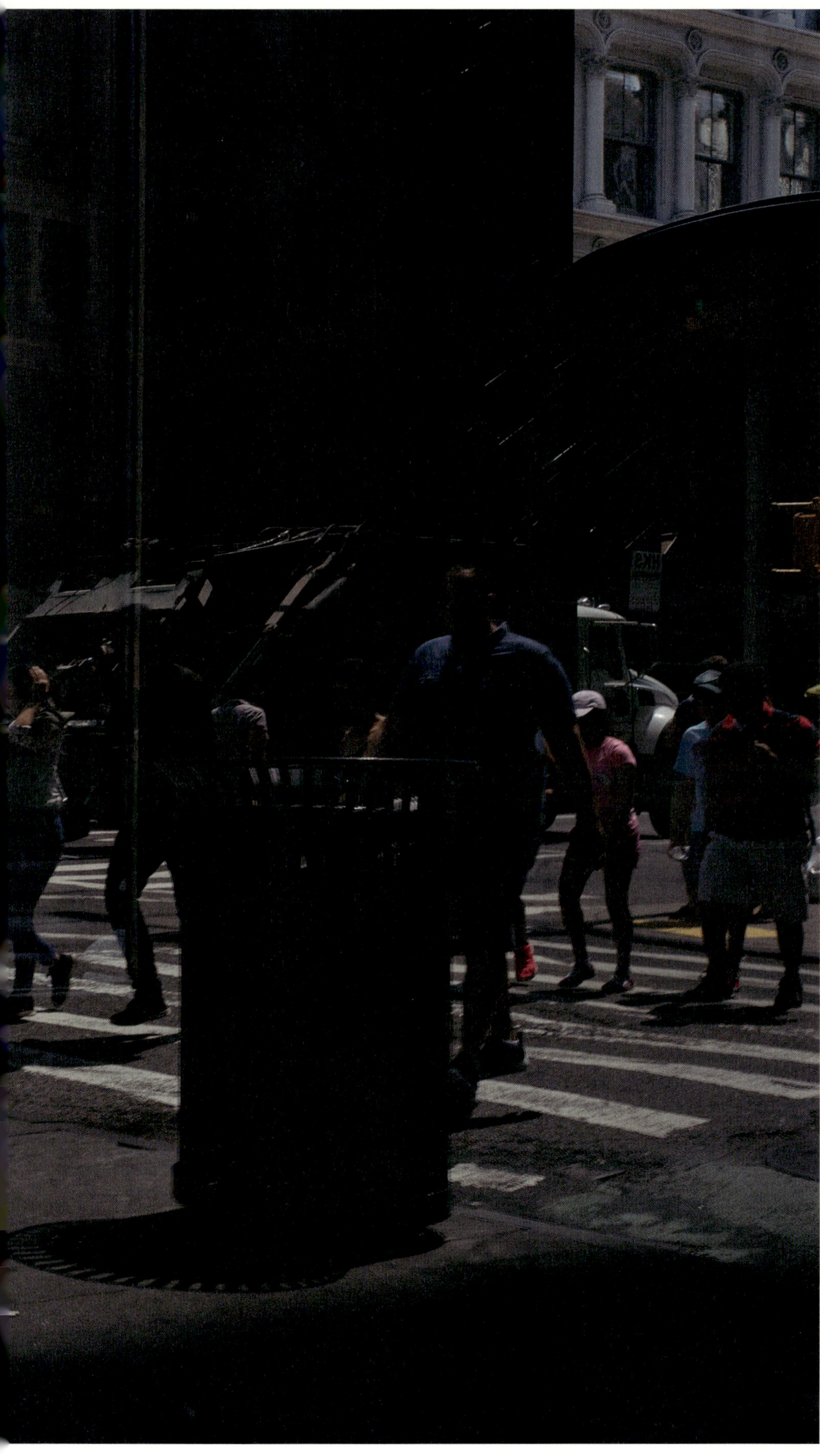

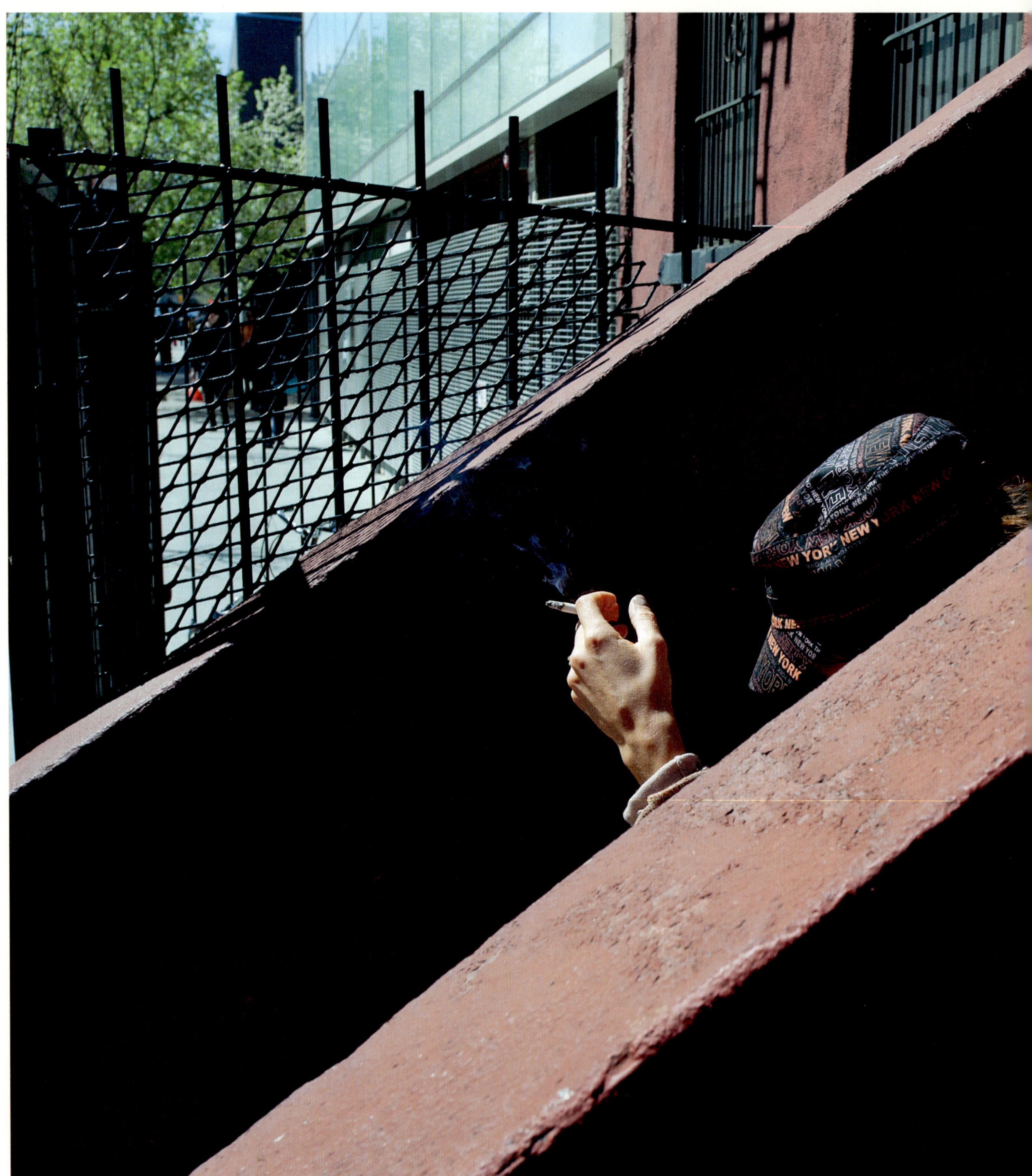

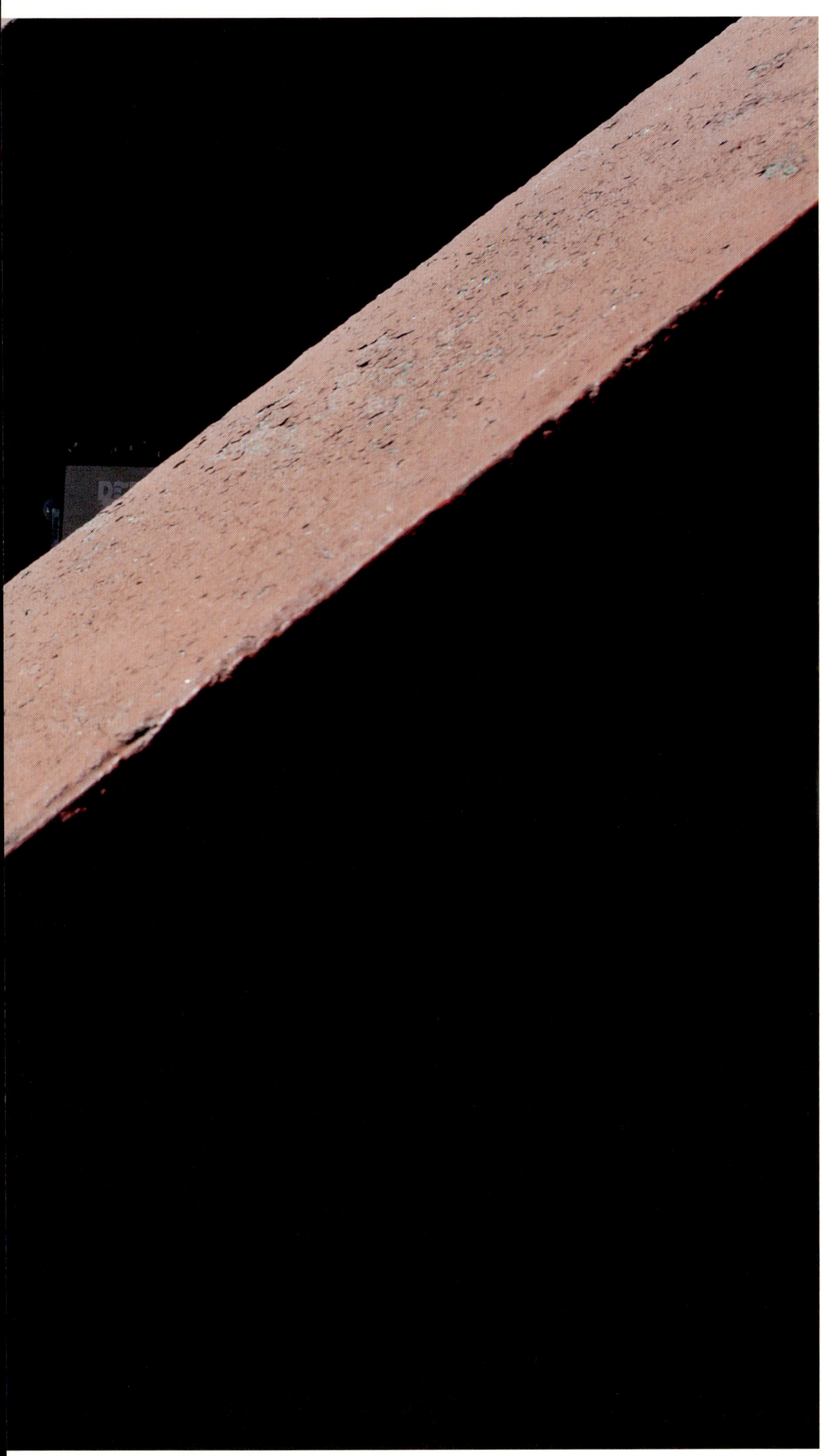

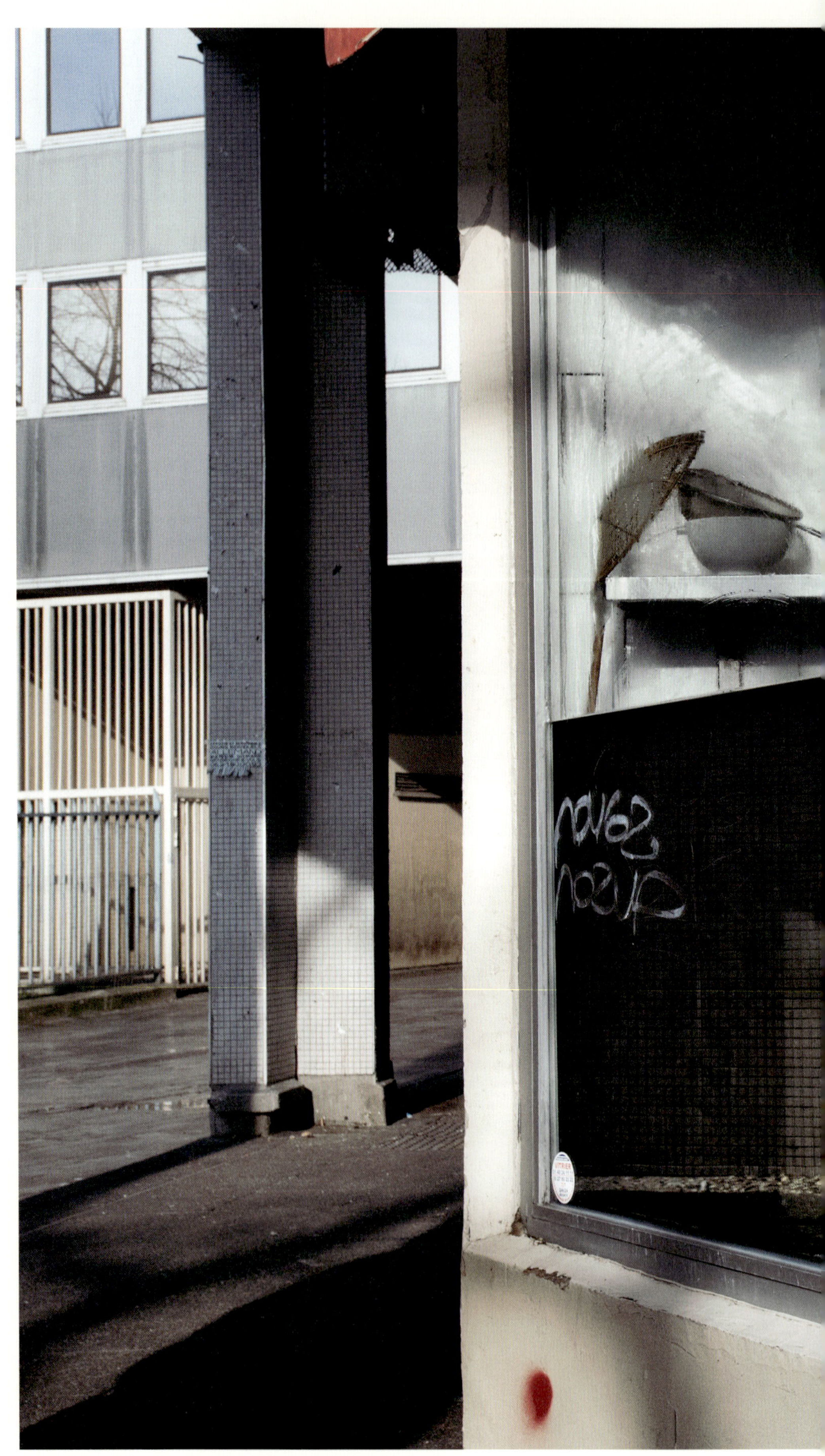

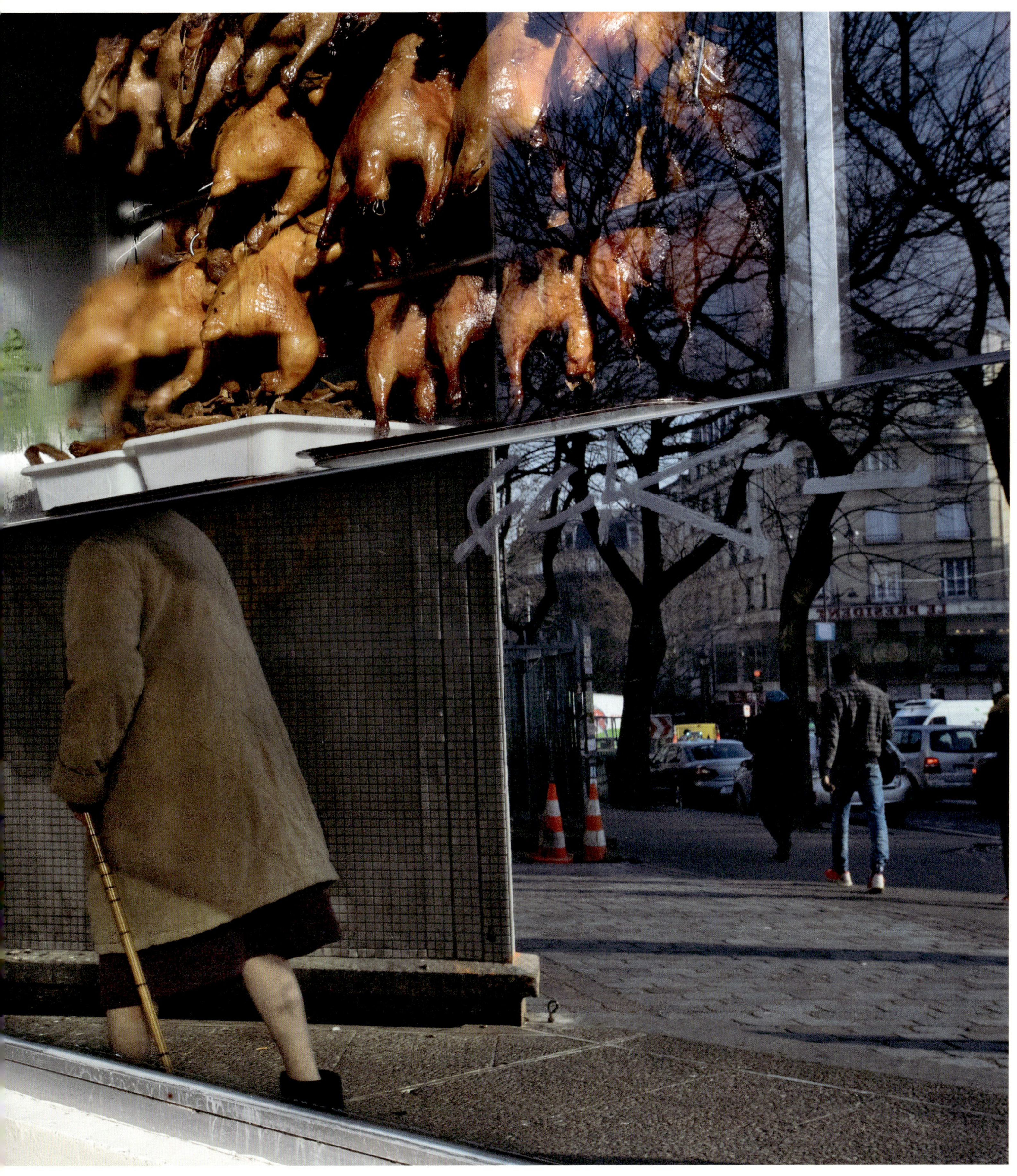

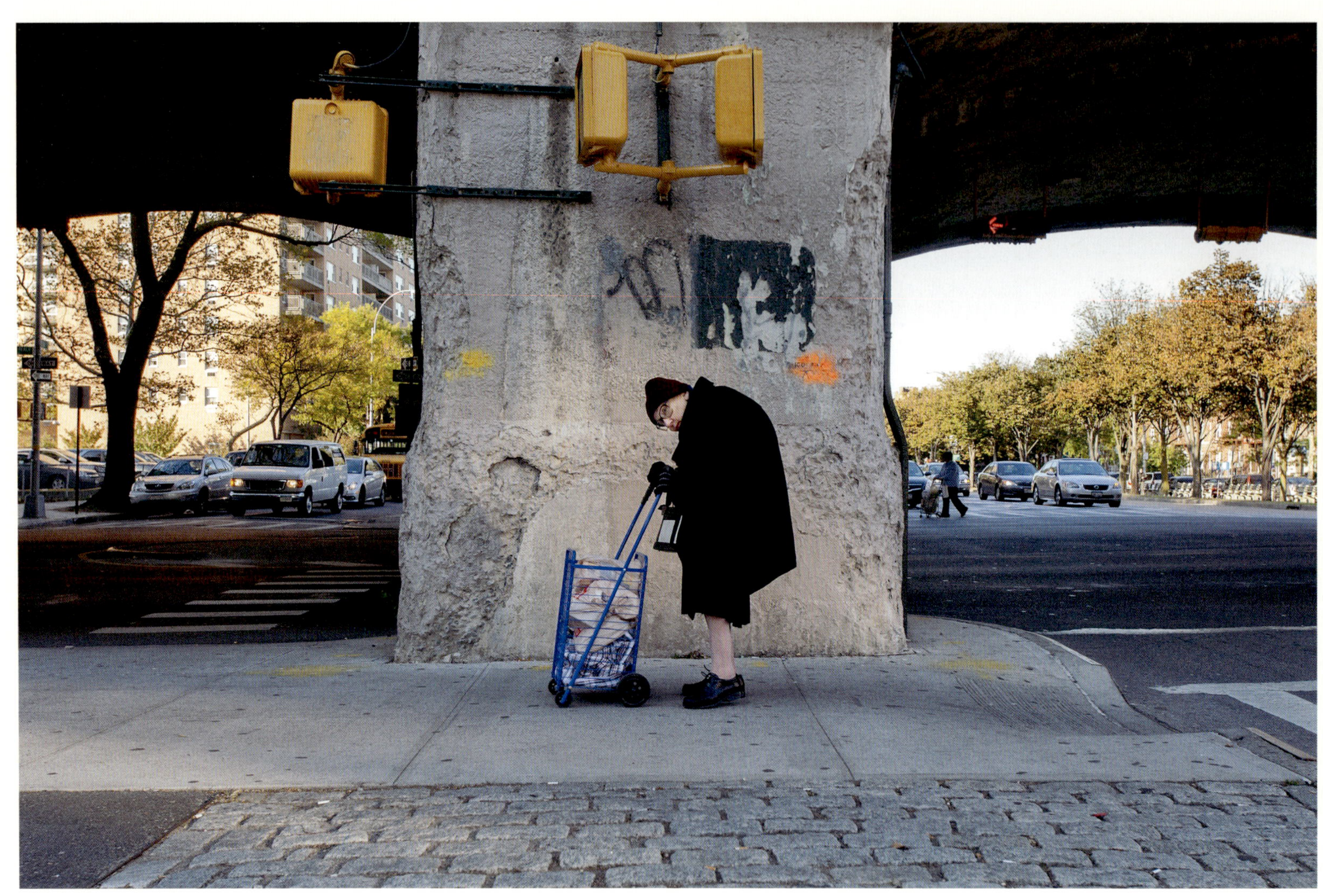

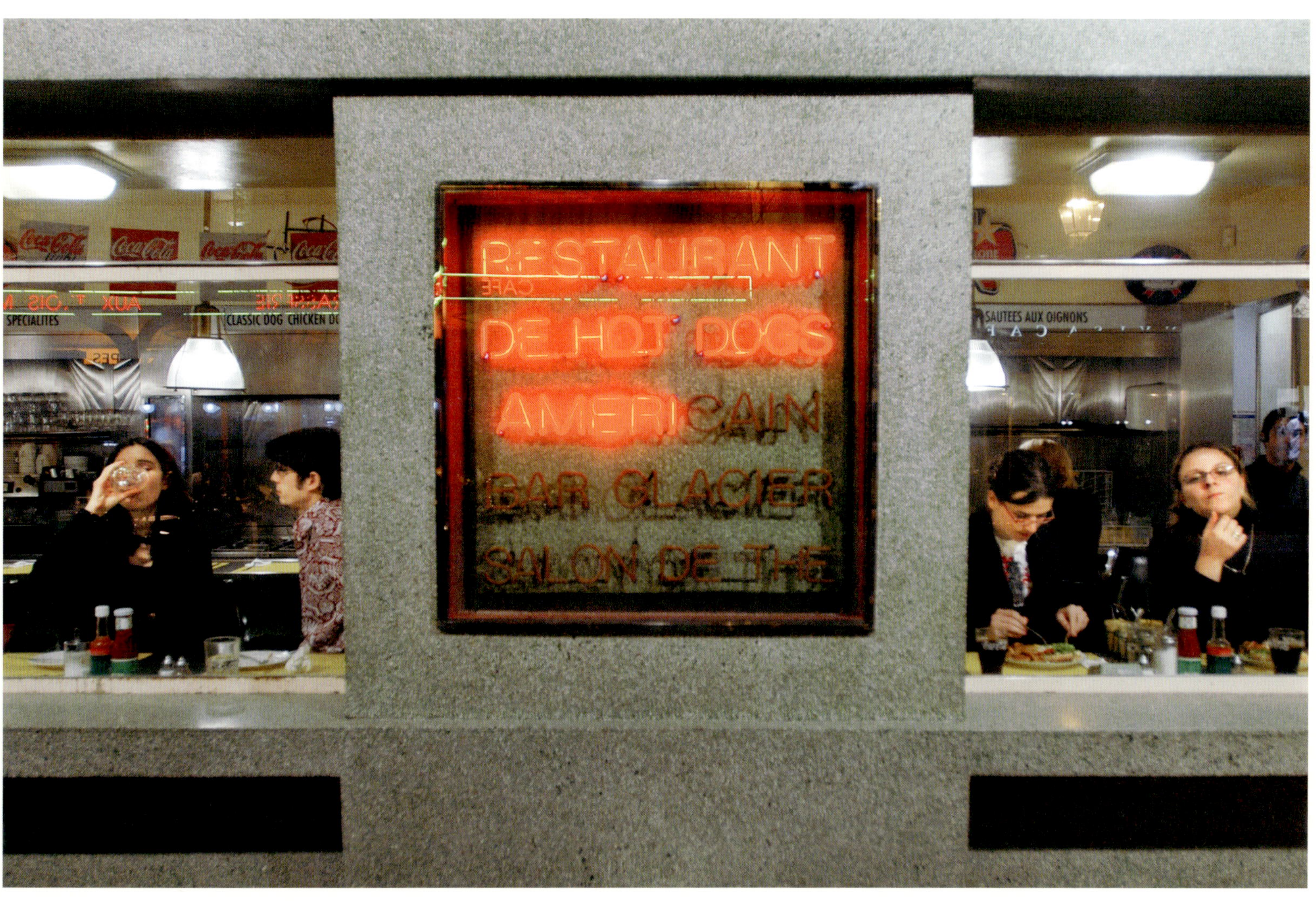
RESTAURANT
DE HOT DOGS
AMERICAIN
BAR GLACIER
SALON DE THE

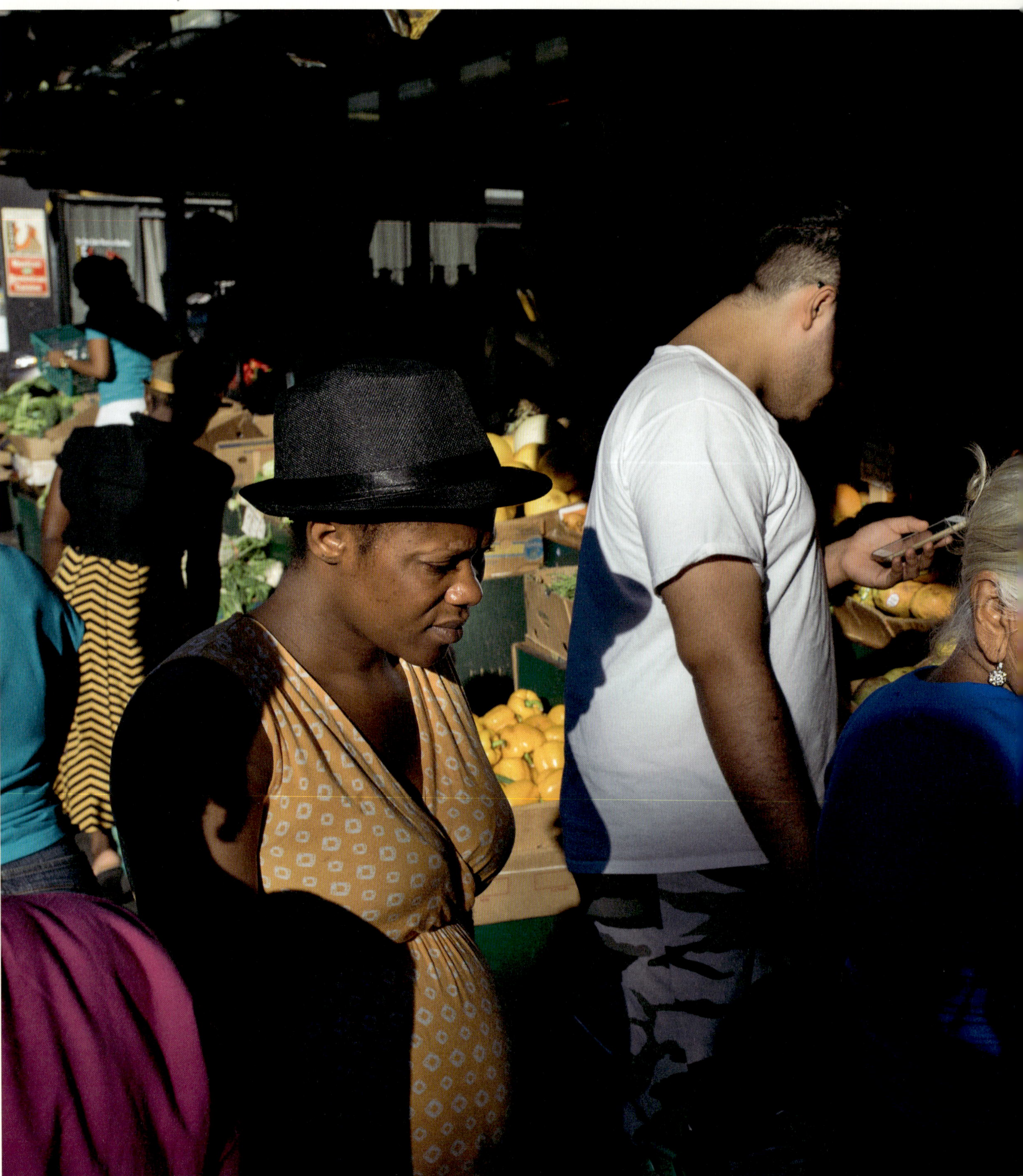

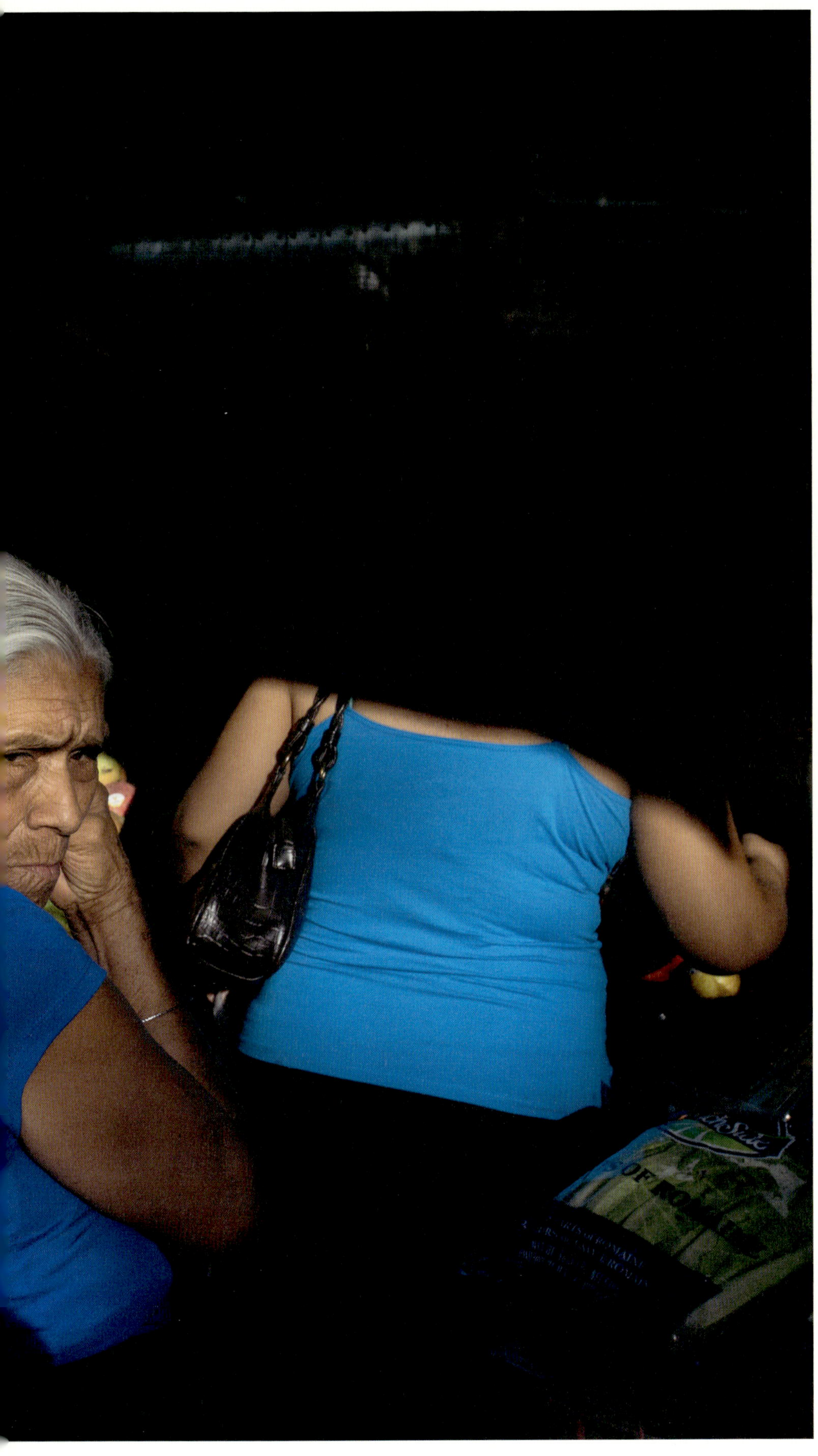

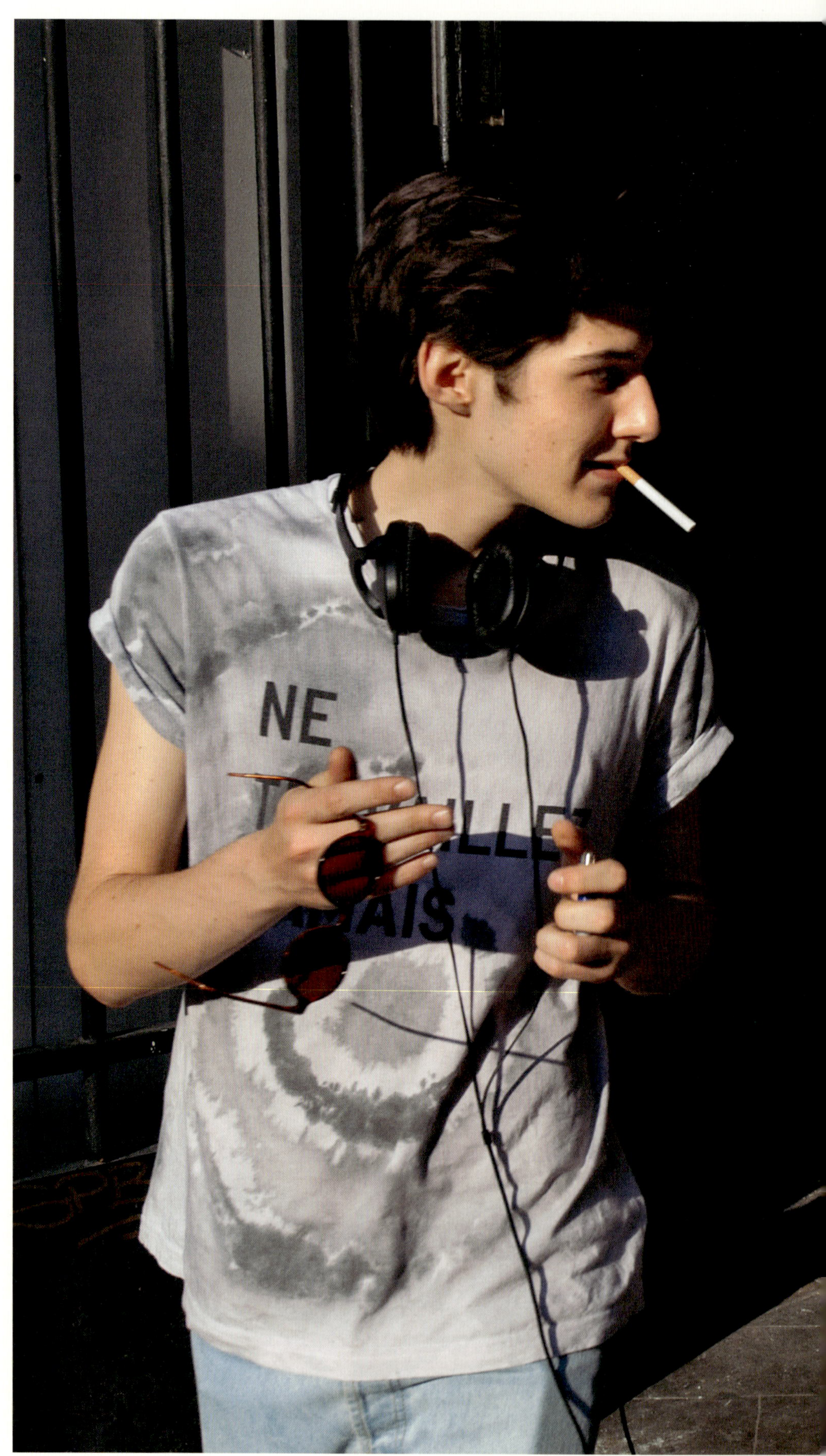
NE
ILLE
AIS

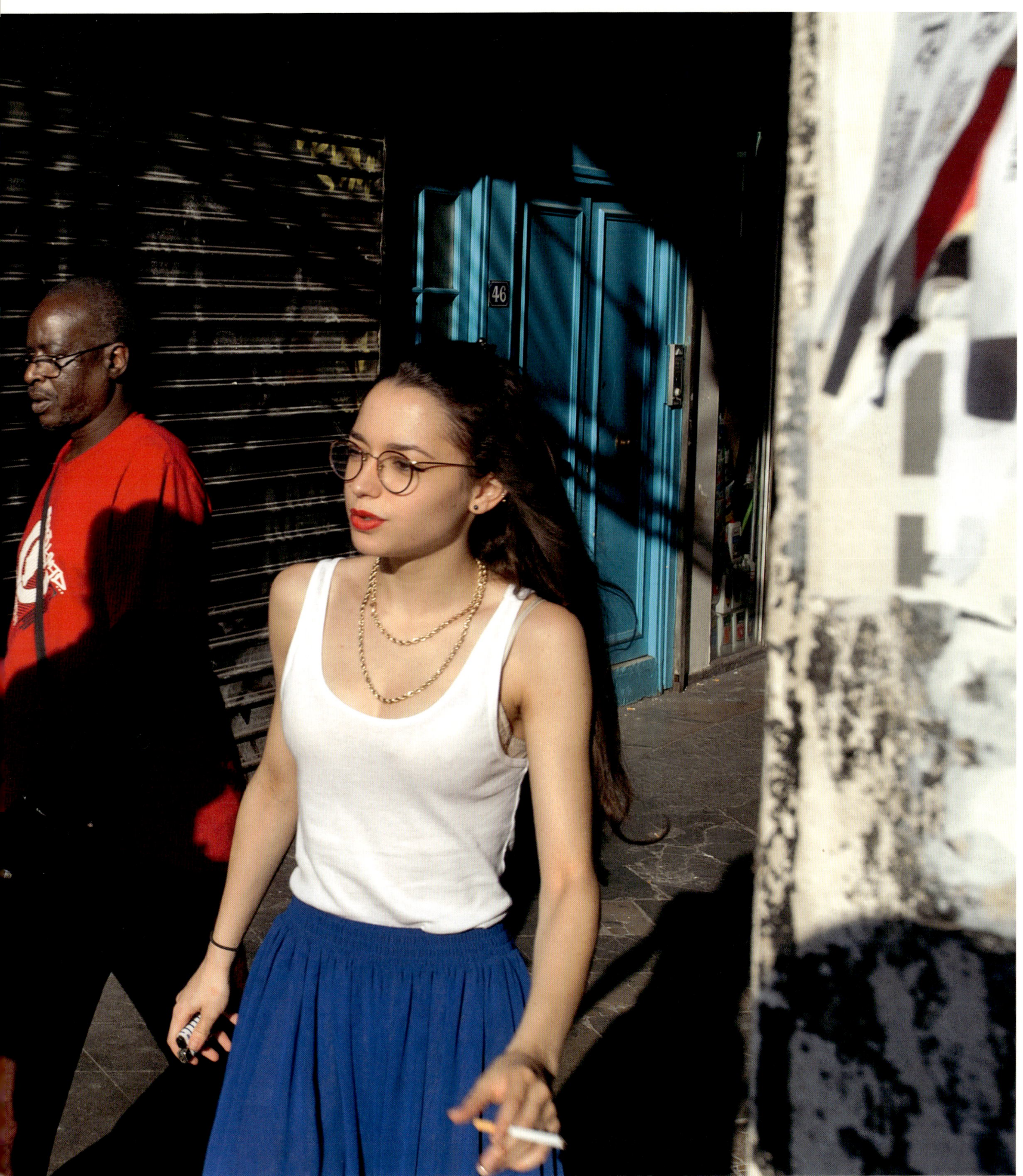

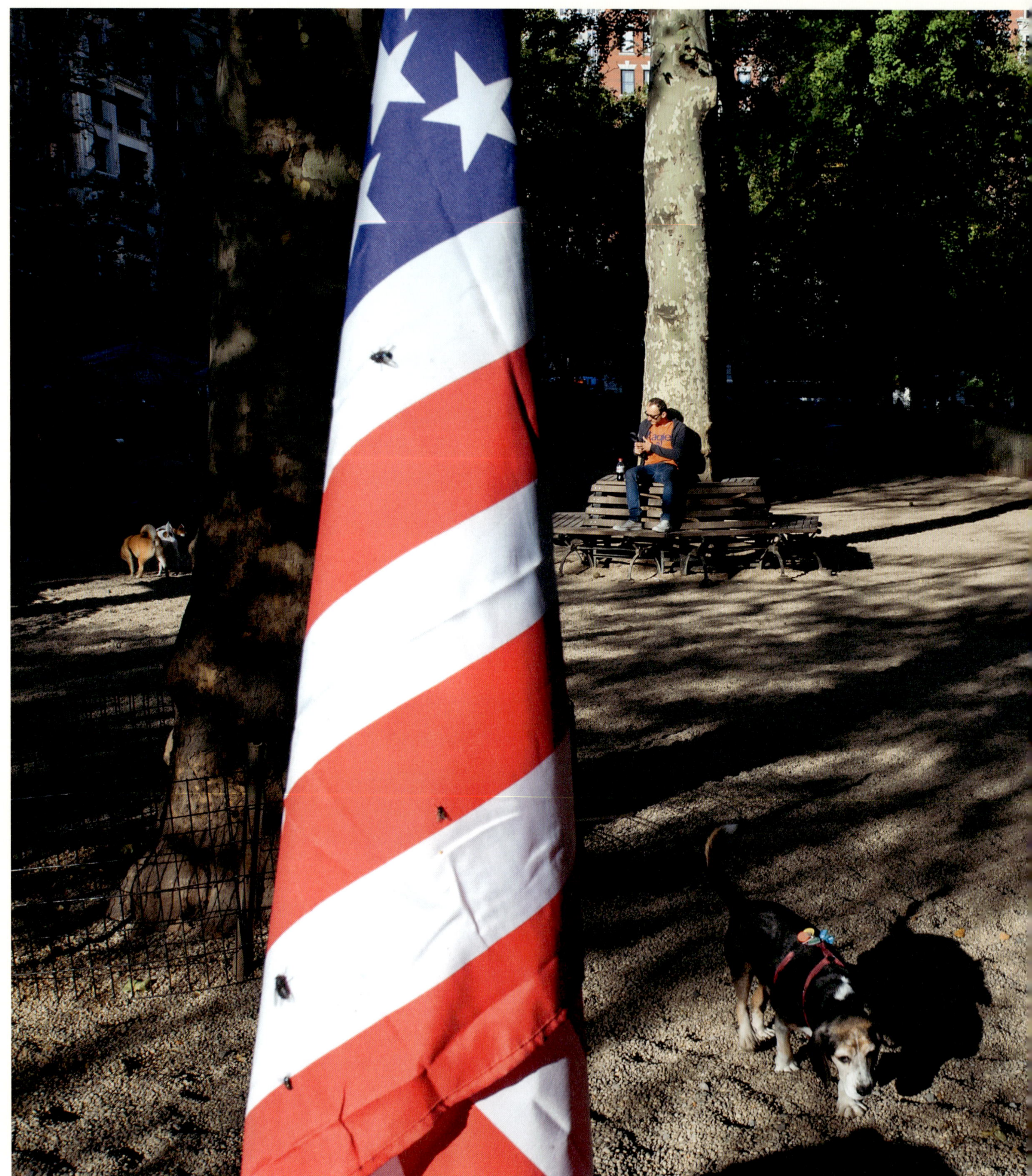

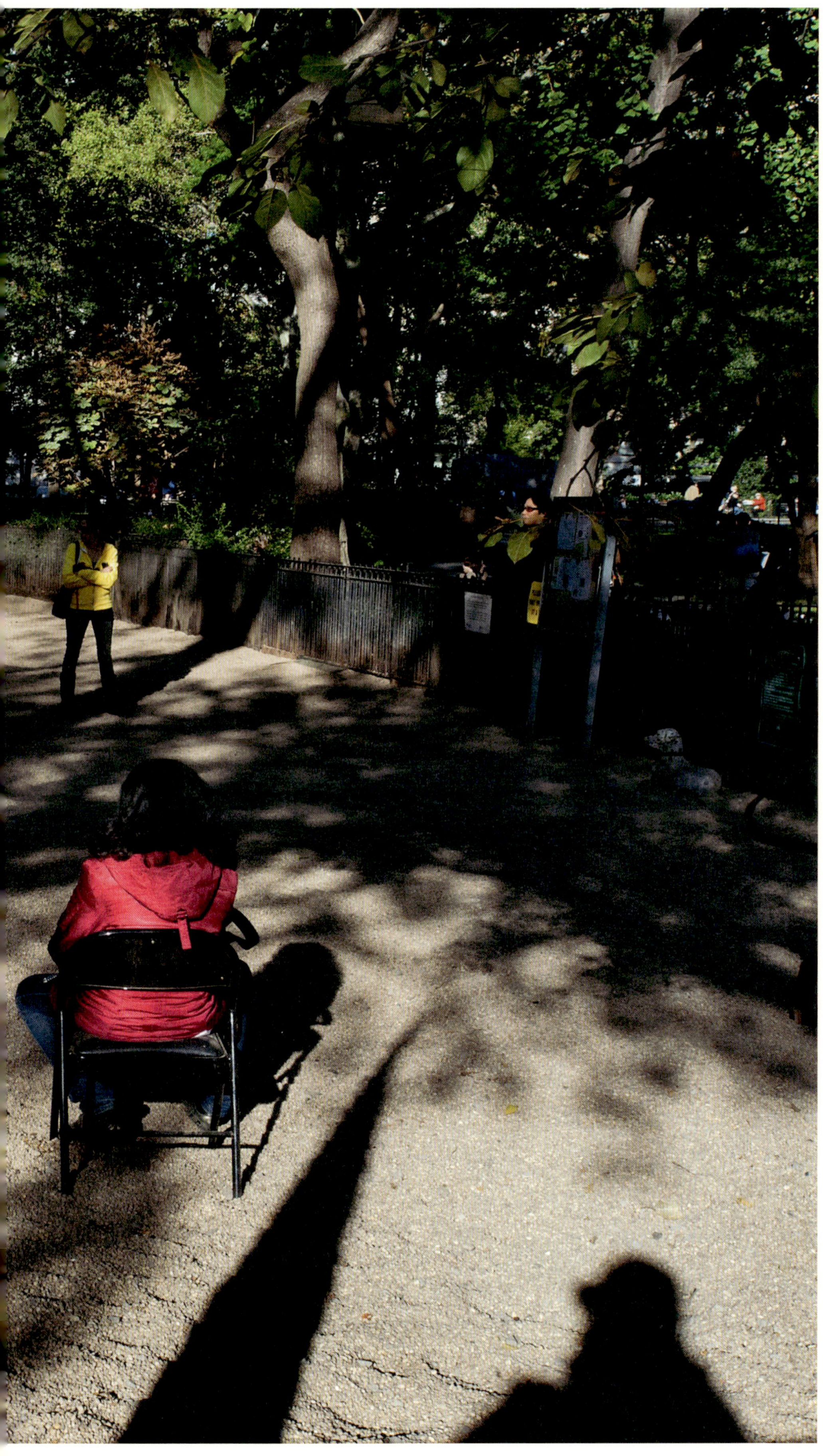

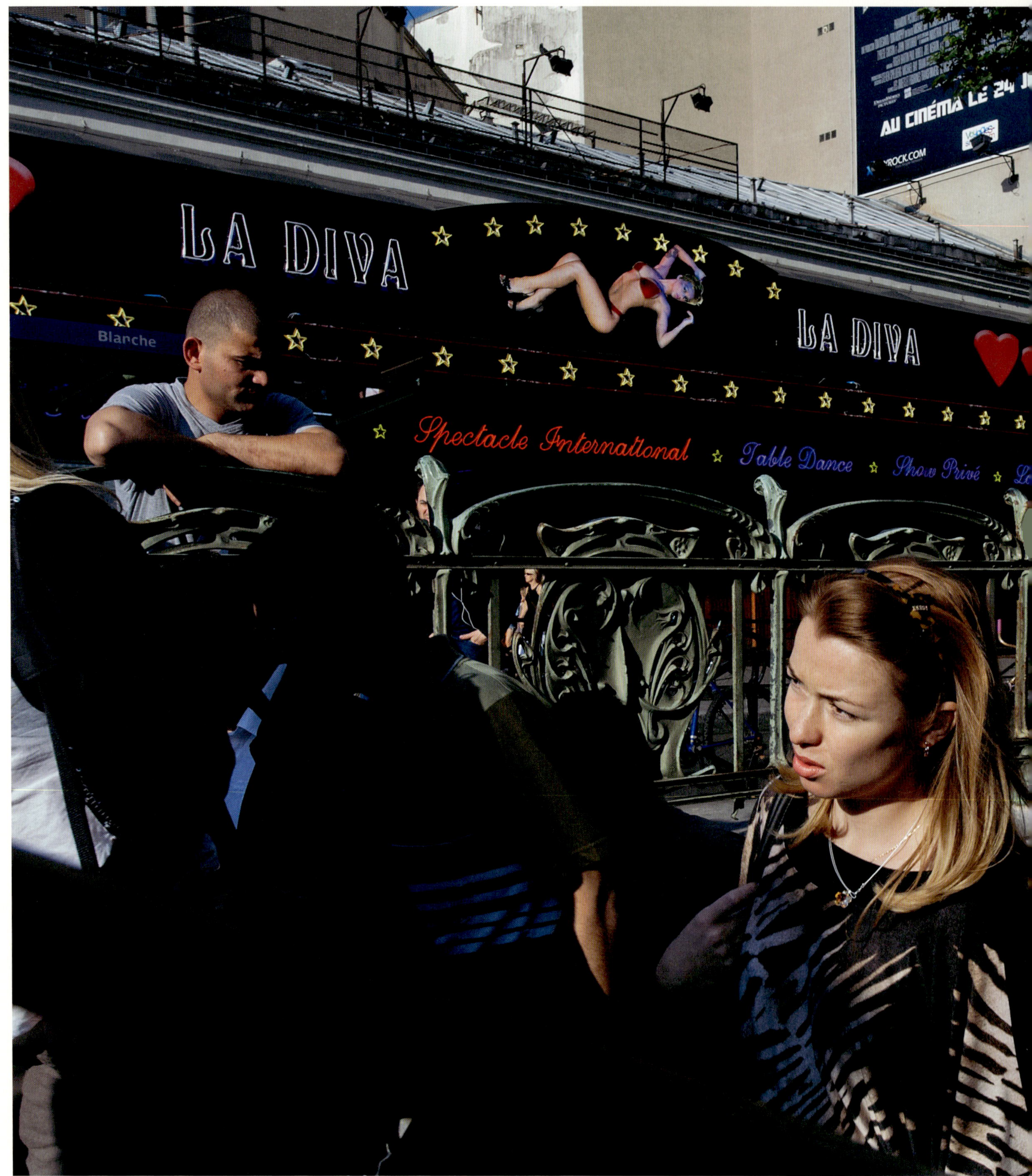
AU CINÉMA LE 24 J
skyrock.com
Blanche
LA DIVA
LA DIVA
Spectacle International
Table Dance
Show Privé

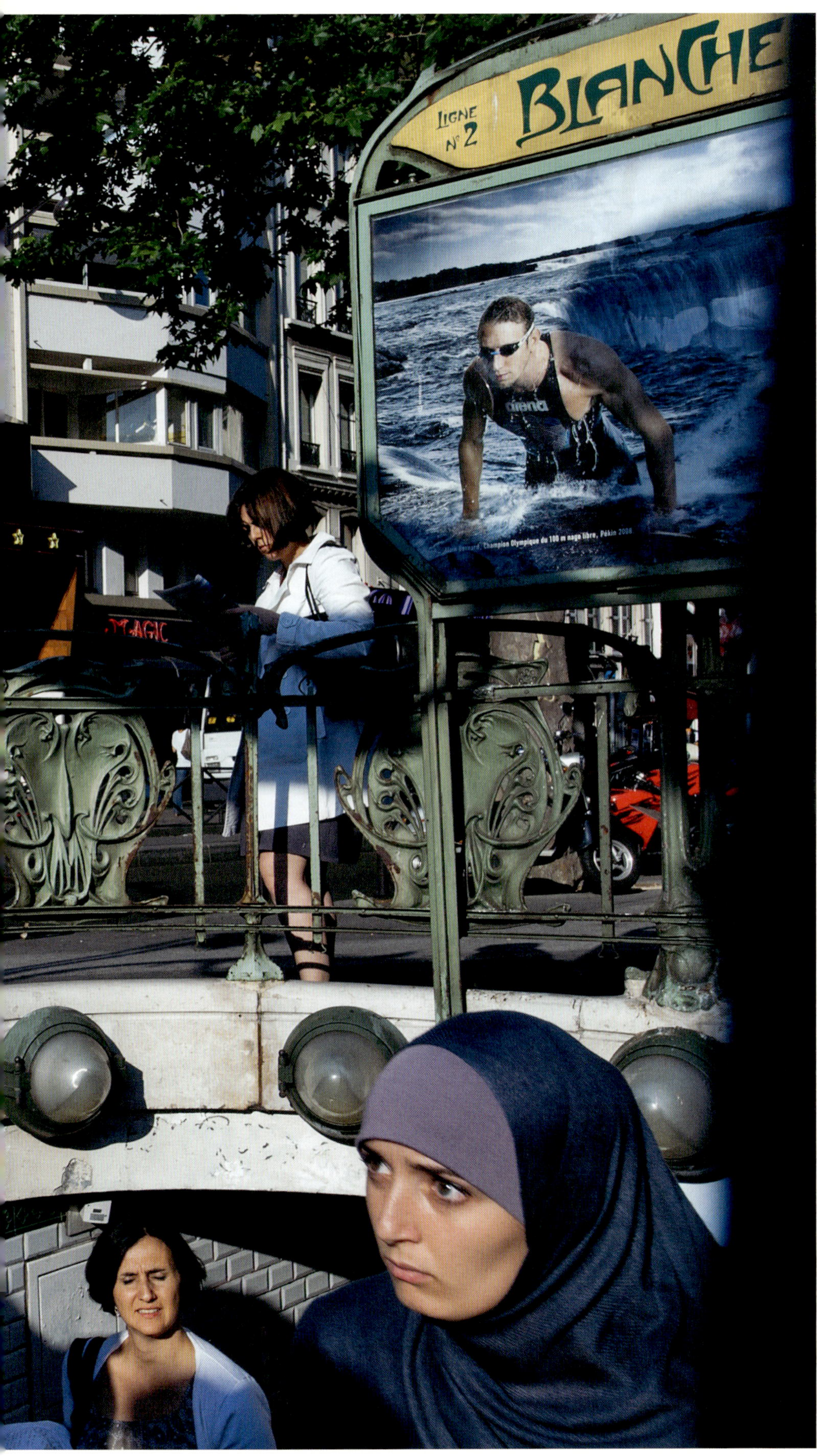

LIGNE
N° 2
BLANCHE

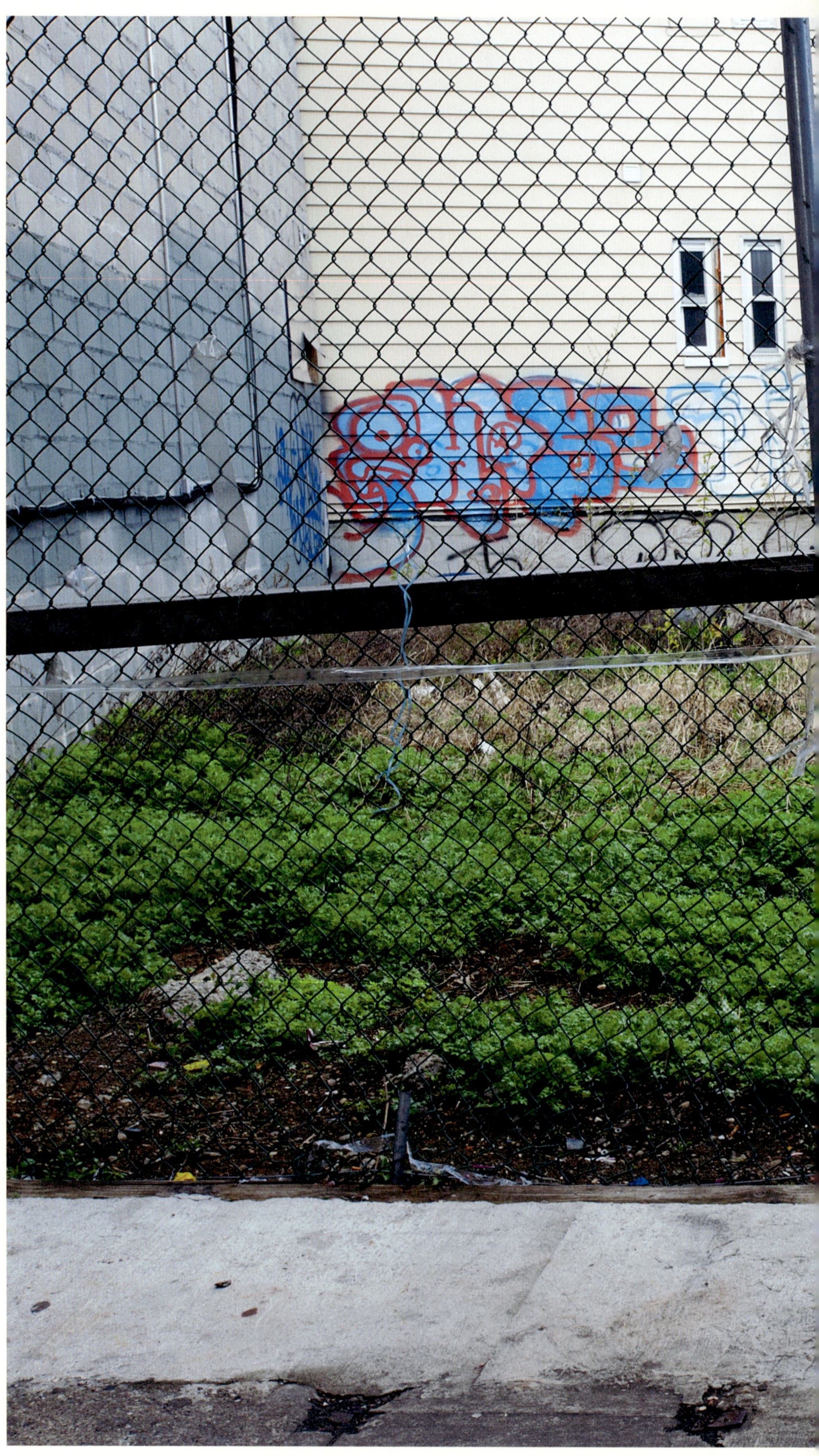

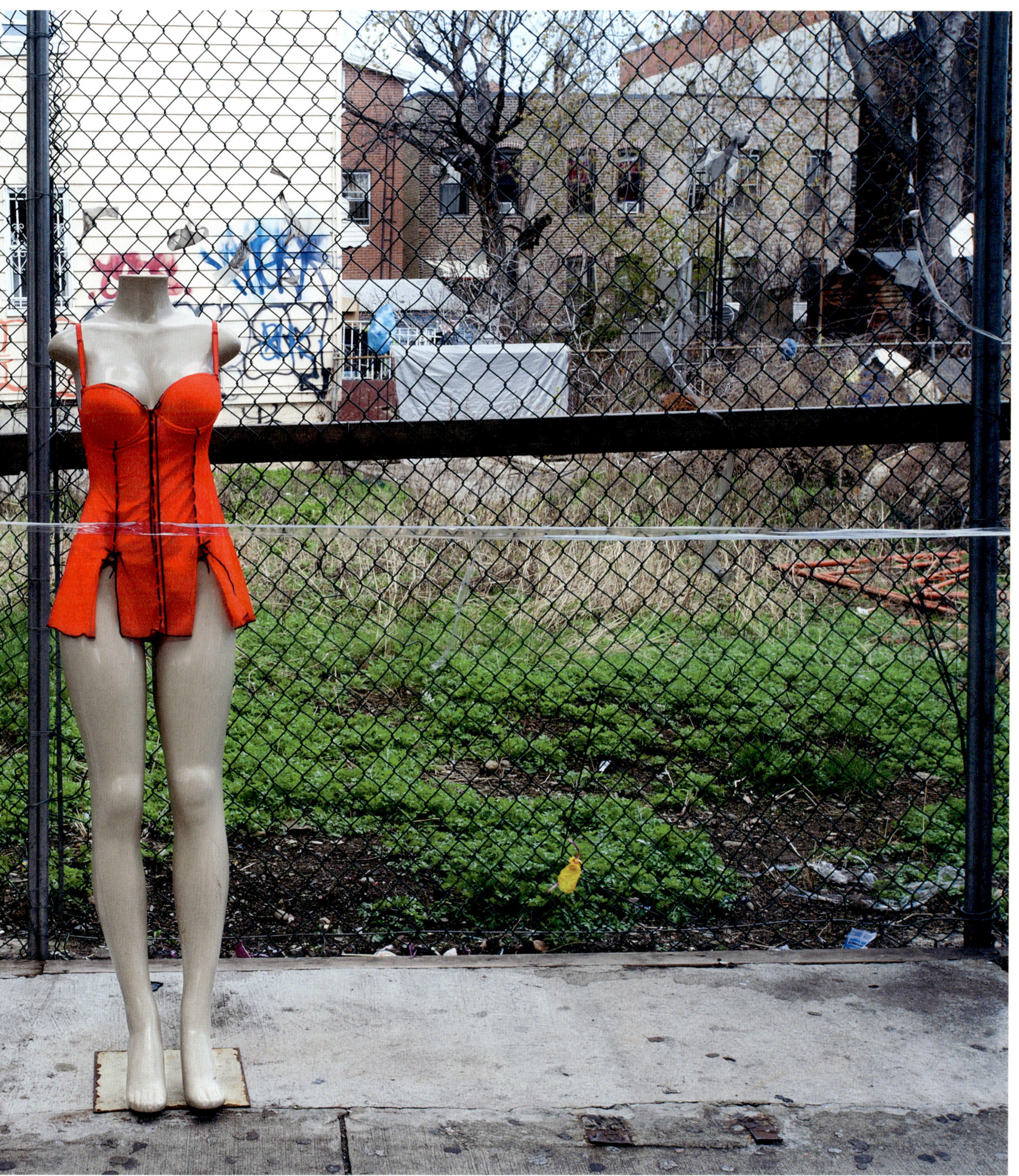

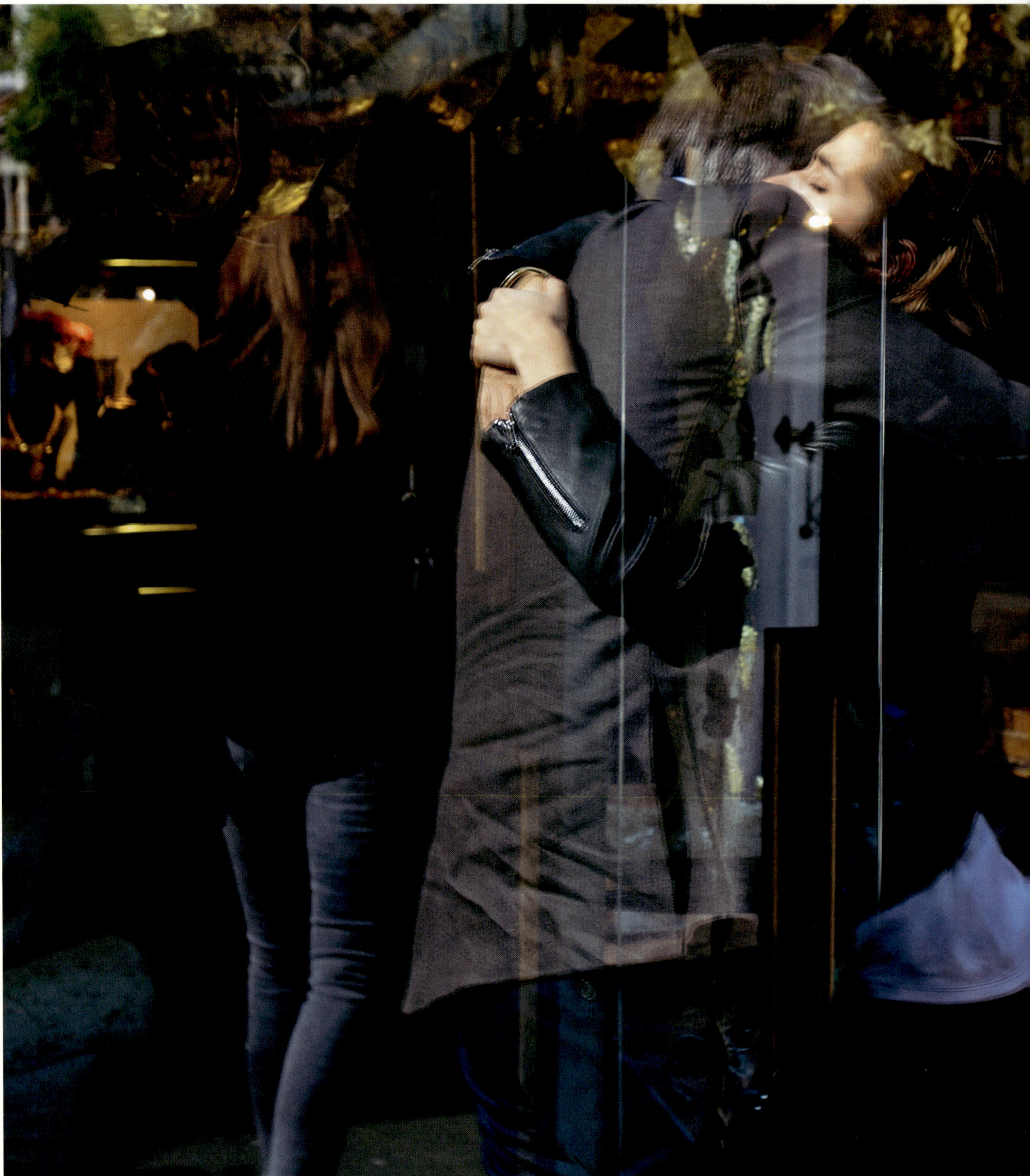

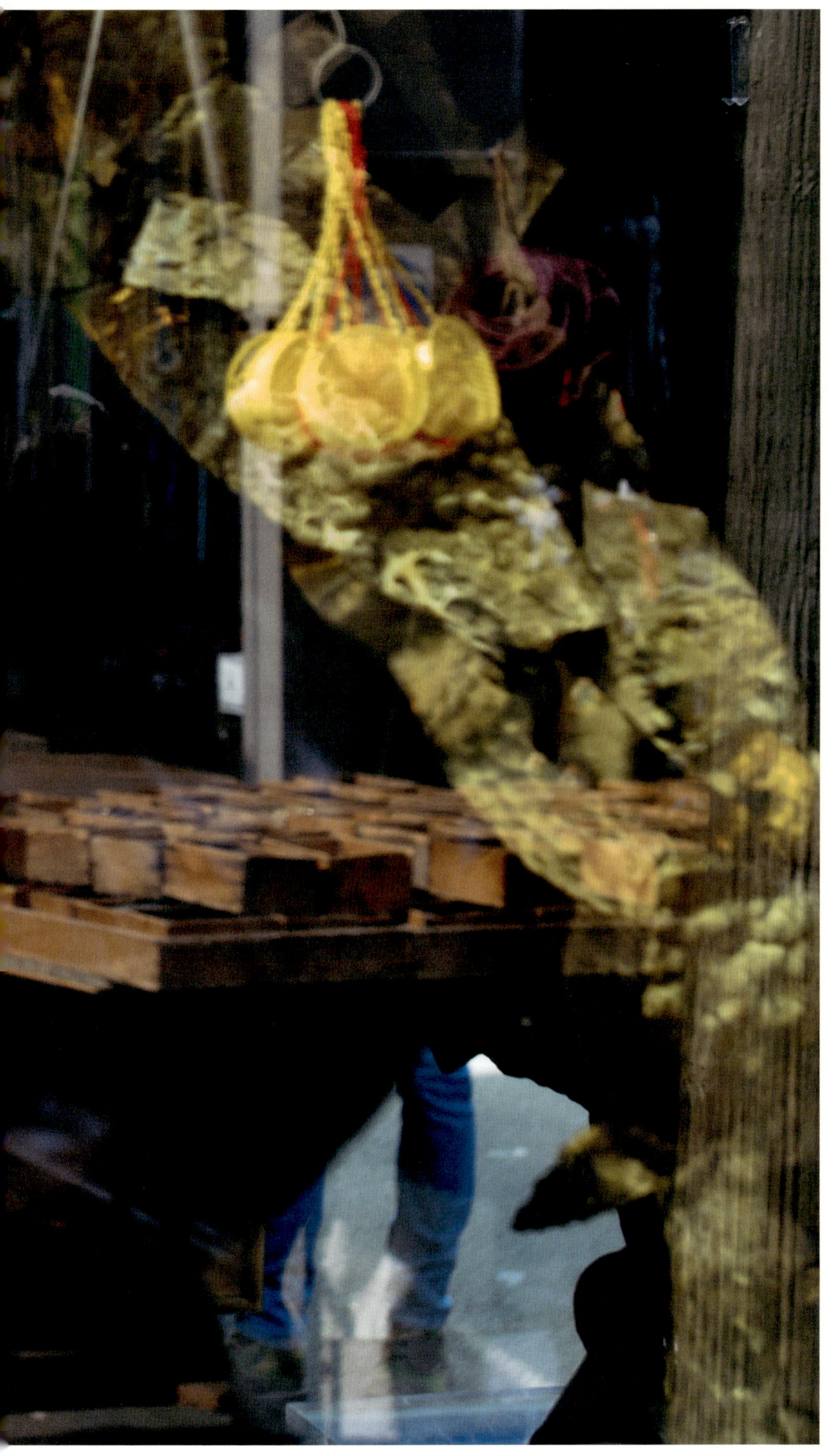

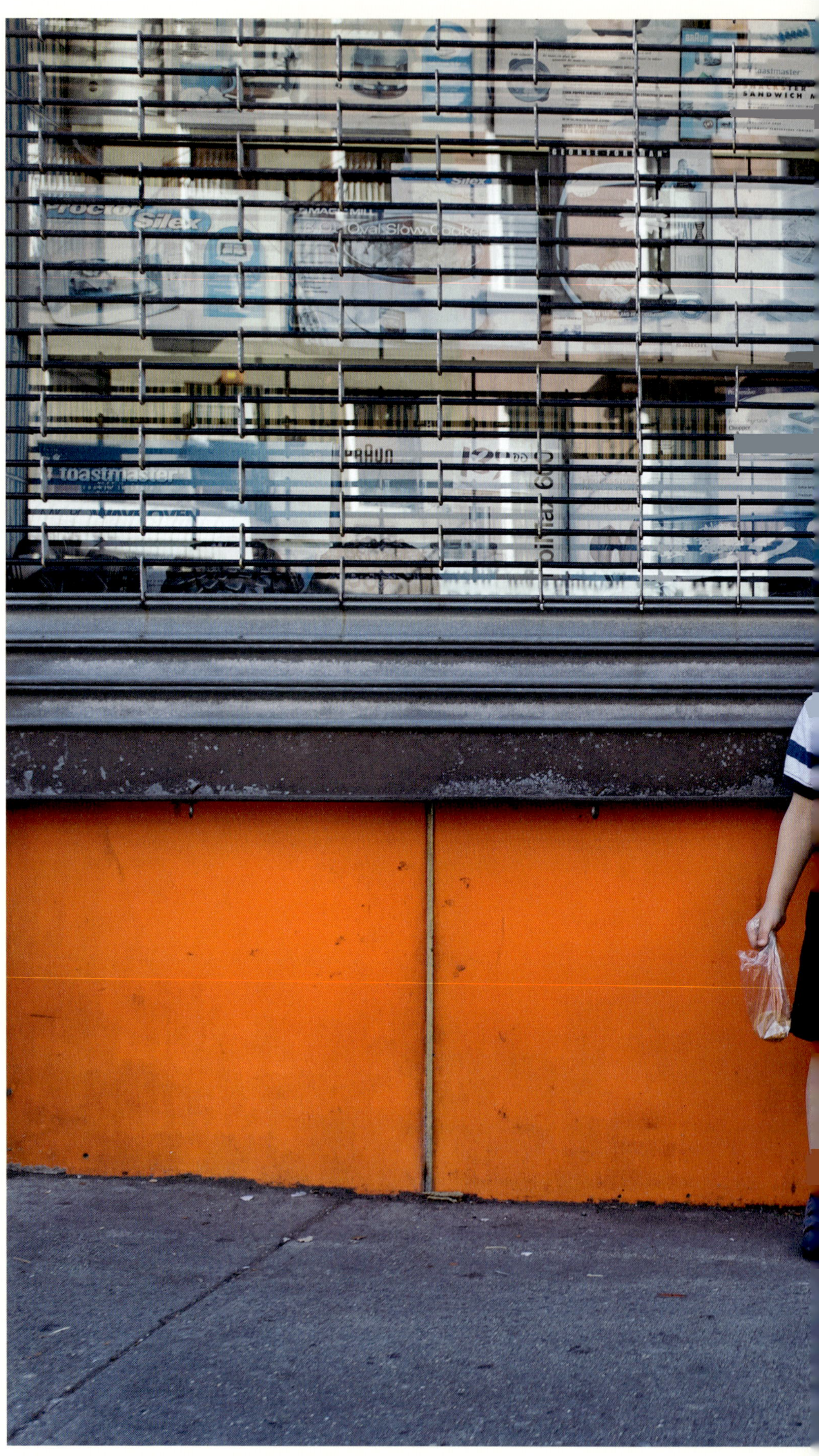

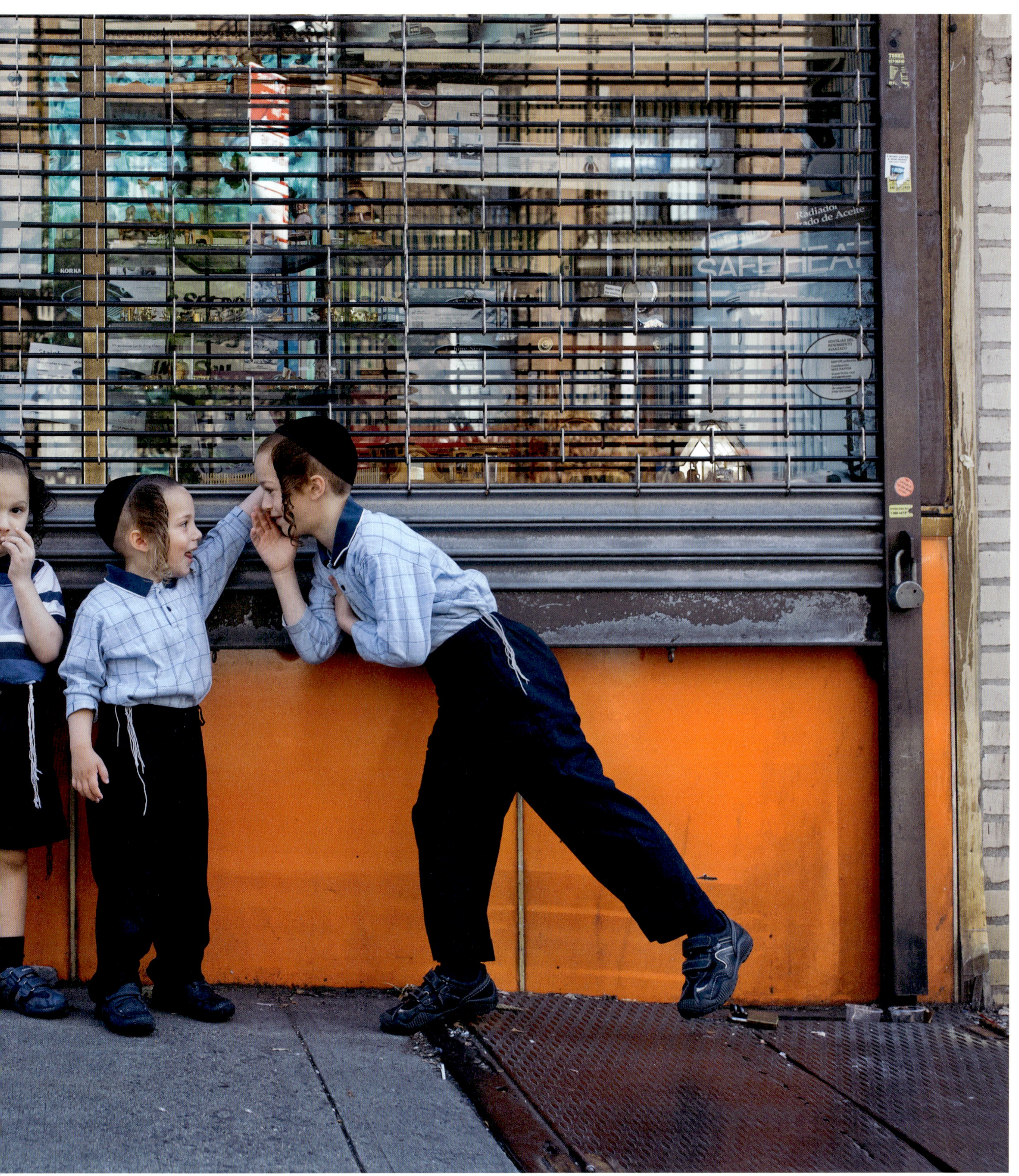

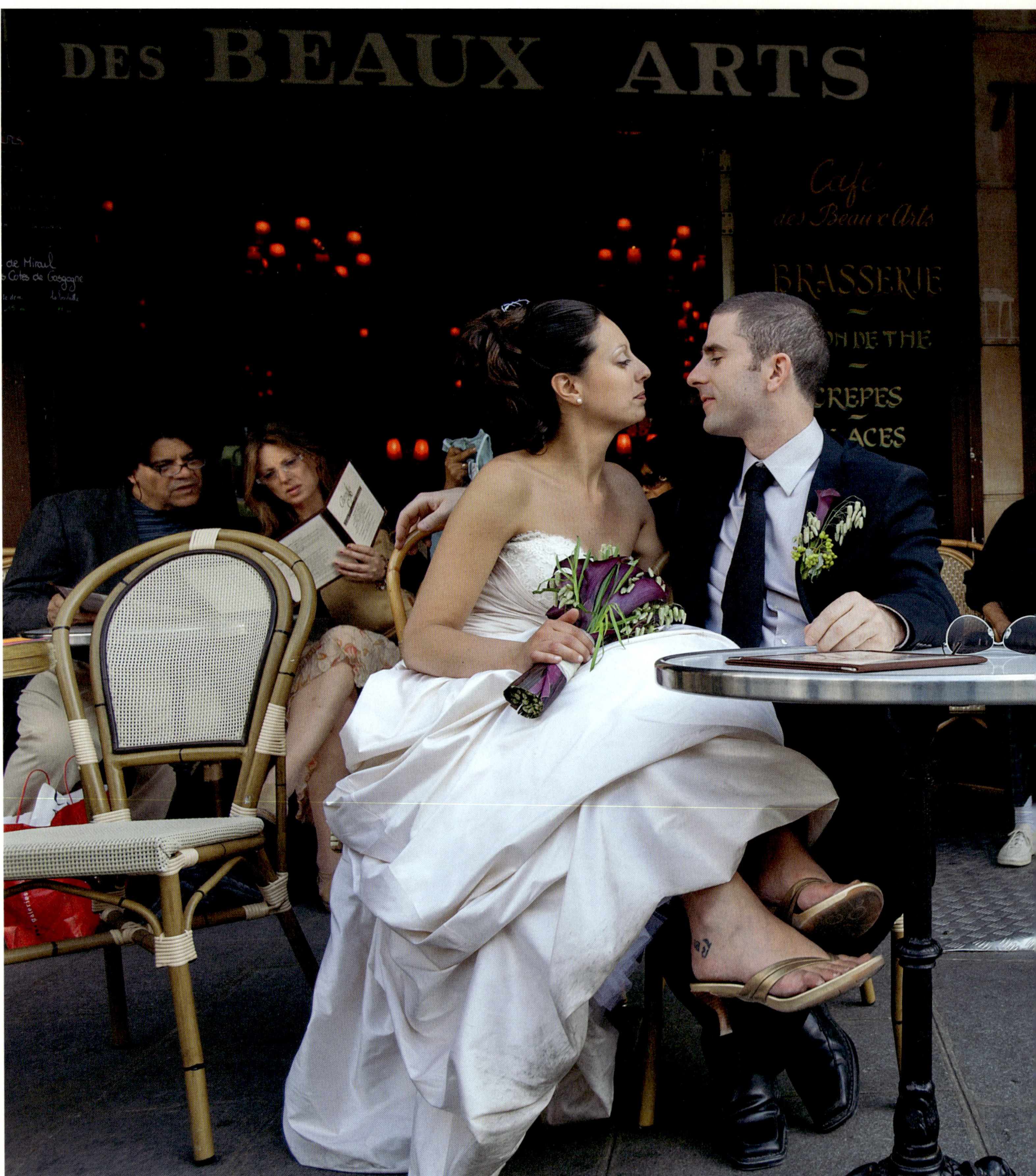
DES BEAUX ARTS
Café
des Beaux Arts
BRASSERIE
CREPES
ACES

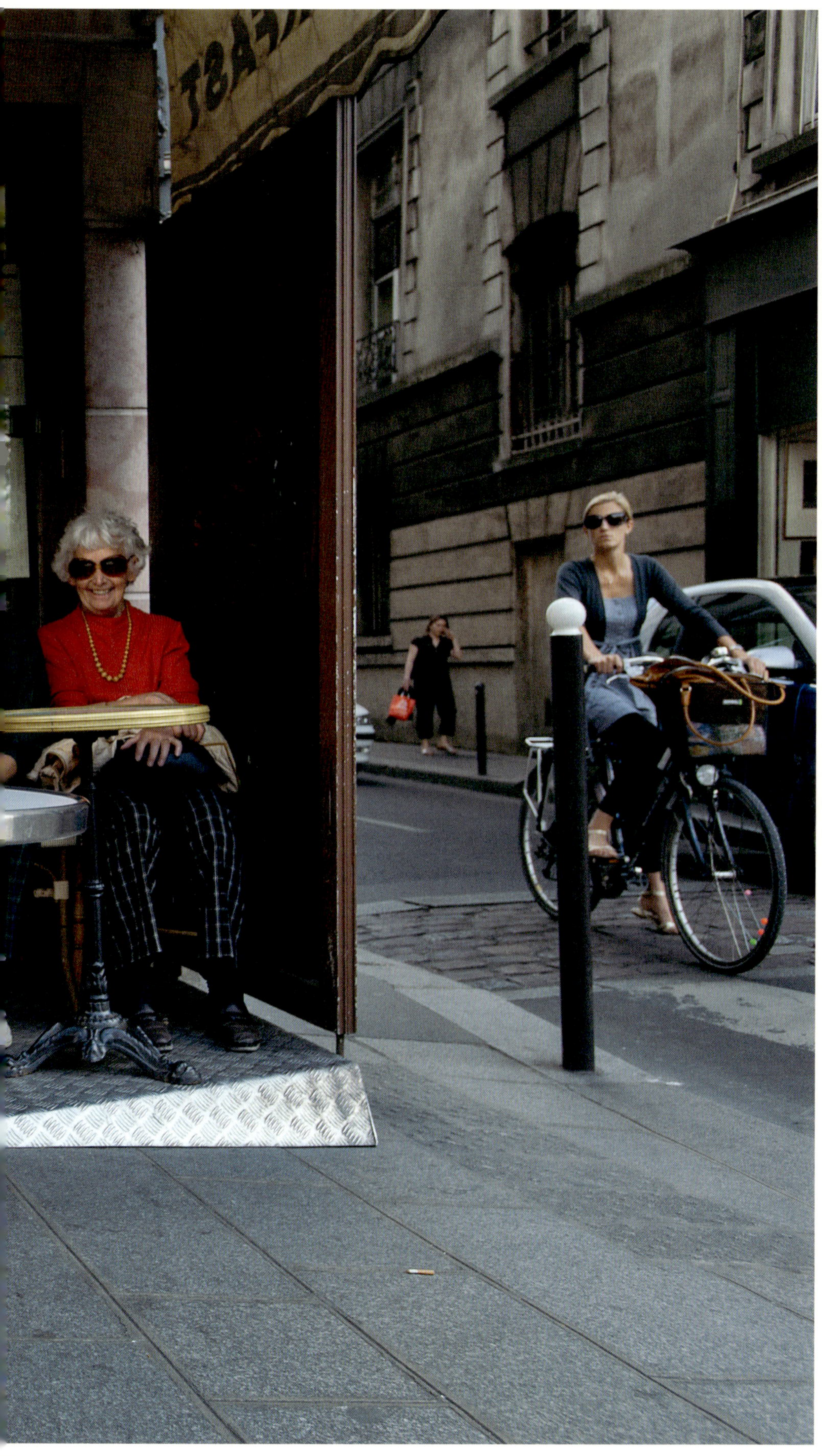

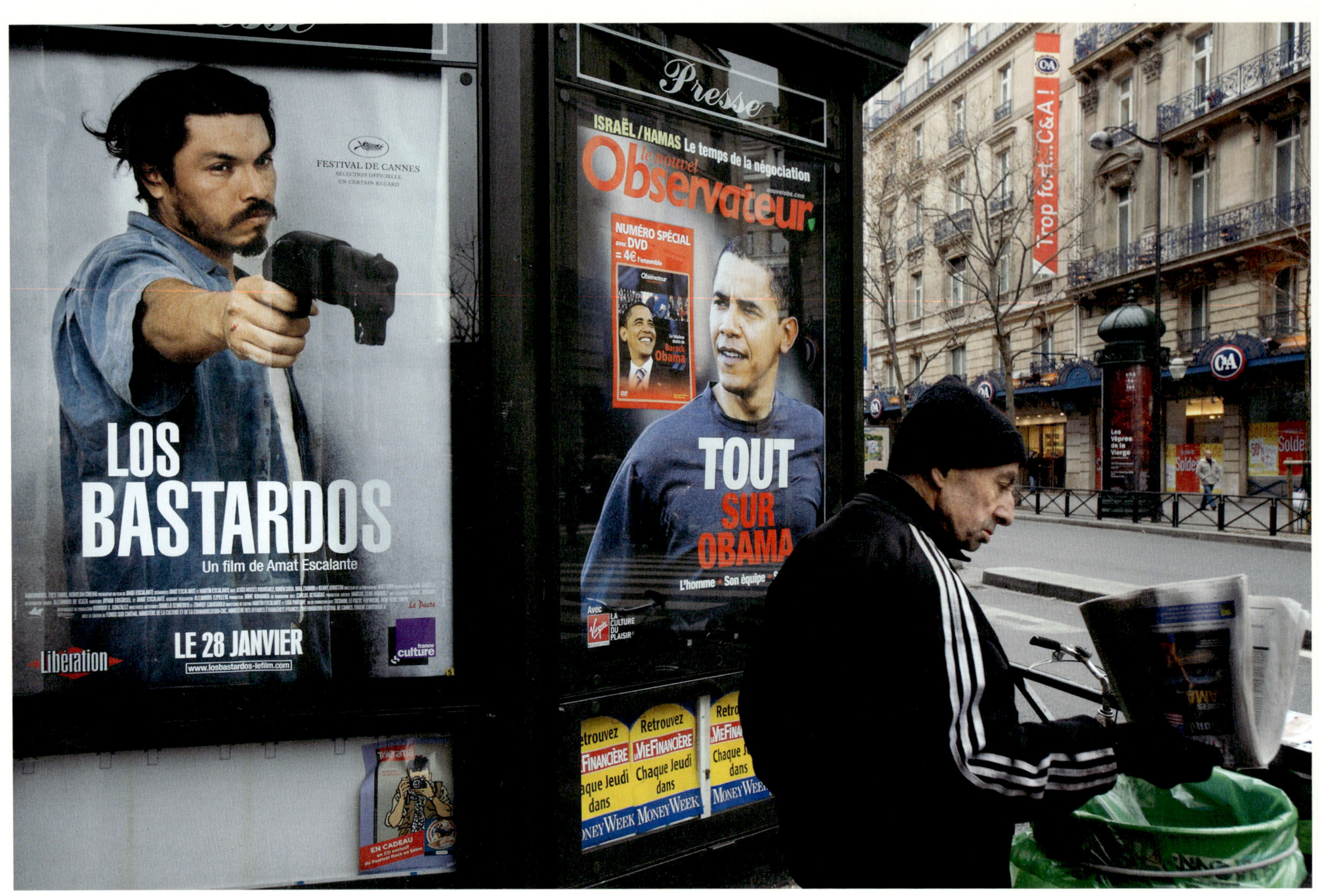
FESTIVAL DE CANNES
SÉLECTION OFFICIELLE
UN CERTAIN REGARD
LOS BASTARDOS
Un film de Amat Escalante
Le Pacte
Libération
LE 28 JANVIER
france culture
www.losbastardos-lefilm.com
Presse
ISRAËL / HAMAS Le temps de la négociation
Le nouvel
Observateur
nouvelobs.com
NUMÉRO SPÉCIAL
avec DVD
= 4€ l'ensemble
Obama
TOUT
SUR
OBAMA
L'homme • Son équipe •
Virgin LA CULTURE DU PLAISIR
Retrouvez
VieFINANCIÈRE
Chaque Jeudi
dans
MoneyWeek
Trop fo..t..C&A !
C&A

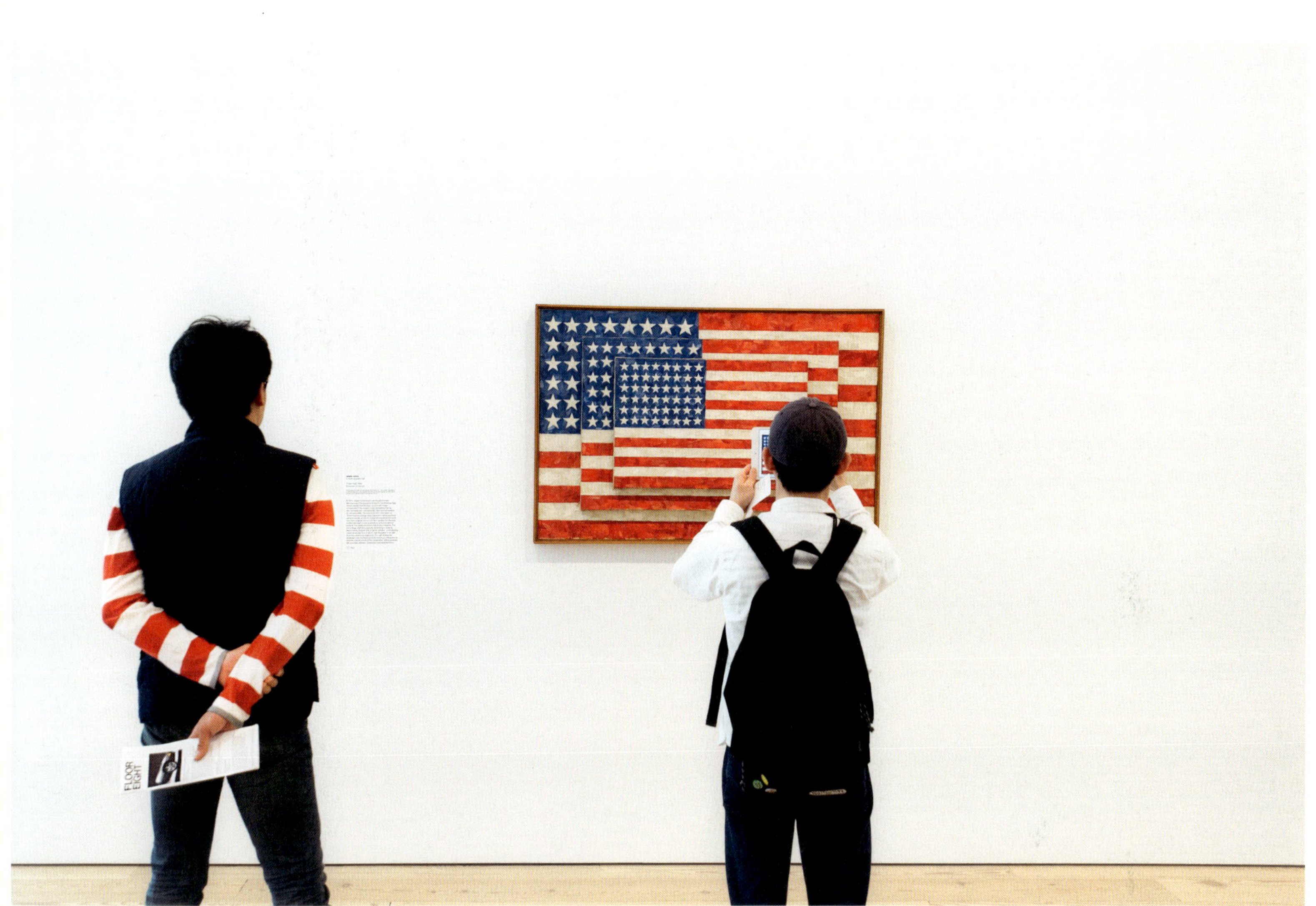

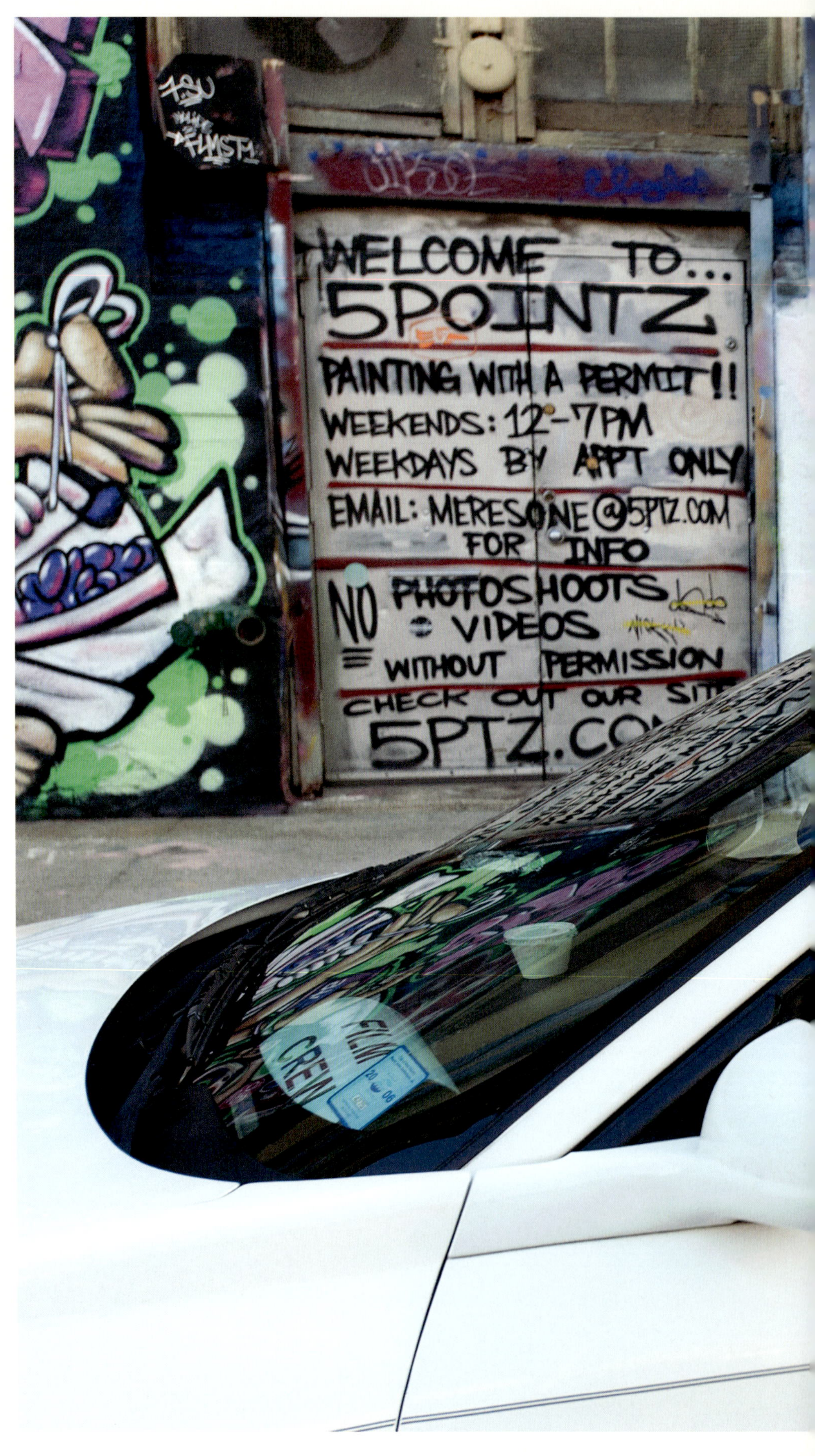

WELCOME TO...
5POINTZ
PAINTING WITH A PERMIT!!
WEEKENDS: 12-7PM
WEEKDAYS BY APPT ONLY
EMAIL: MERESONE @5PTZ.COM
FOR INFO
NO PHOTOSHOOTS
◉ VIDEOS
WITHOUT PERMISSION
CHECK OUT OUR SITE
5PTZ.COM
FILM CREW

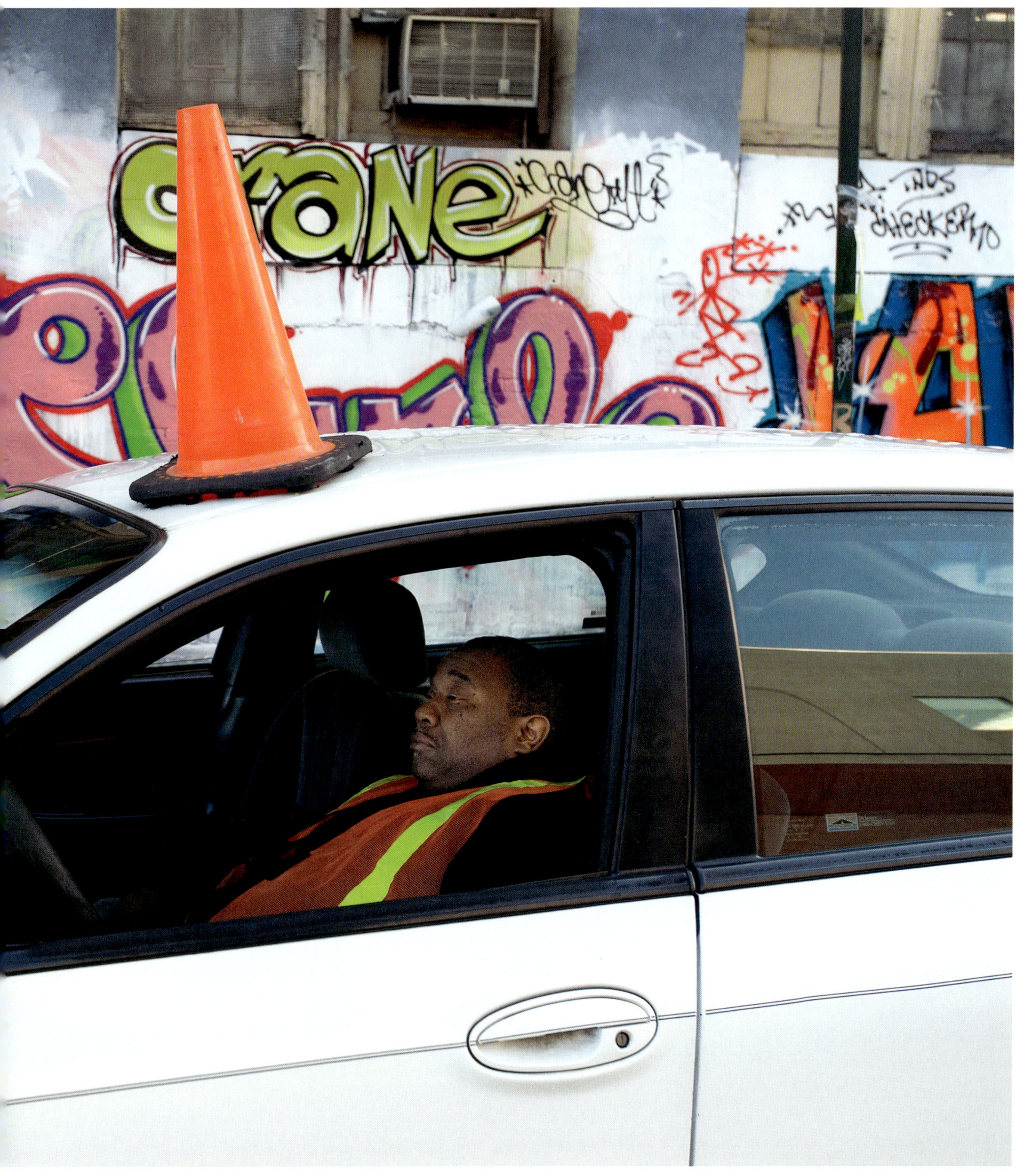
CRANE
CHECKER

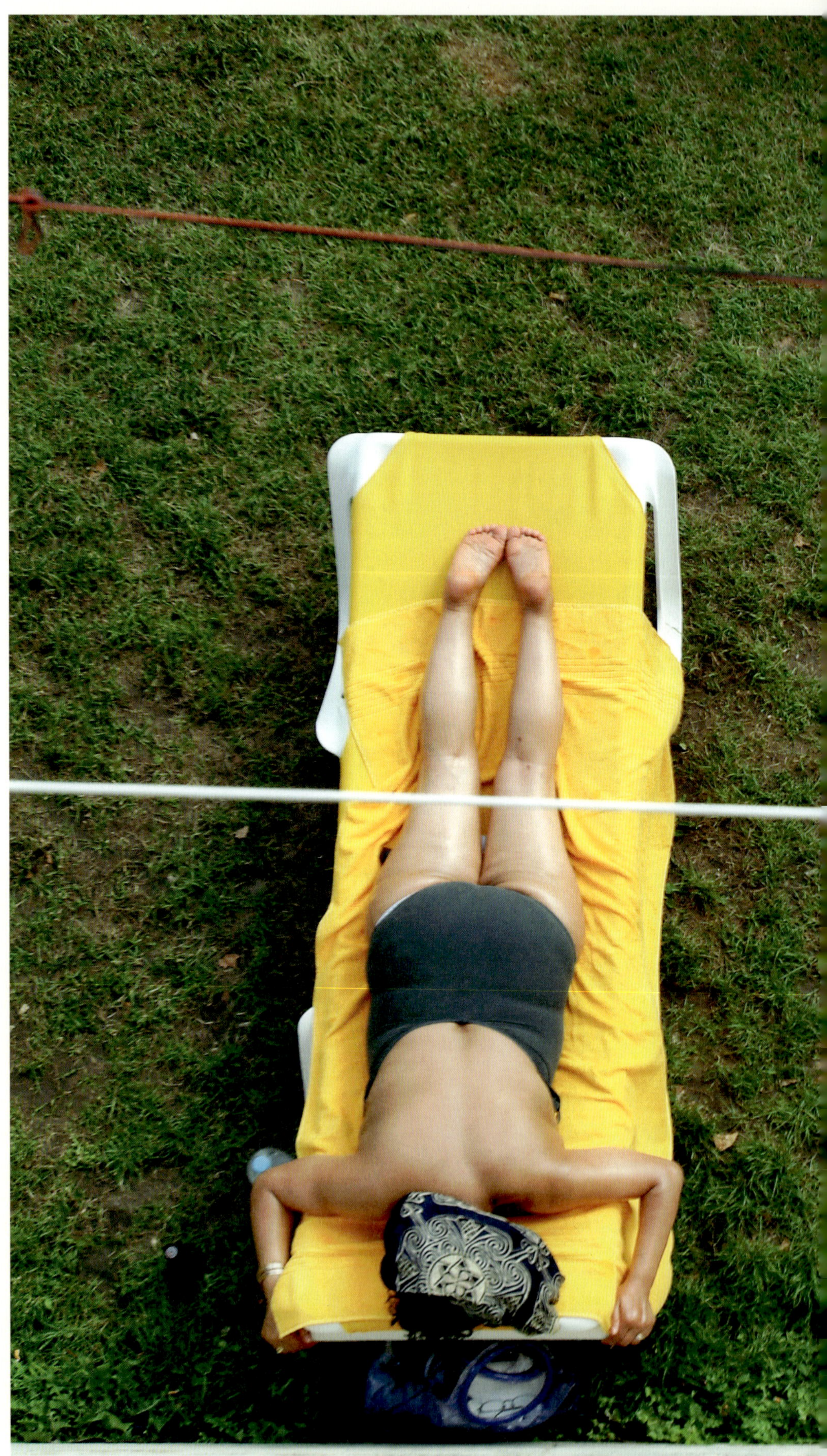

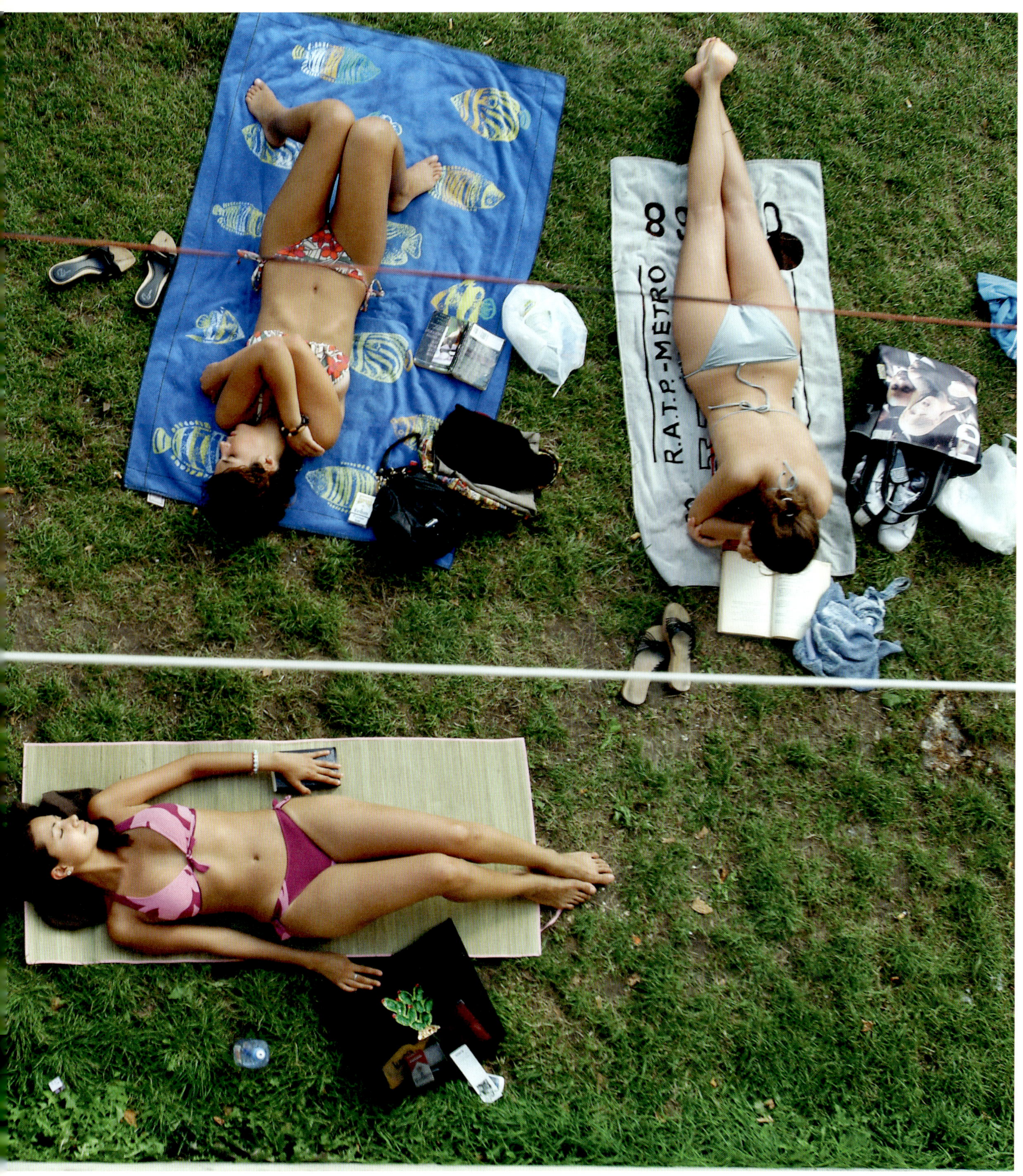

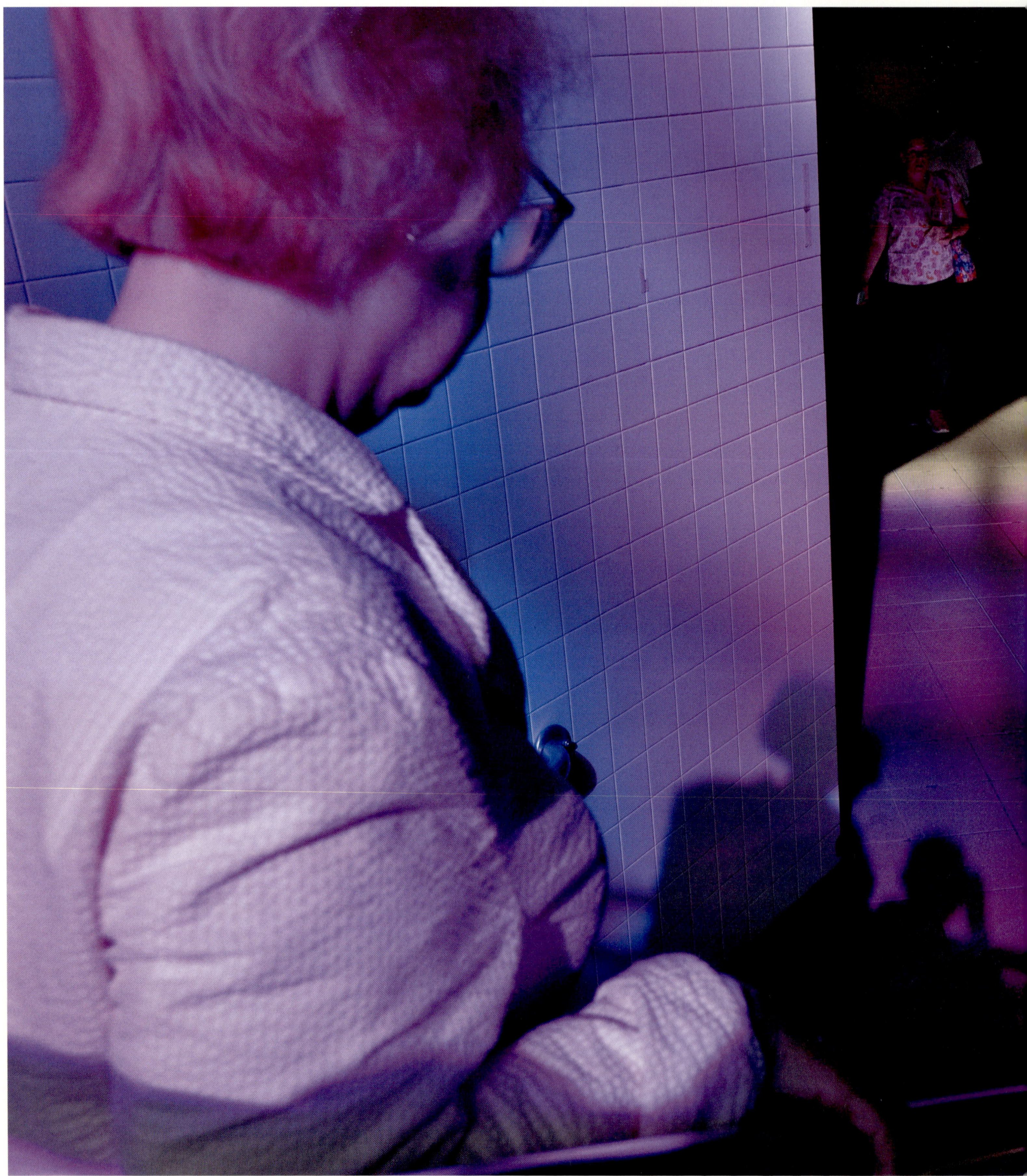

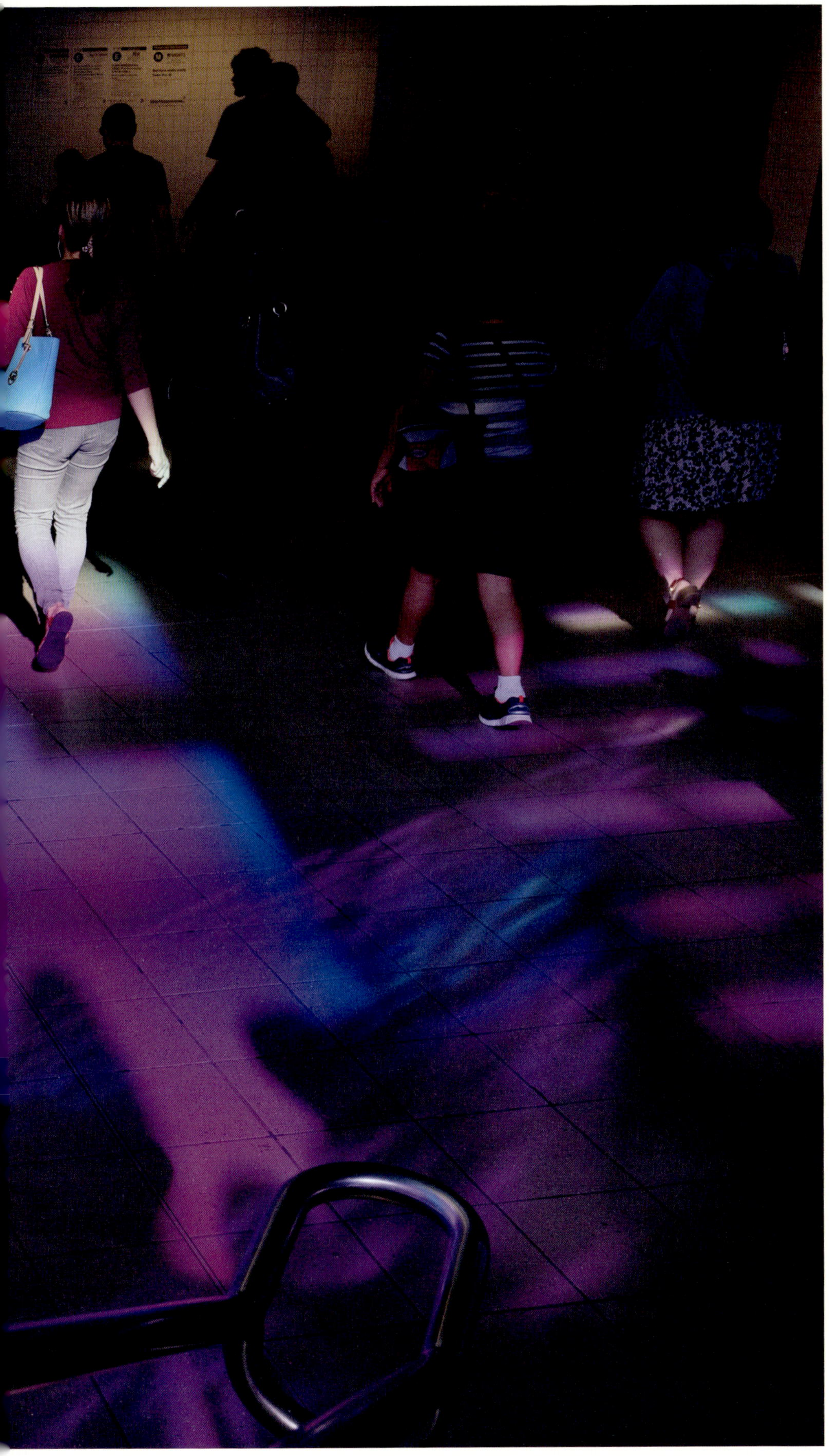

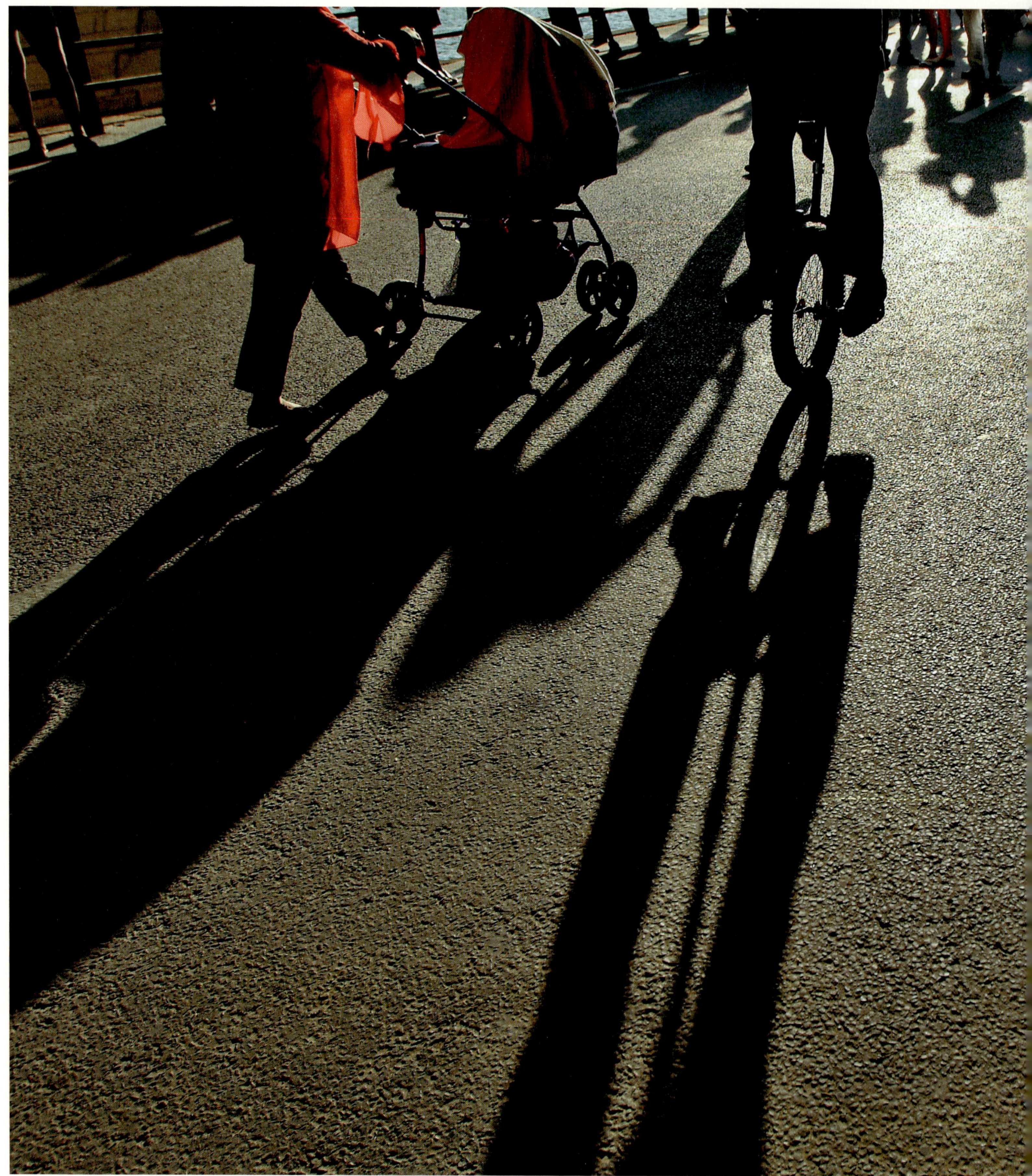

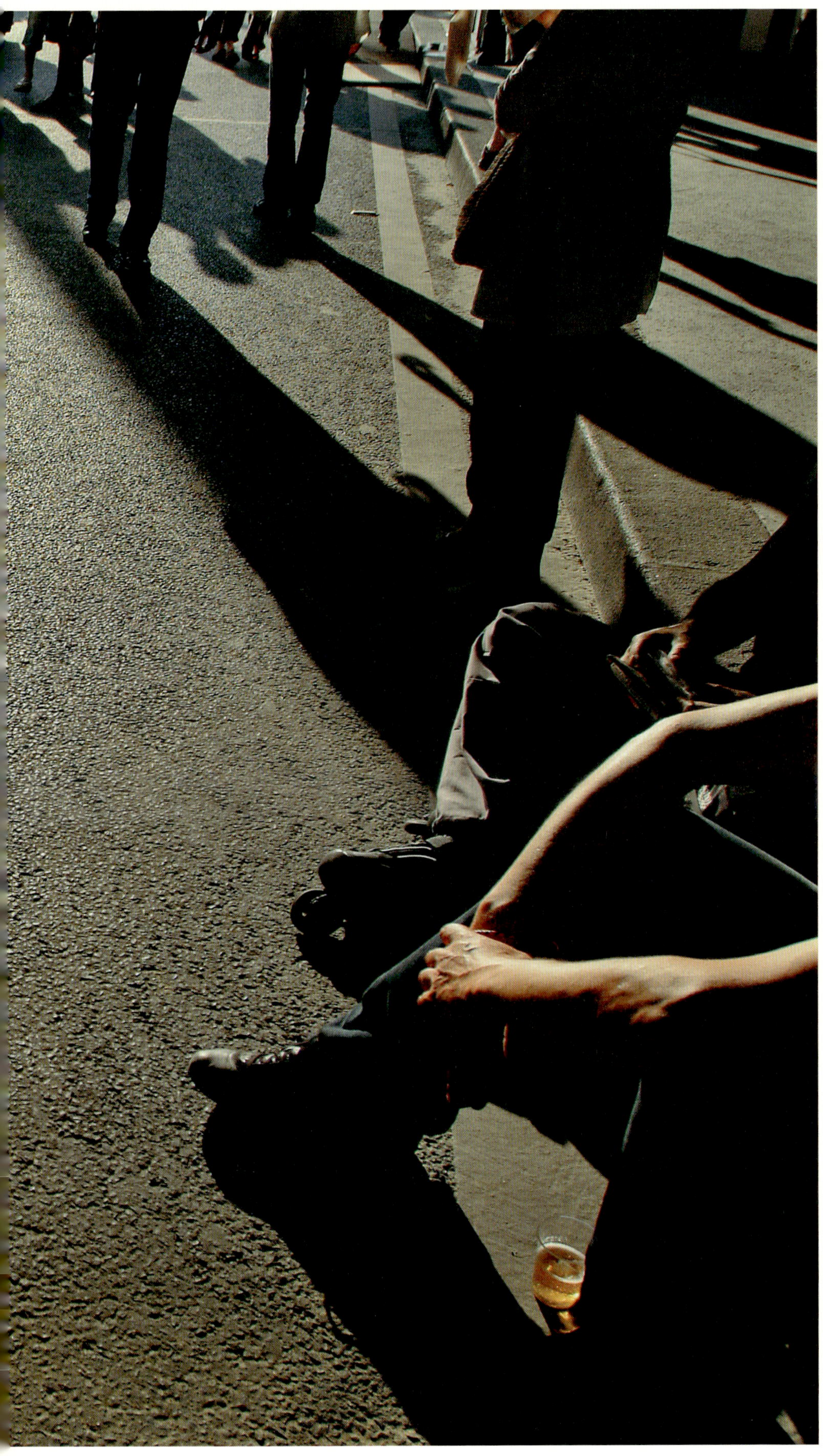

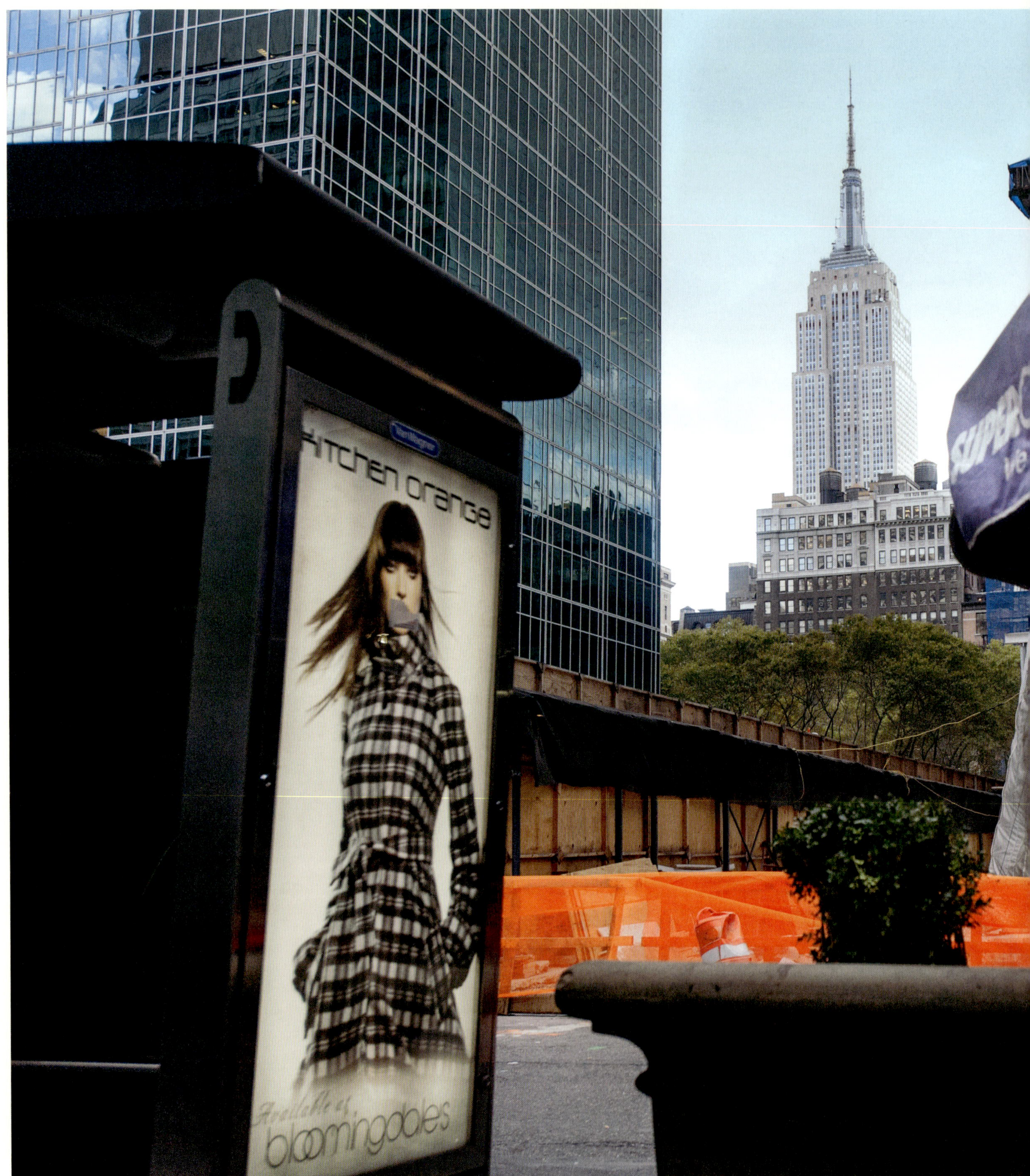

kitchen orange
Available at
bloomingdales

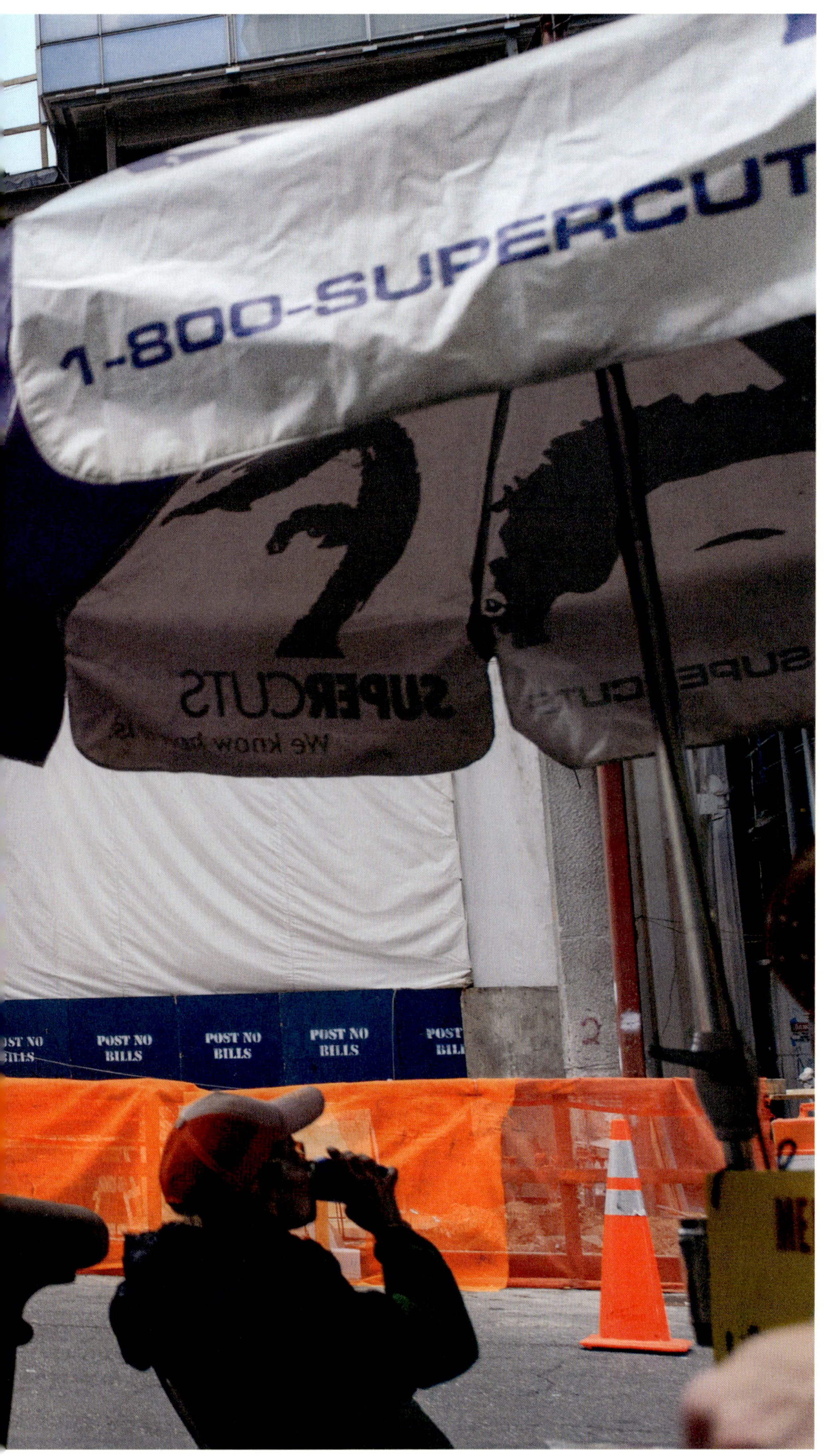

1-800-SUPERCUT
SUPERCUTS
We know how to...
SUPERCUTS
POST NO BILLS
POST NO BILLS
POST NO BILLS
POST NO BILLS
POST NO BILLS

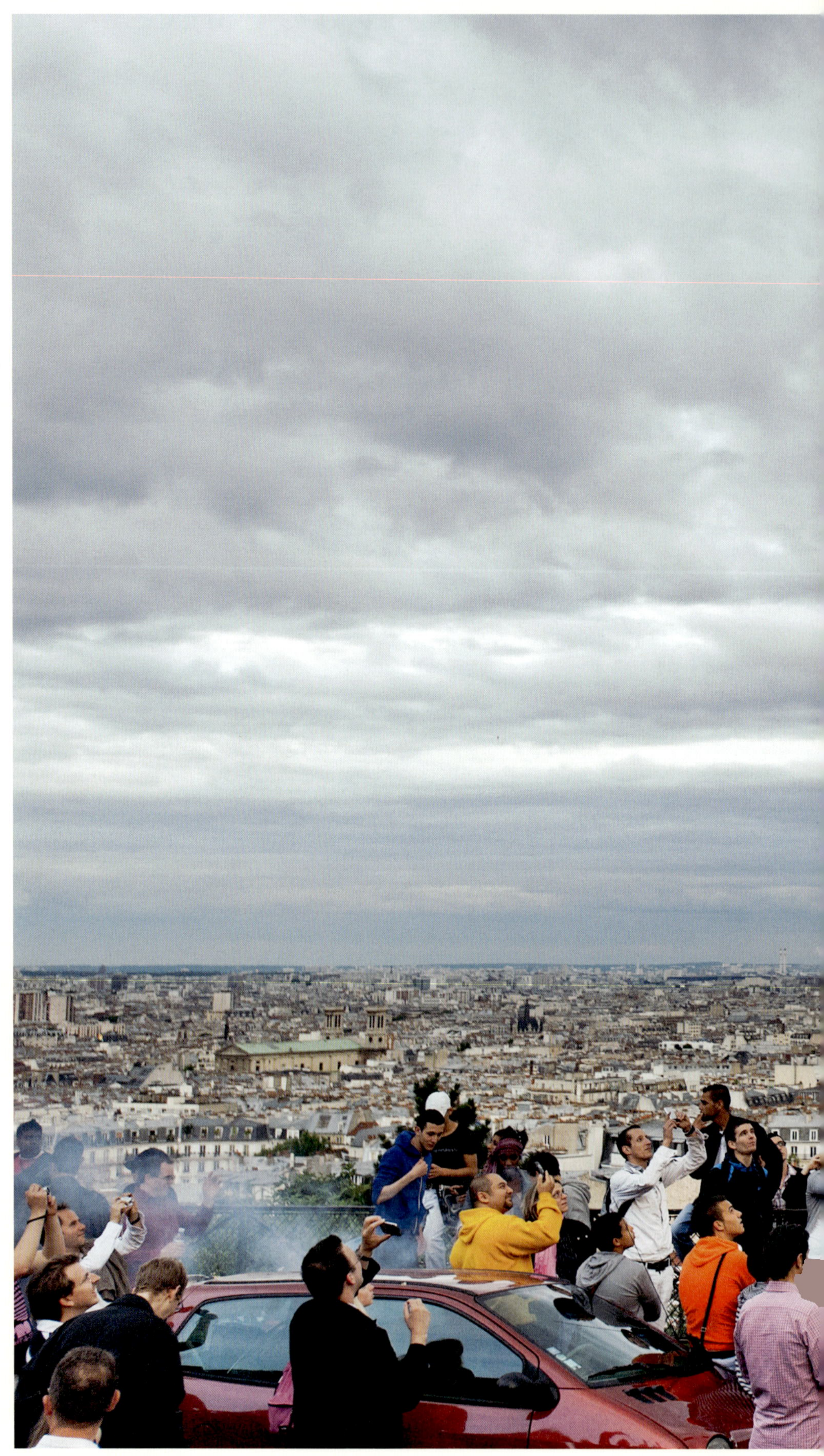

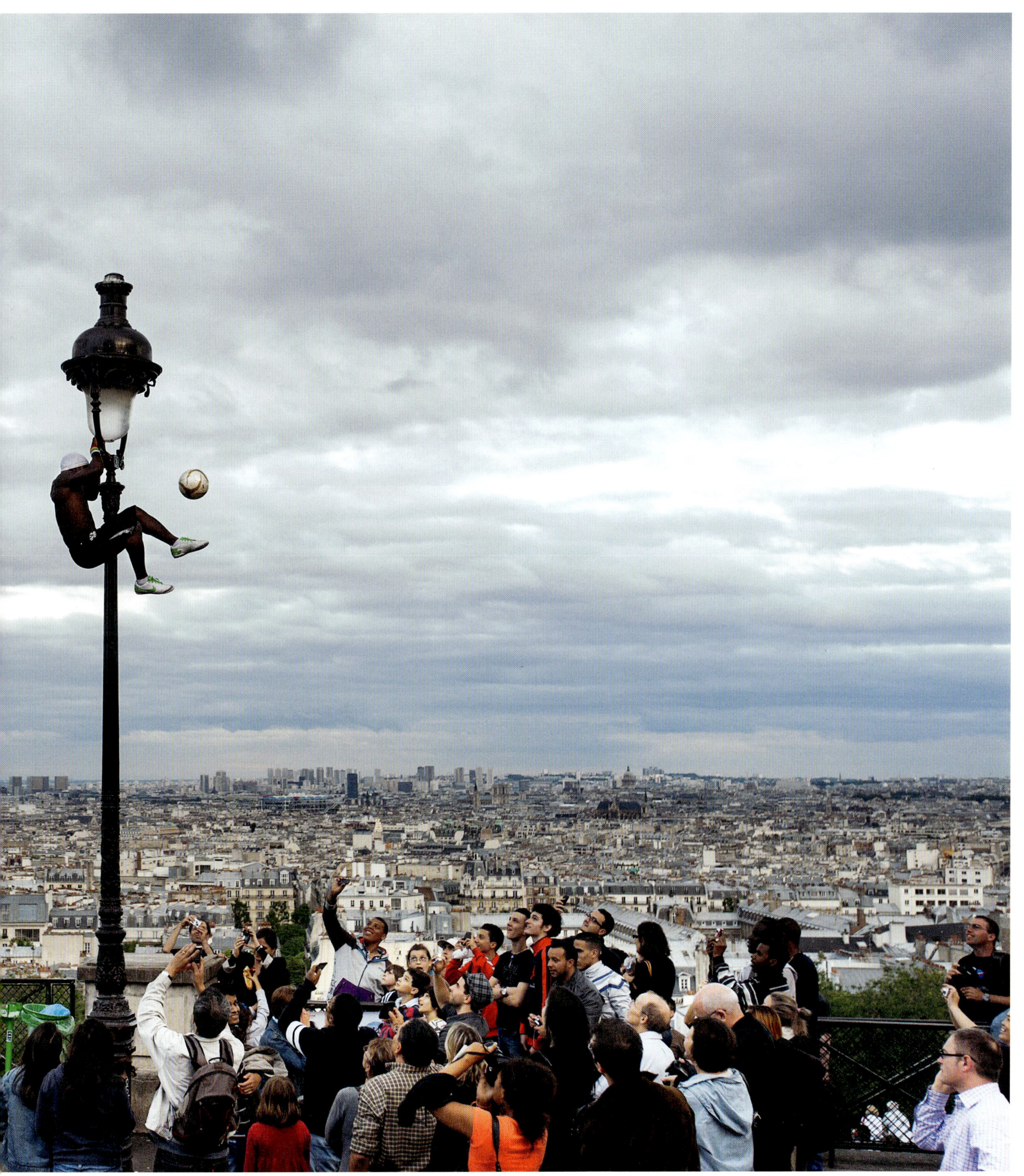

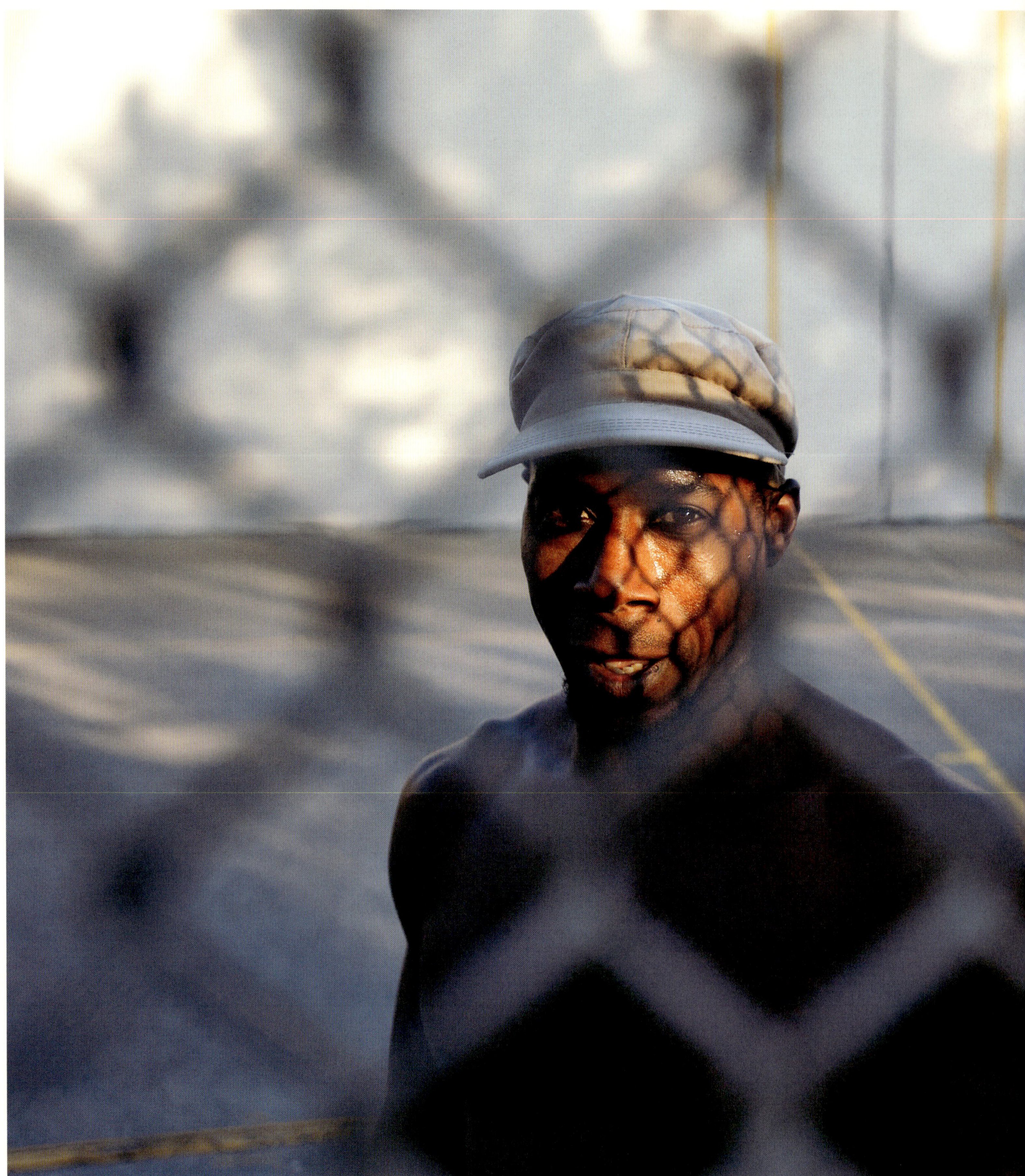

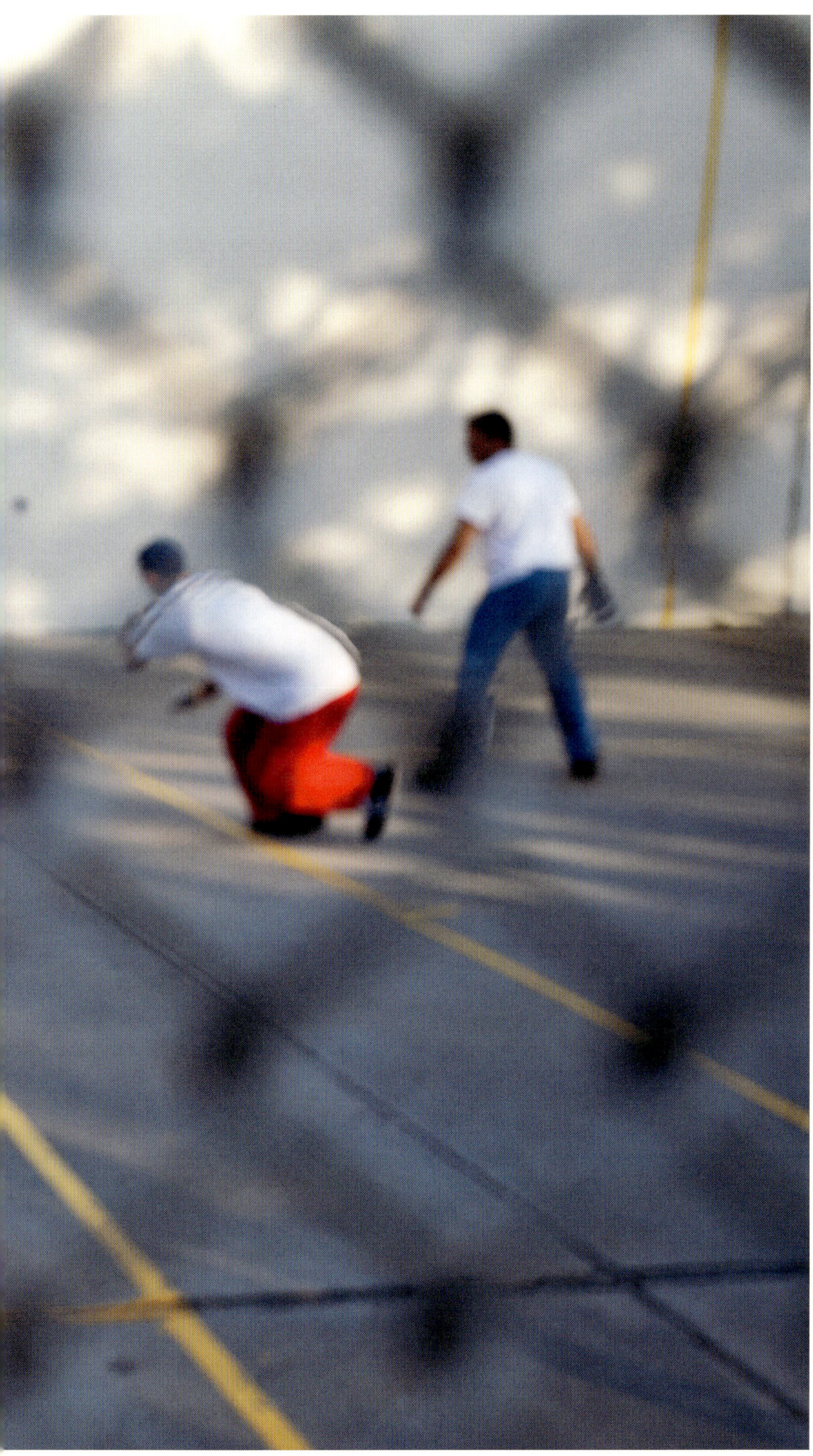

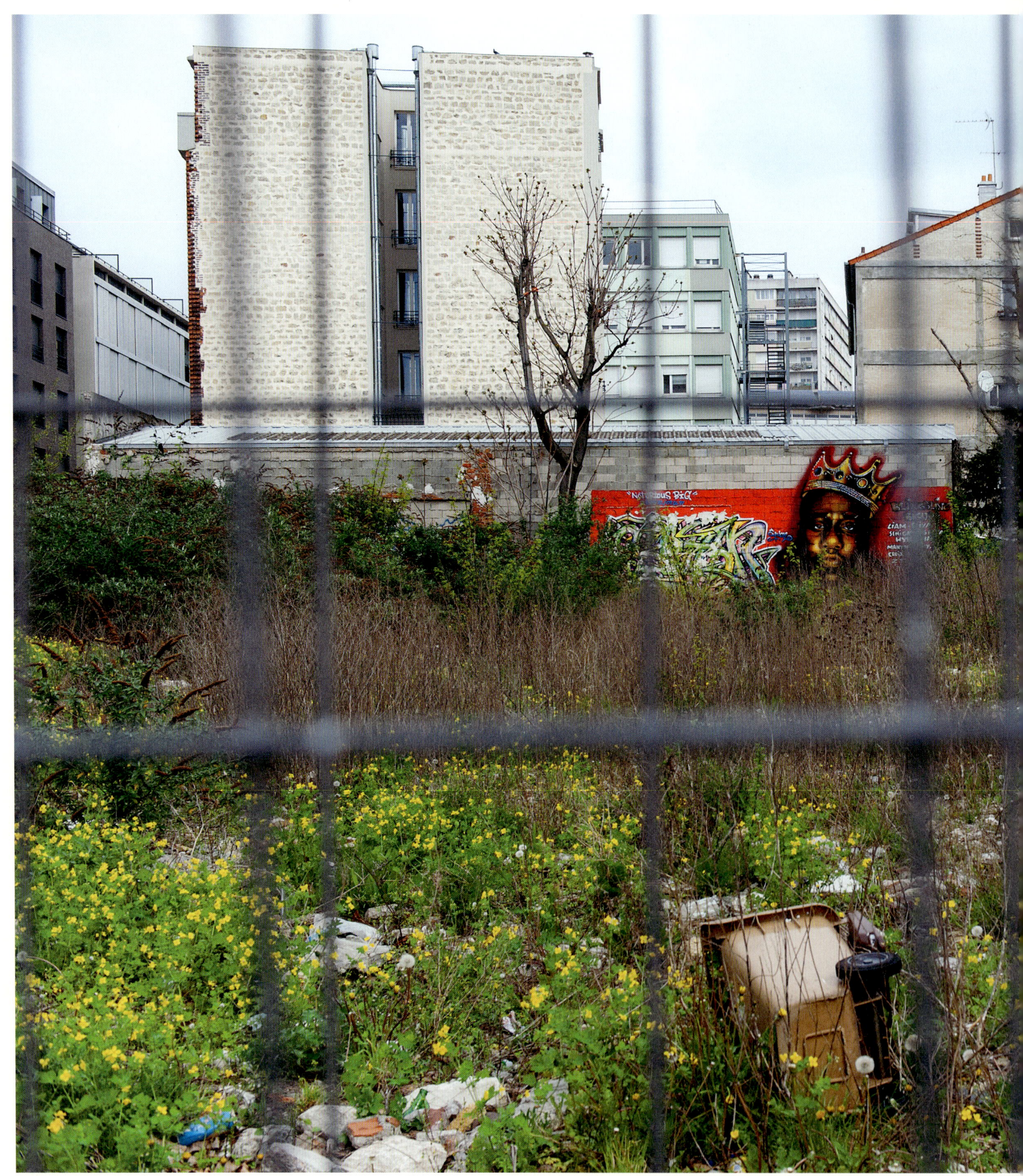

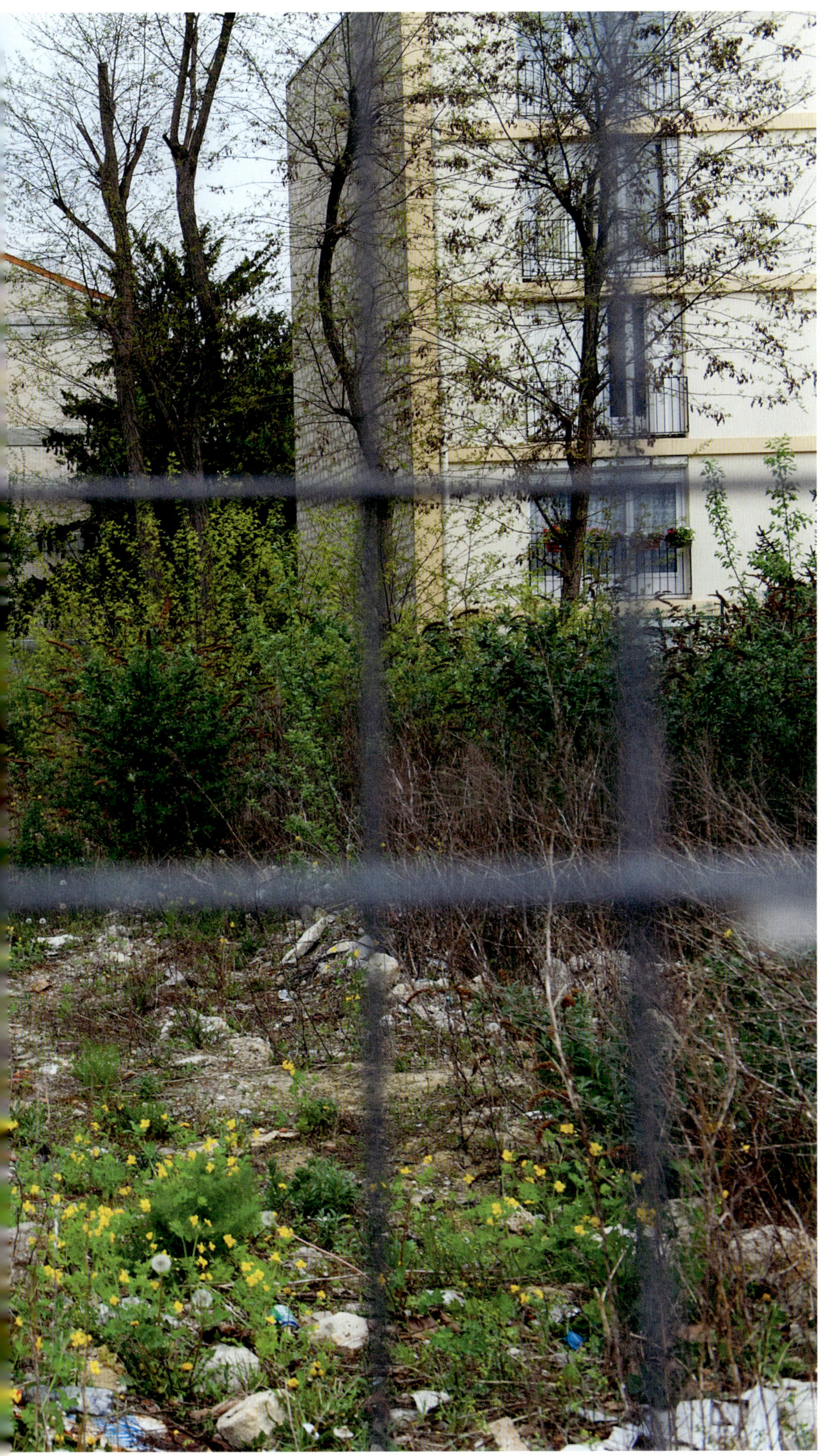

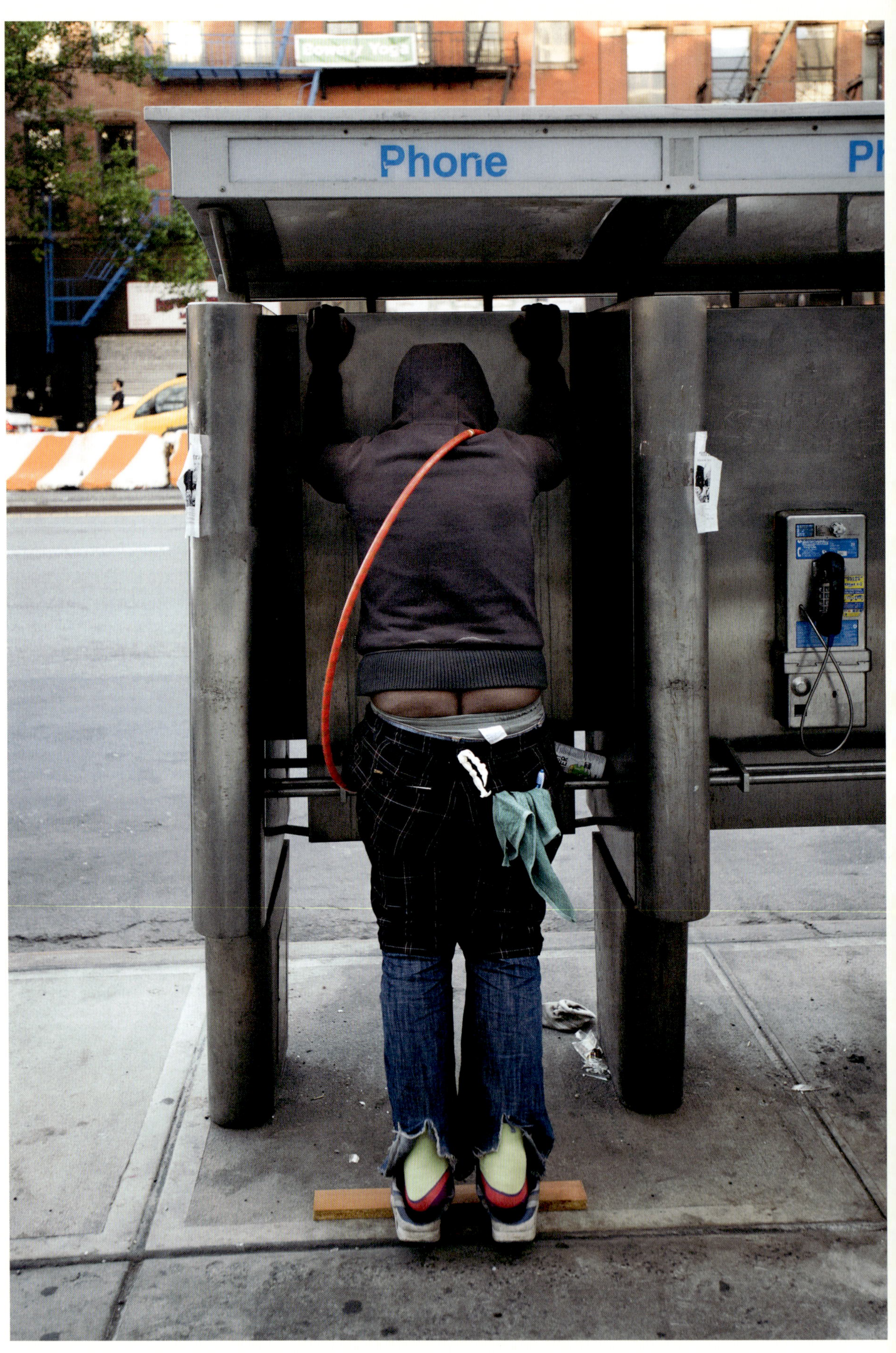
Phone
Ph

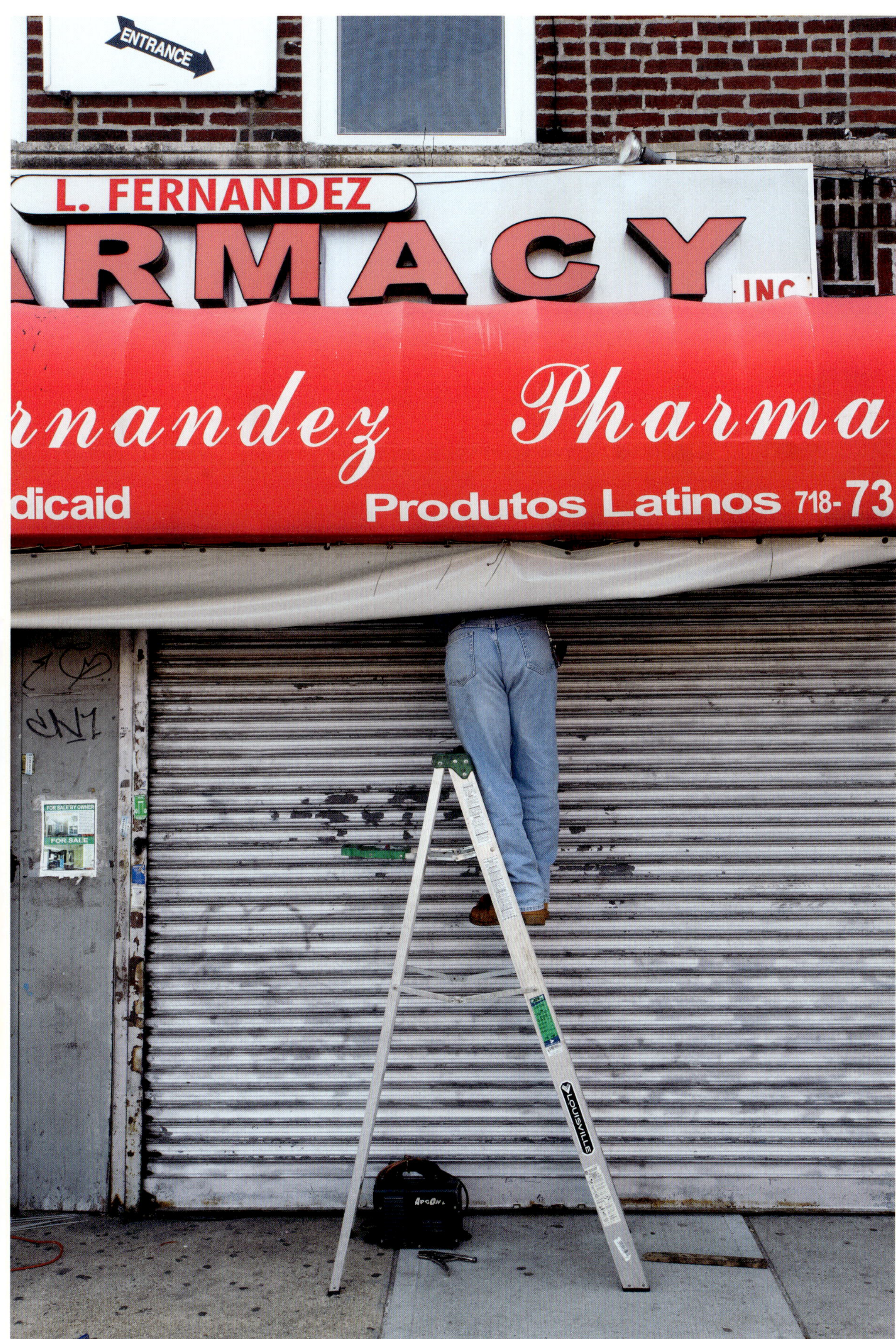

ENTRANCE
L. FERNANDEZ
RMACY
INC
rnandez Pharma
dicaid   Produtos Latinos 718-73
FOR SALE BY OWNER
FOR SALE
LOUISVILLE

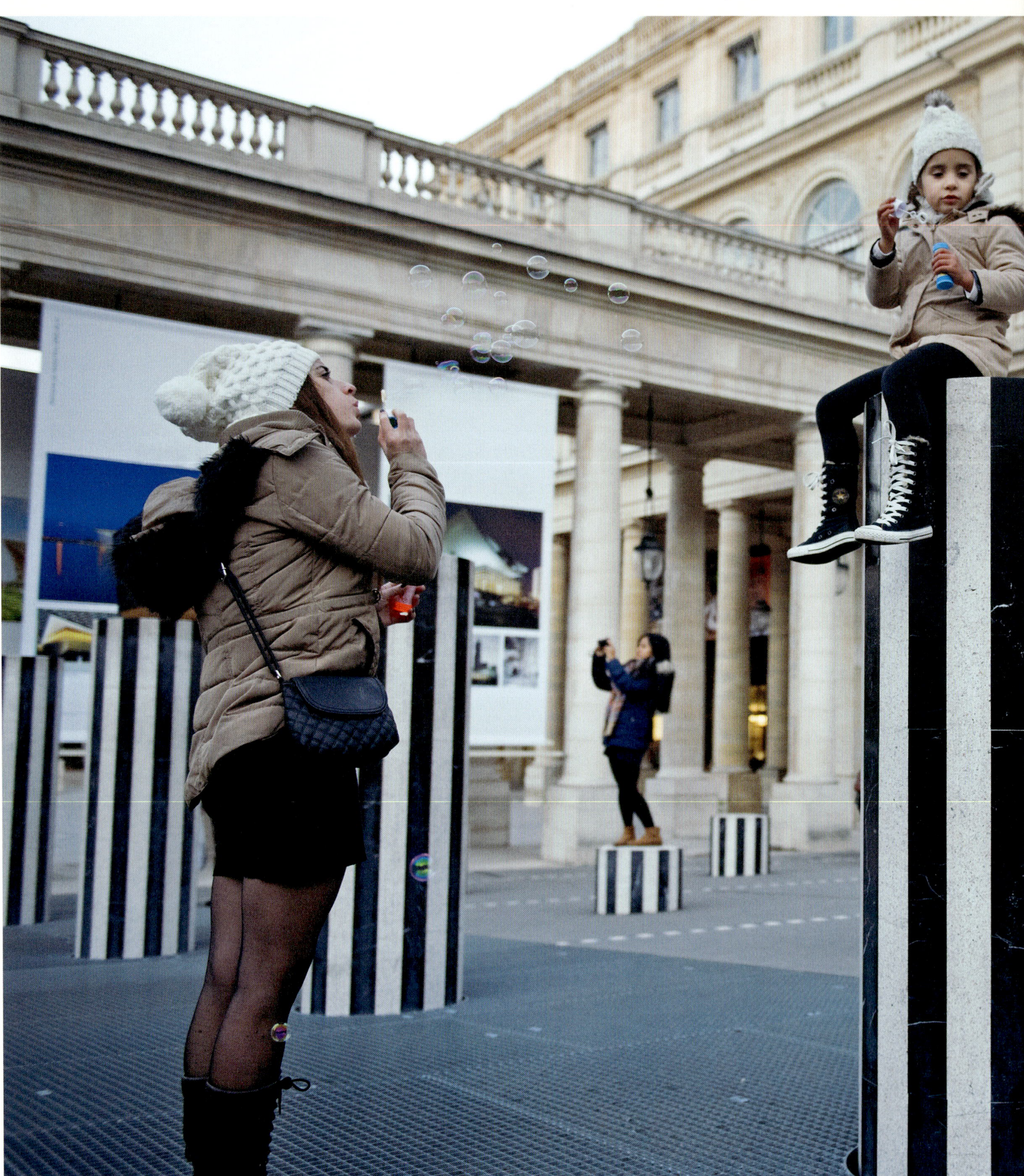

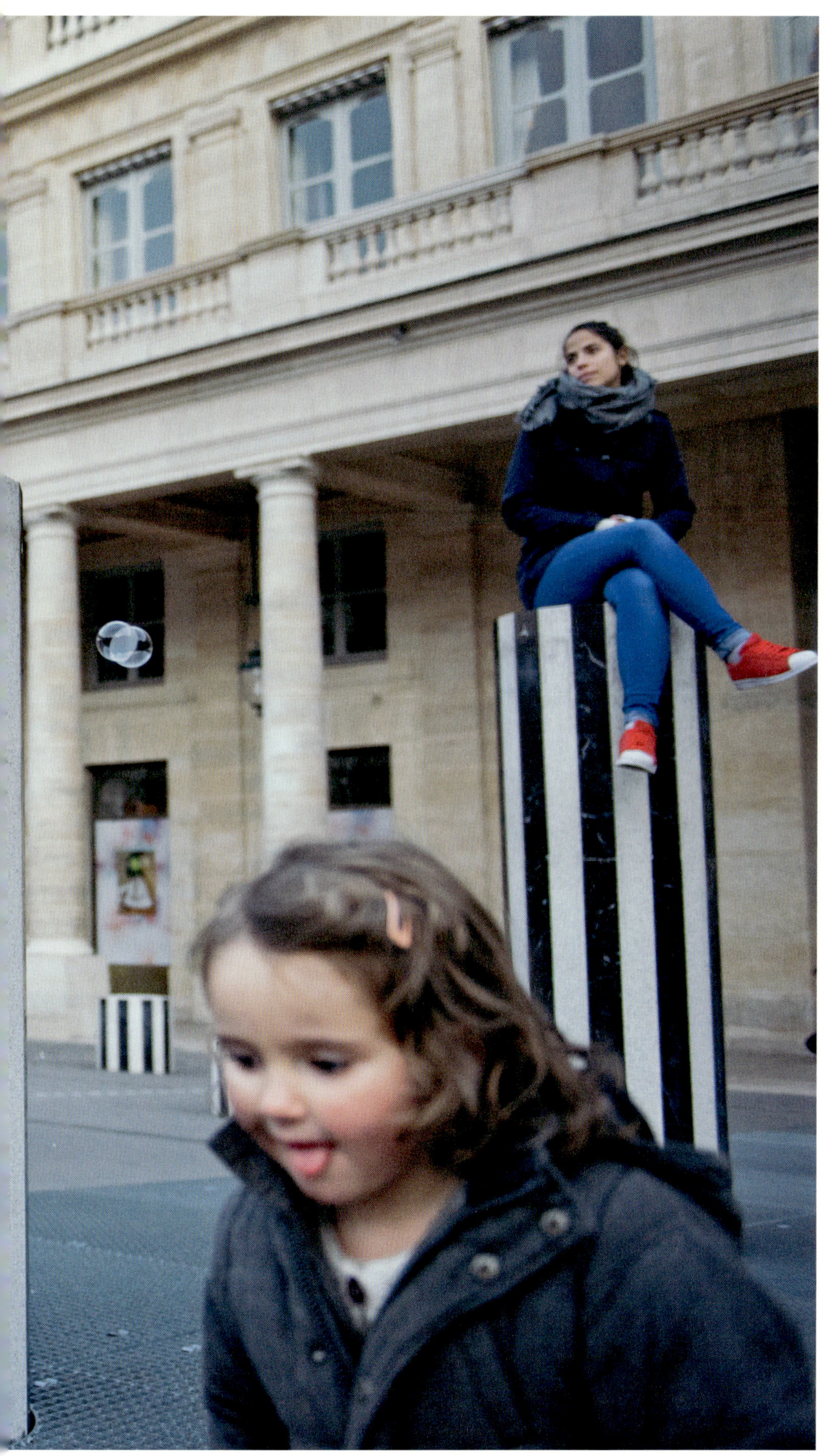

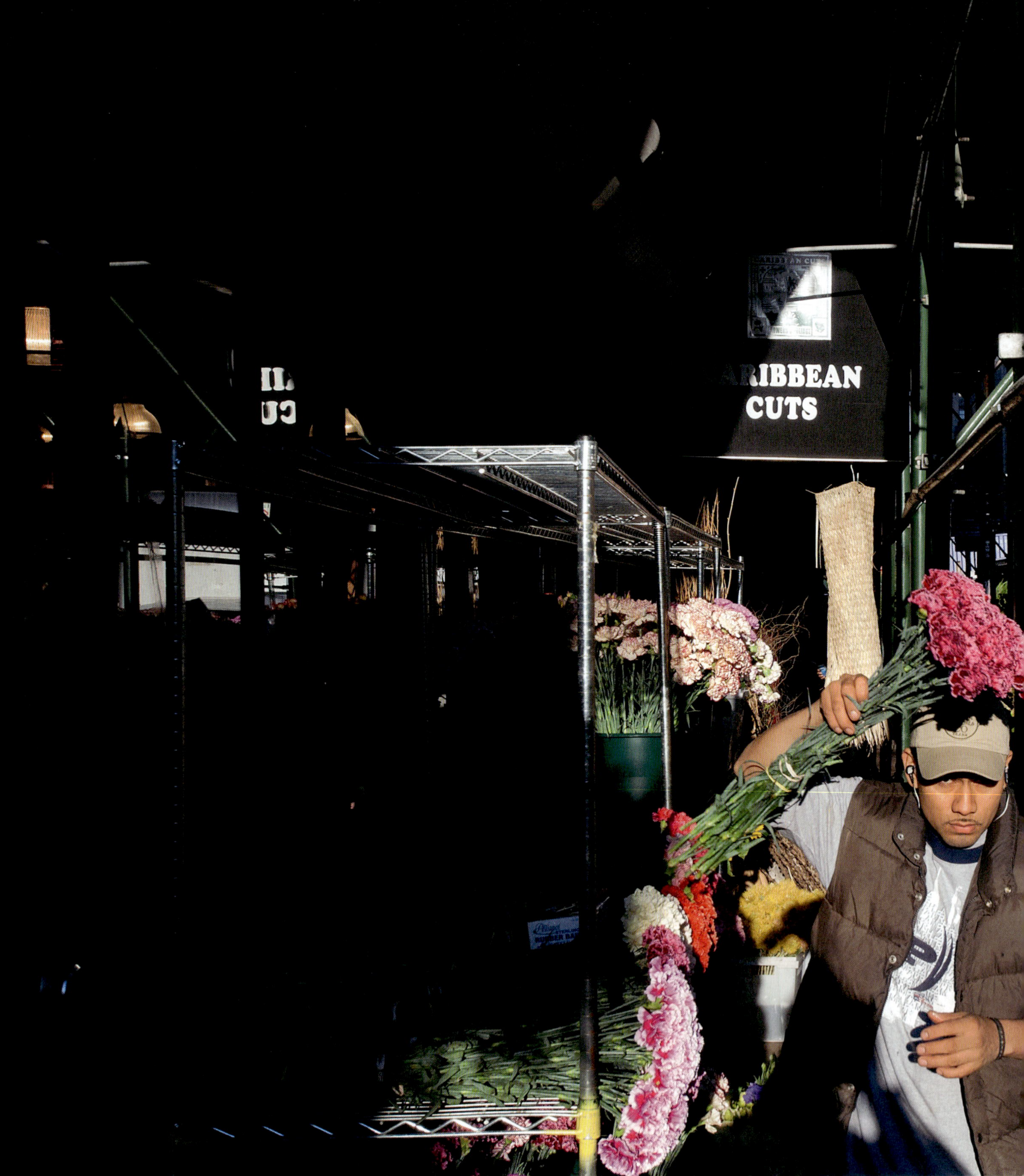

ARIBBEAN
CUTS

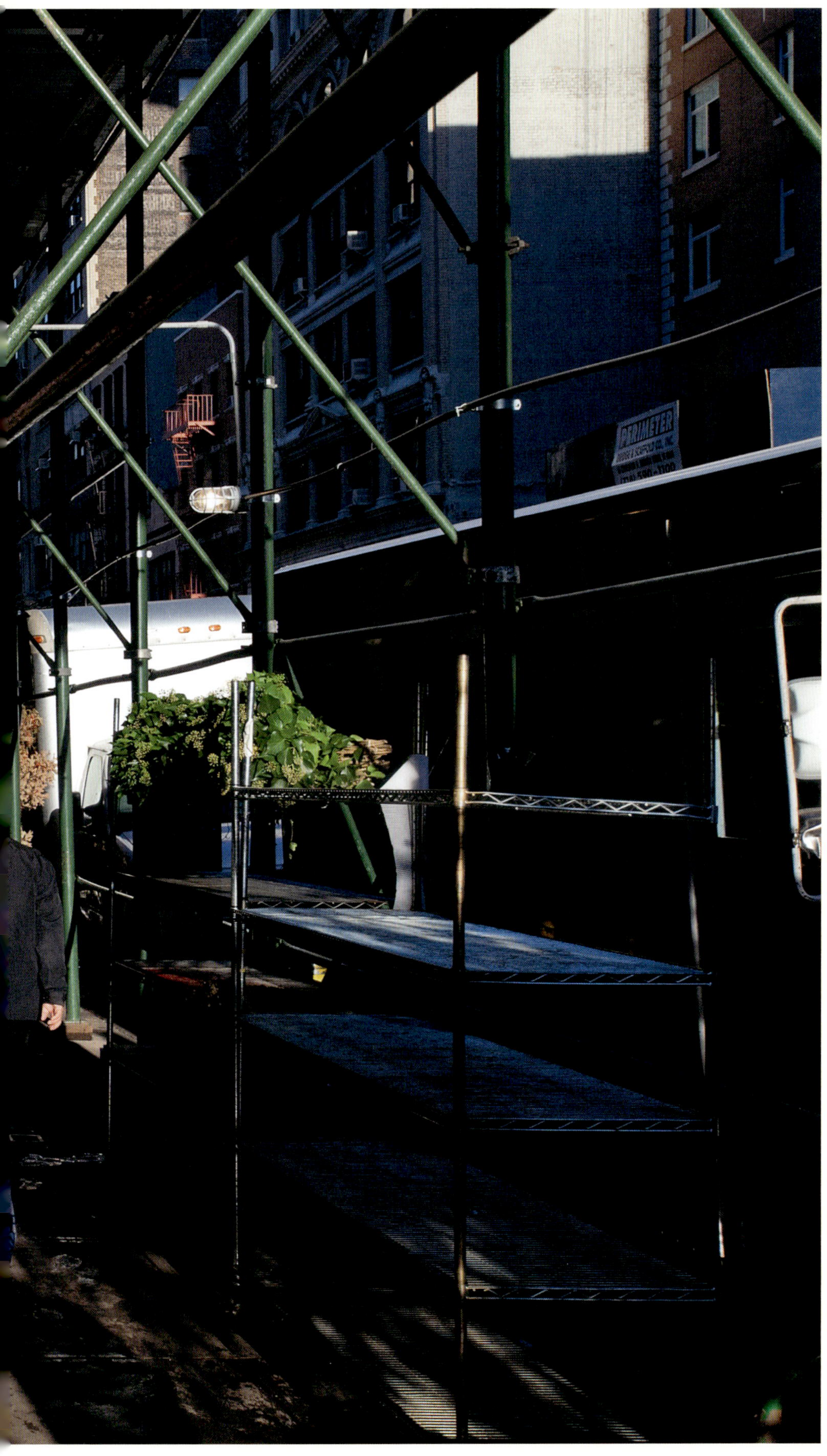

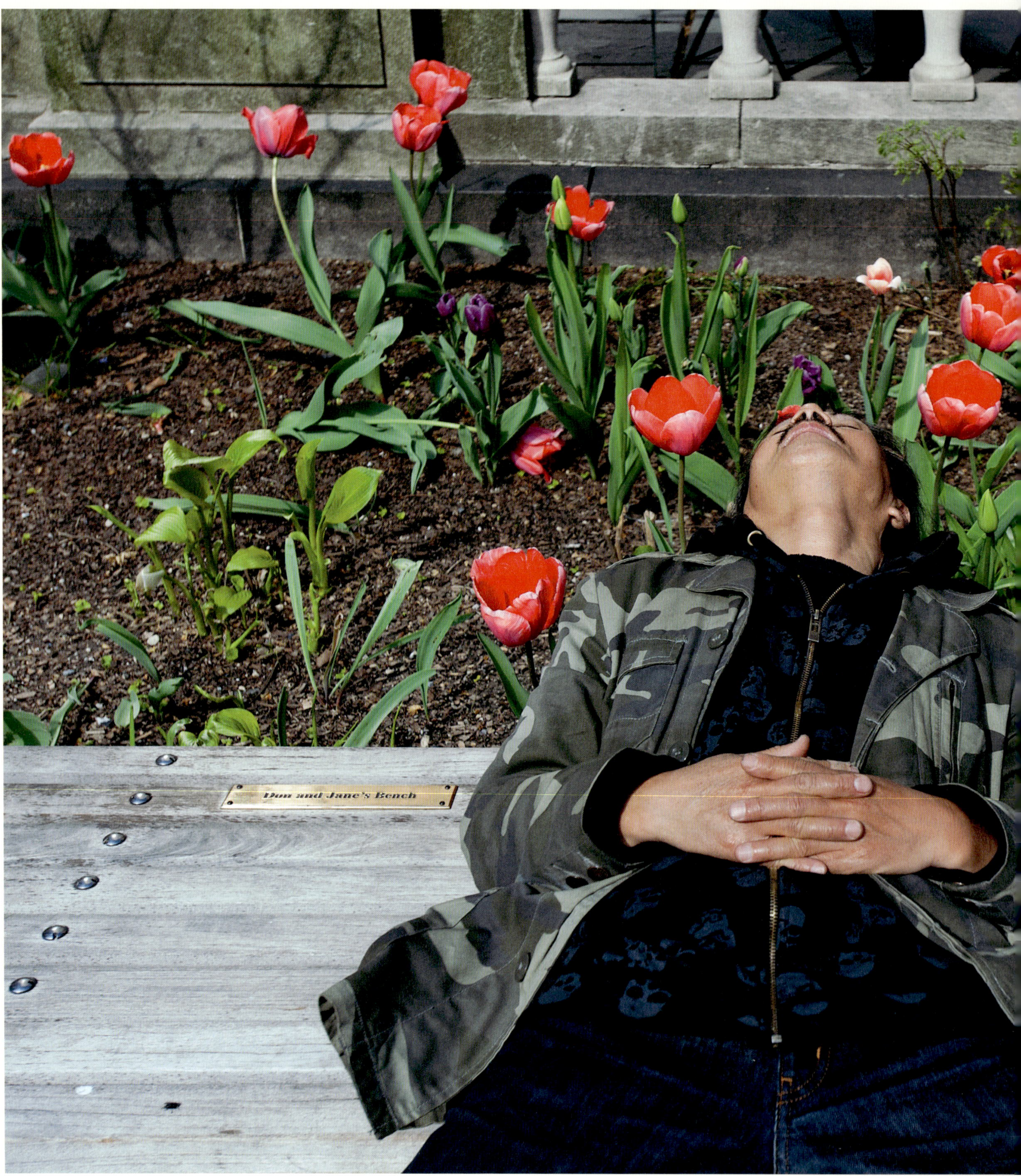
Don and Jane's Bench

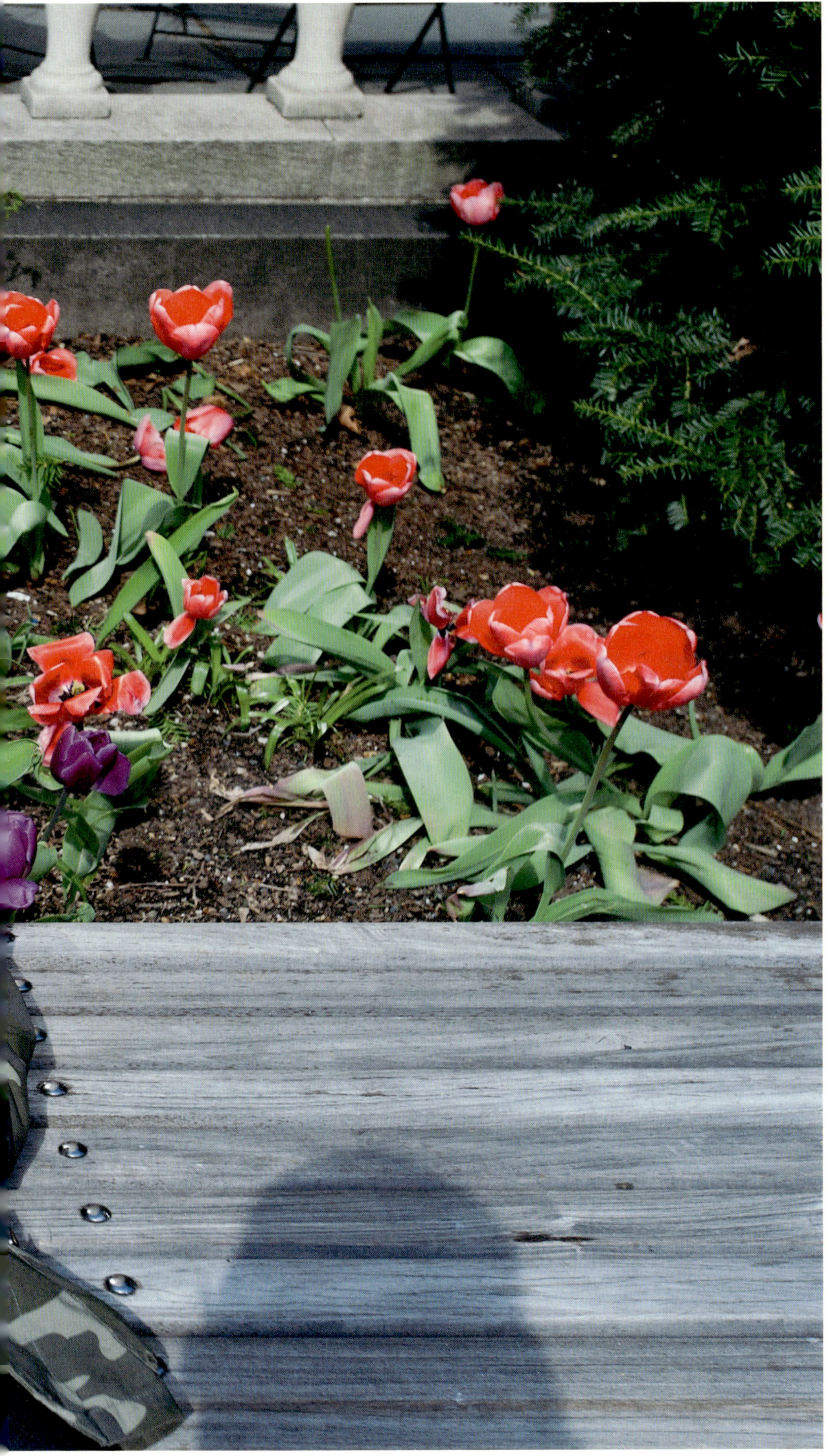

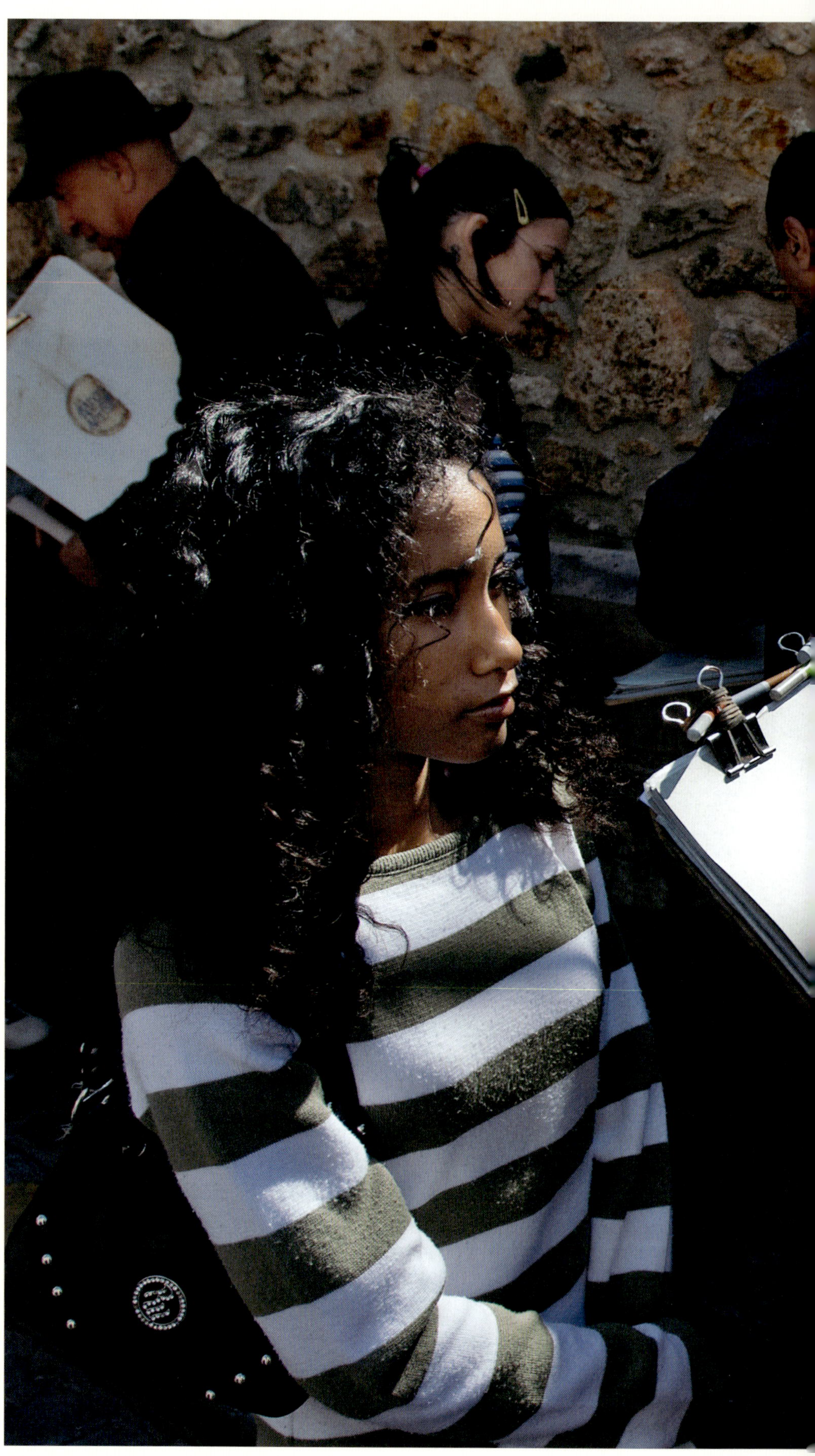

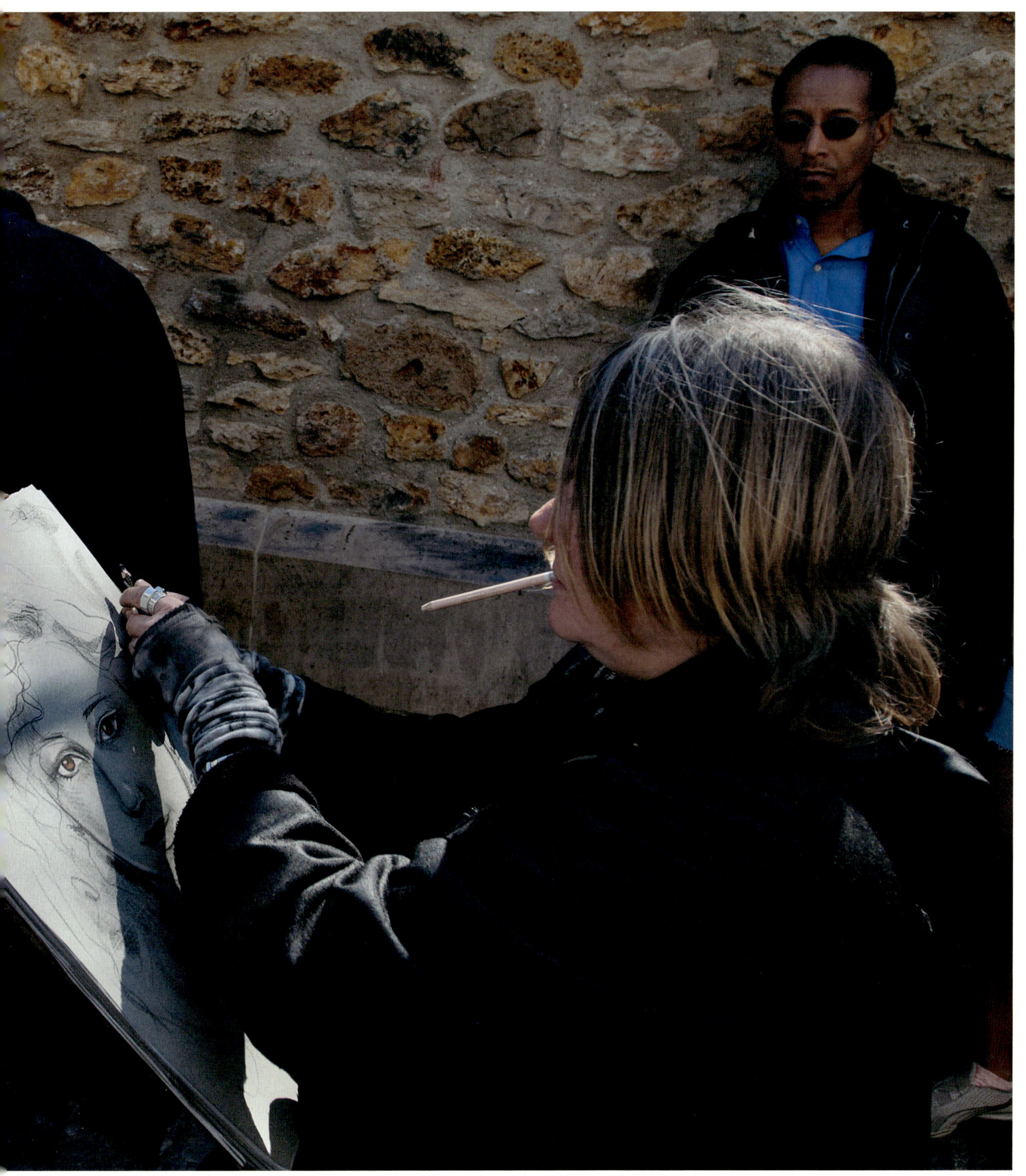

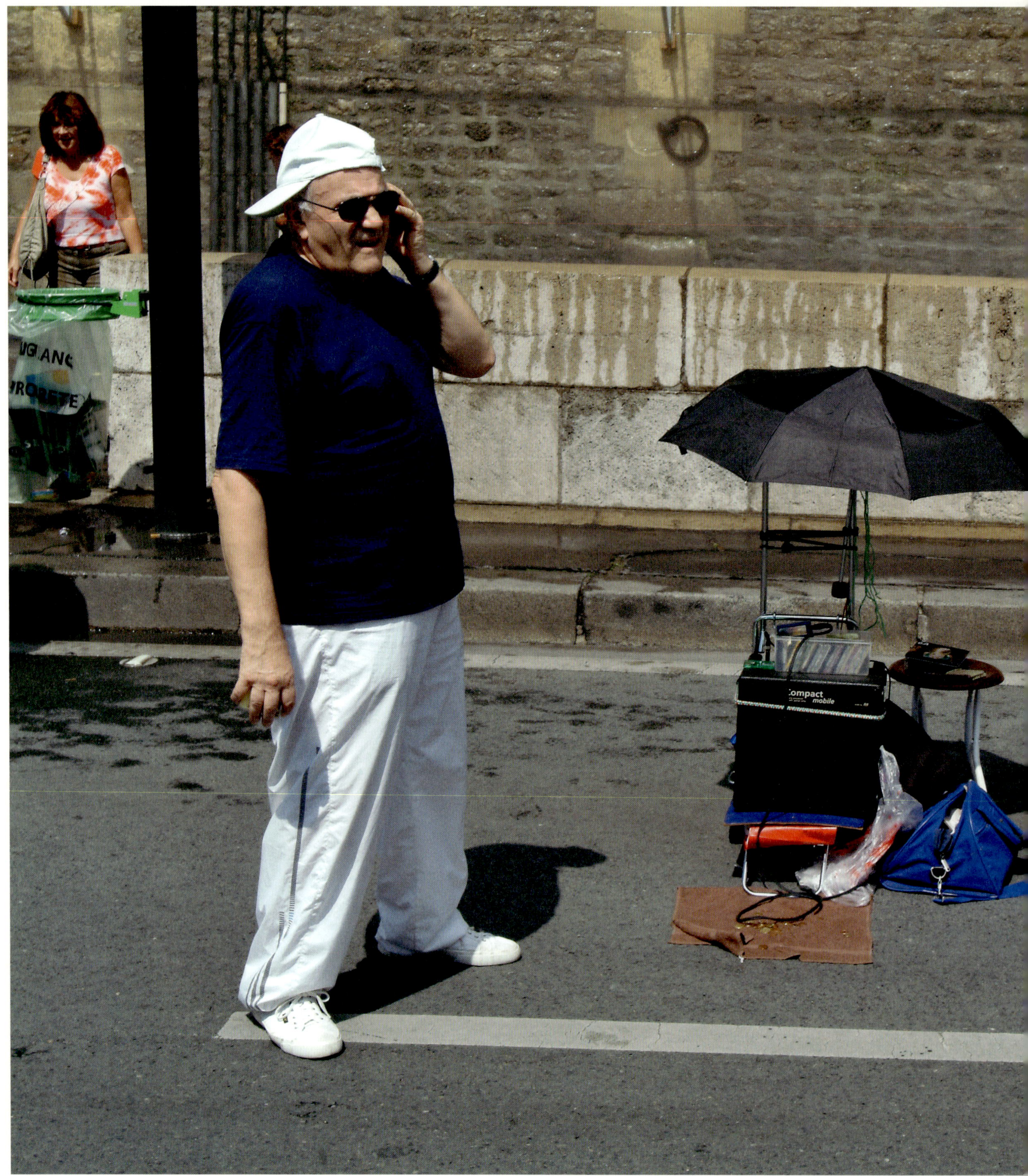

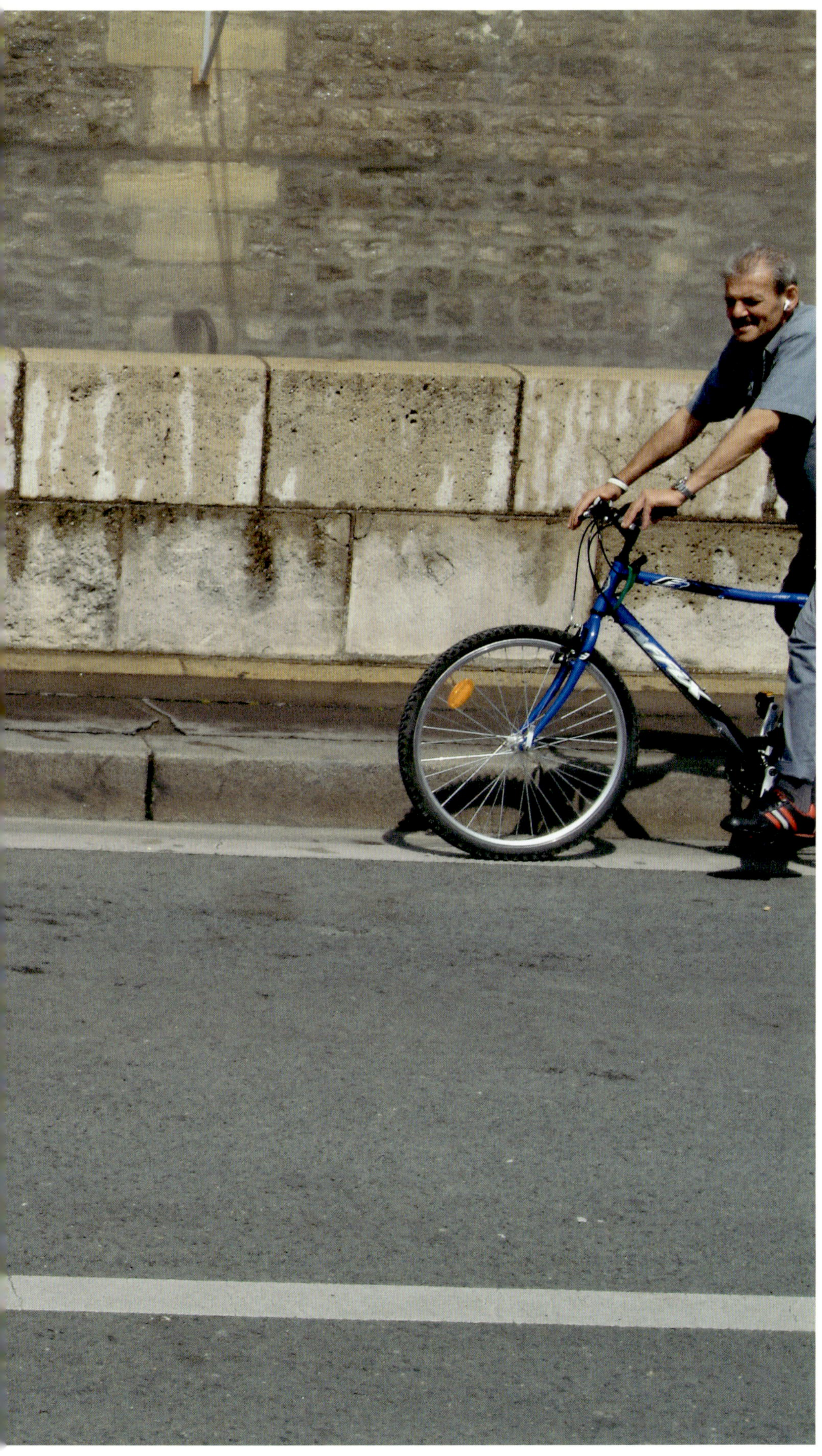

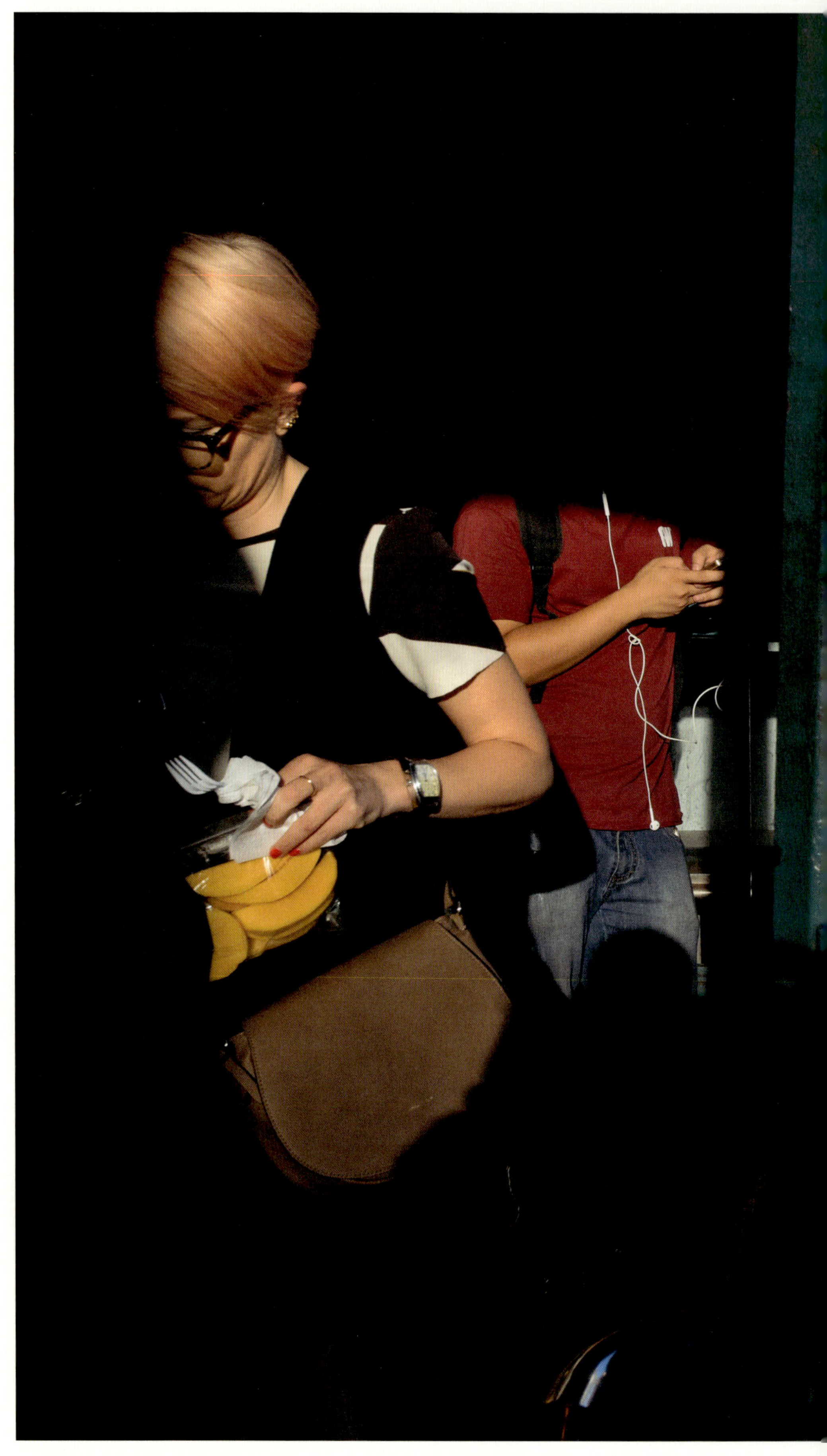

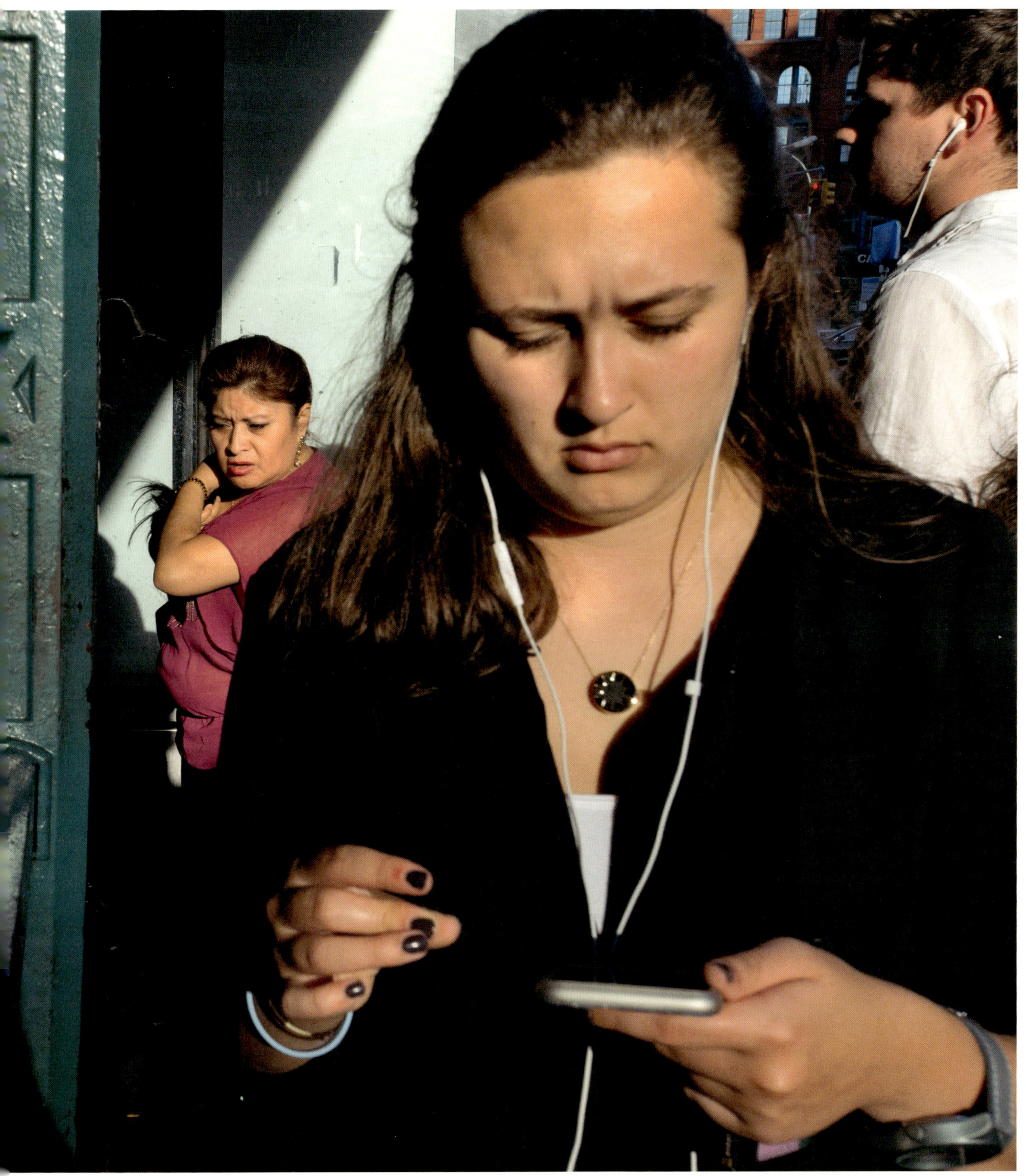

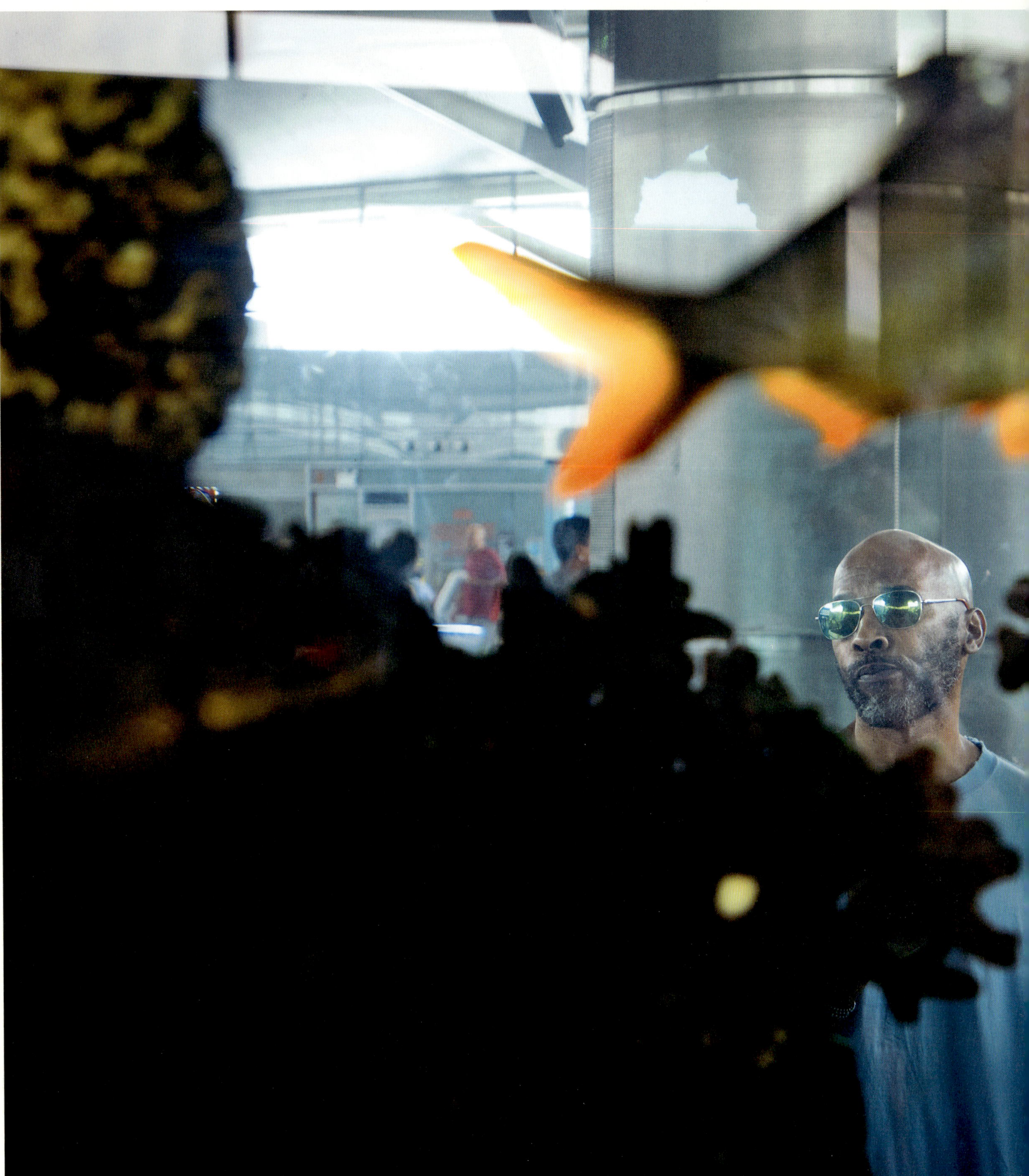

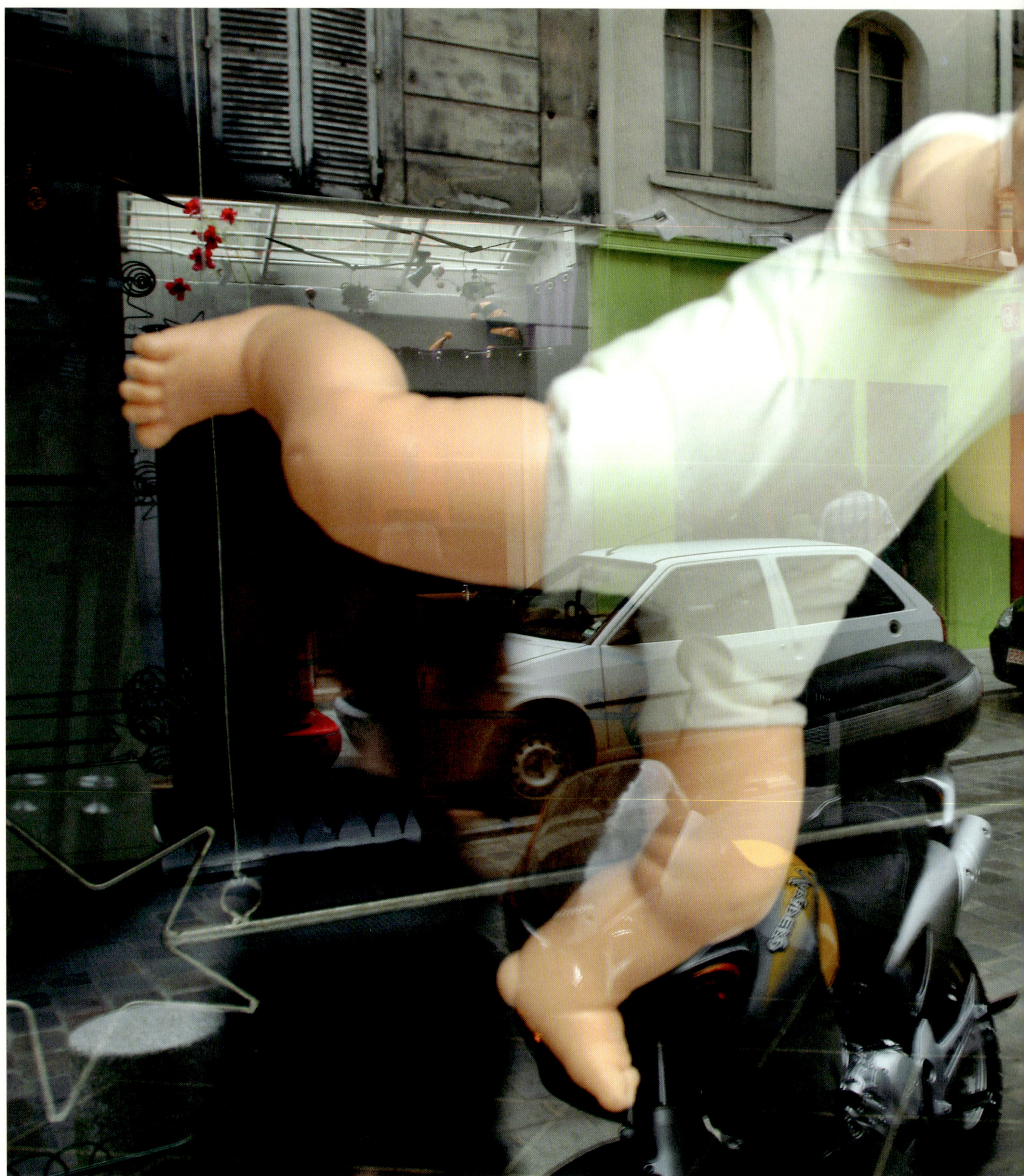

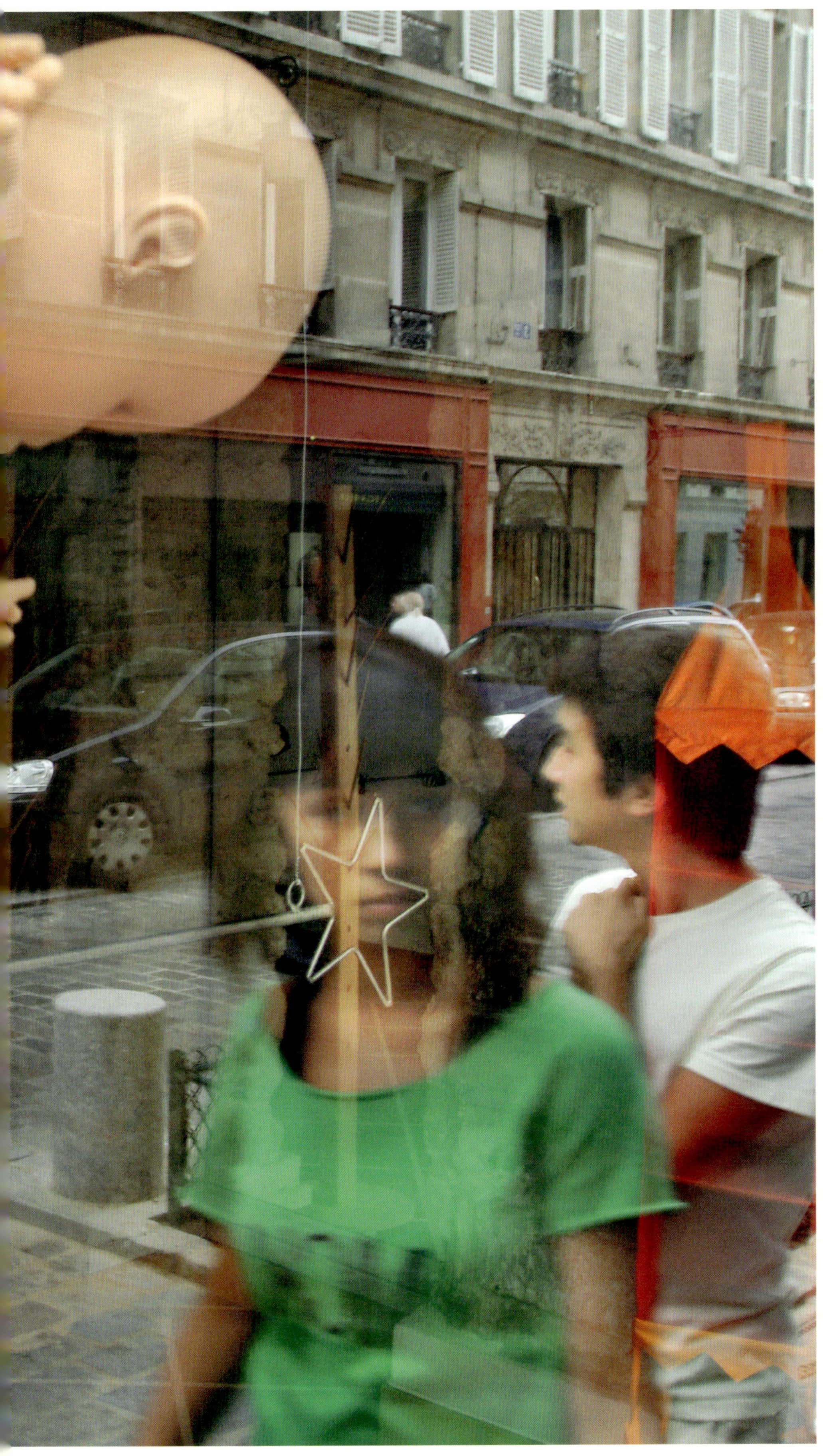

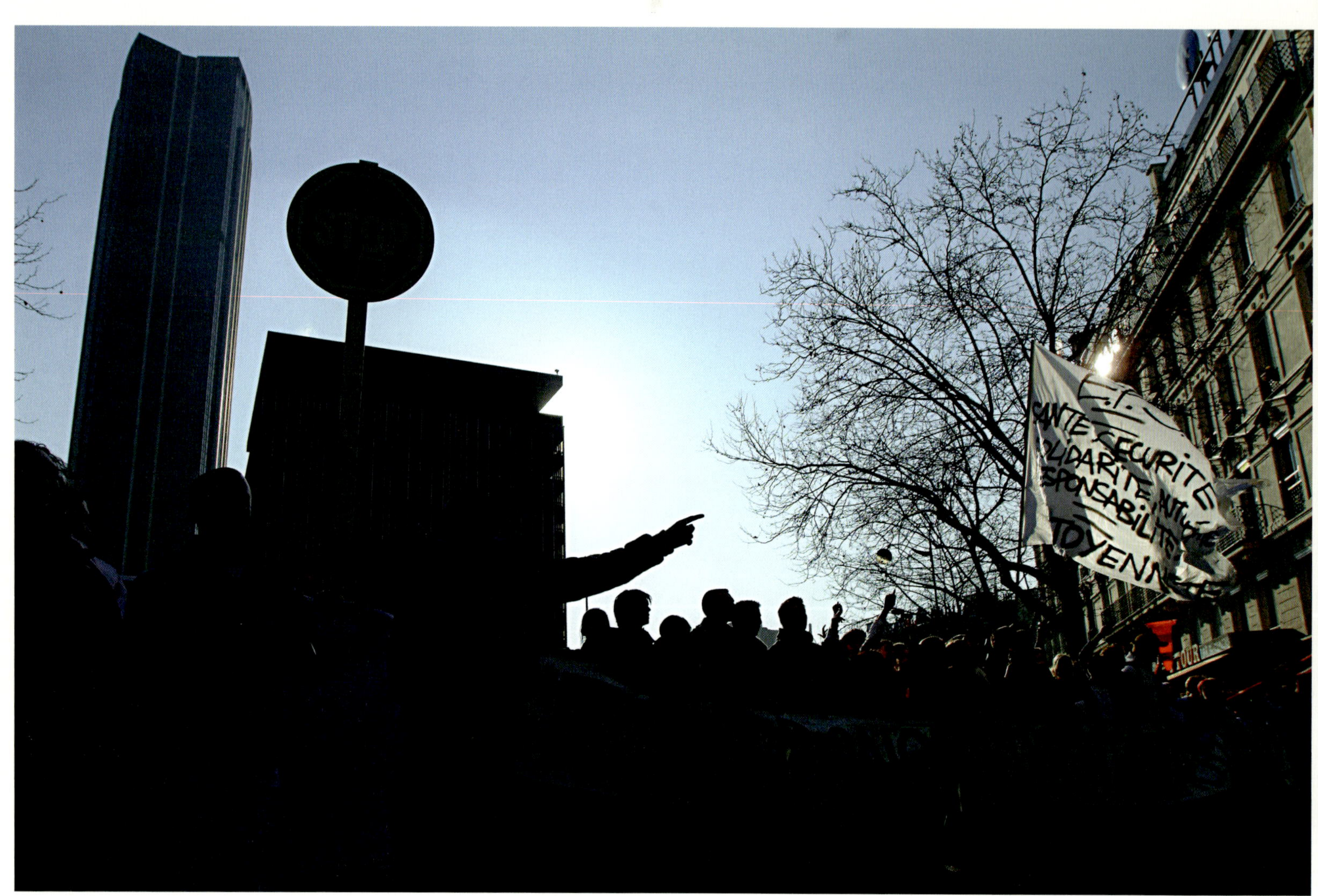
SANTE SECURITE
SOLIDARITE
RESPONSABILITE
CITOYENN

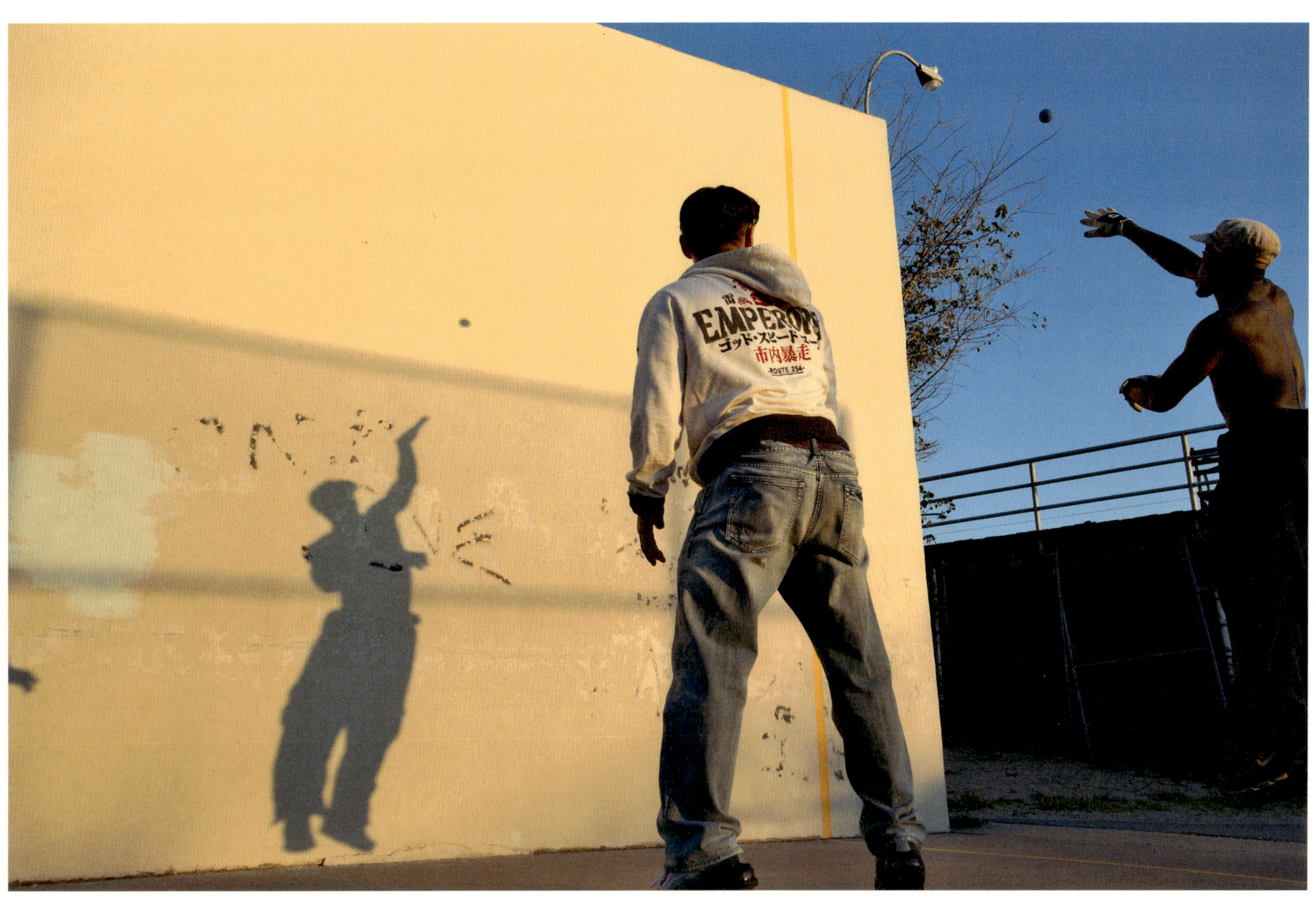

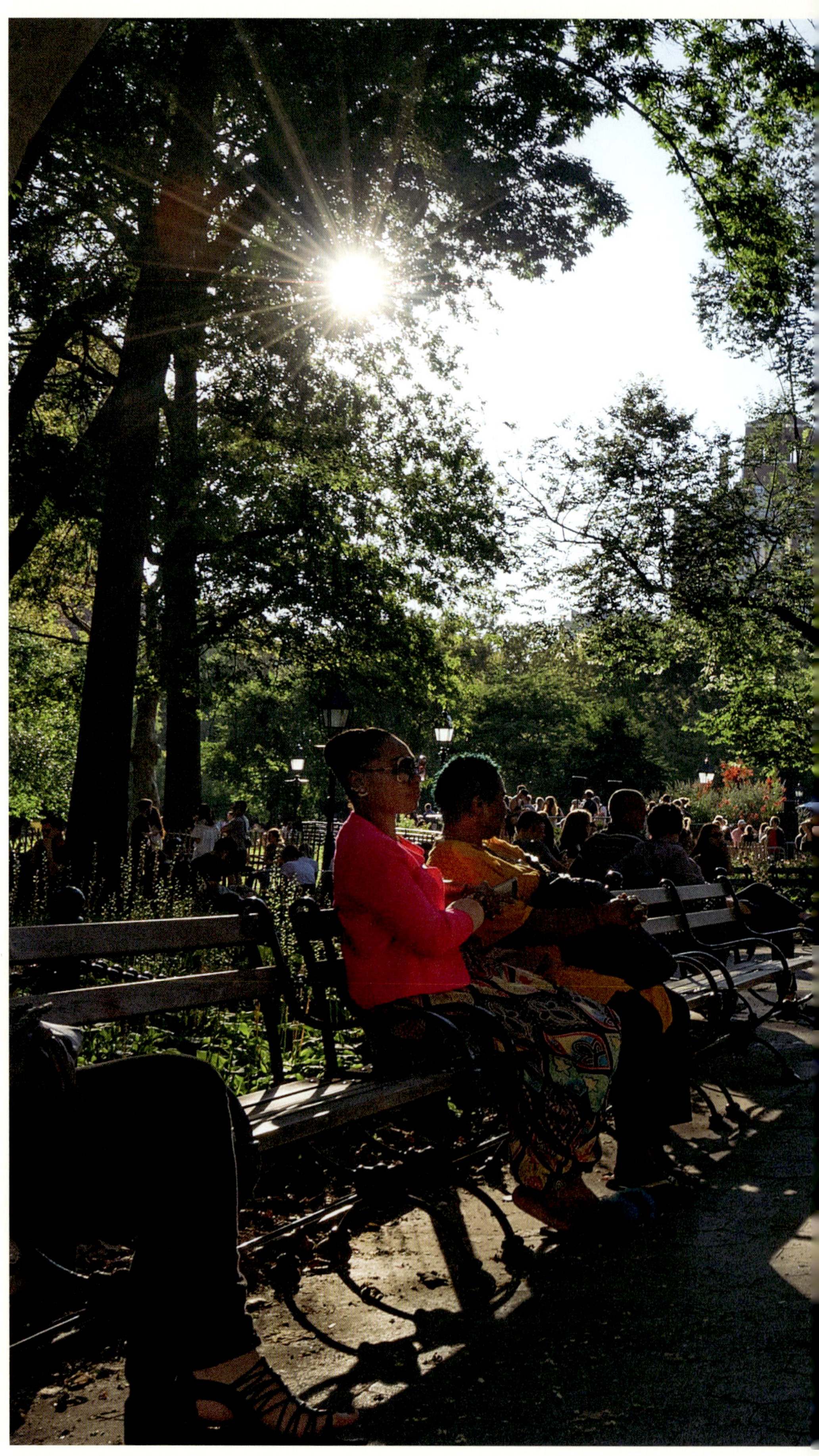

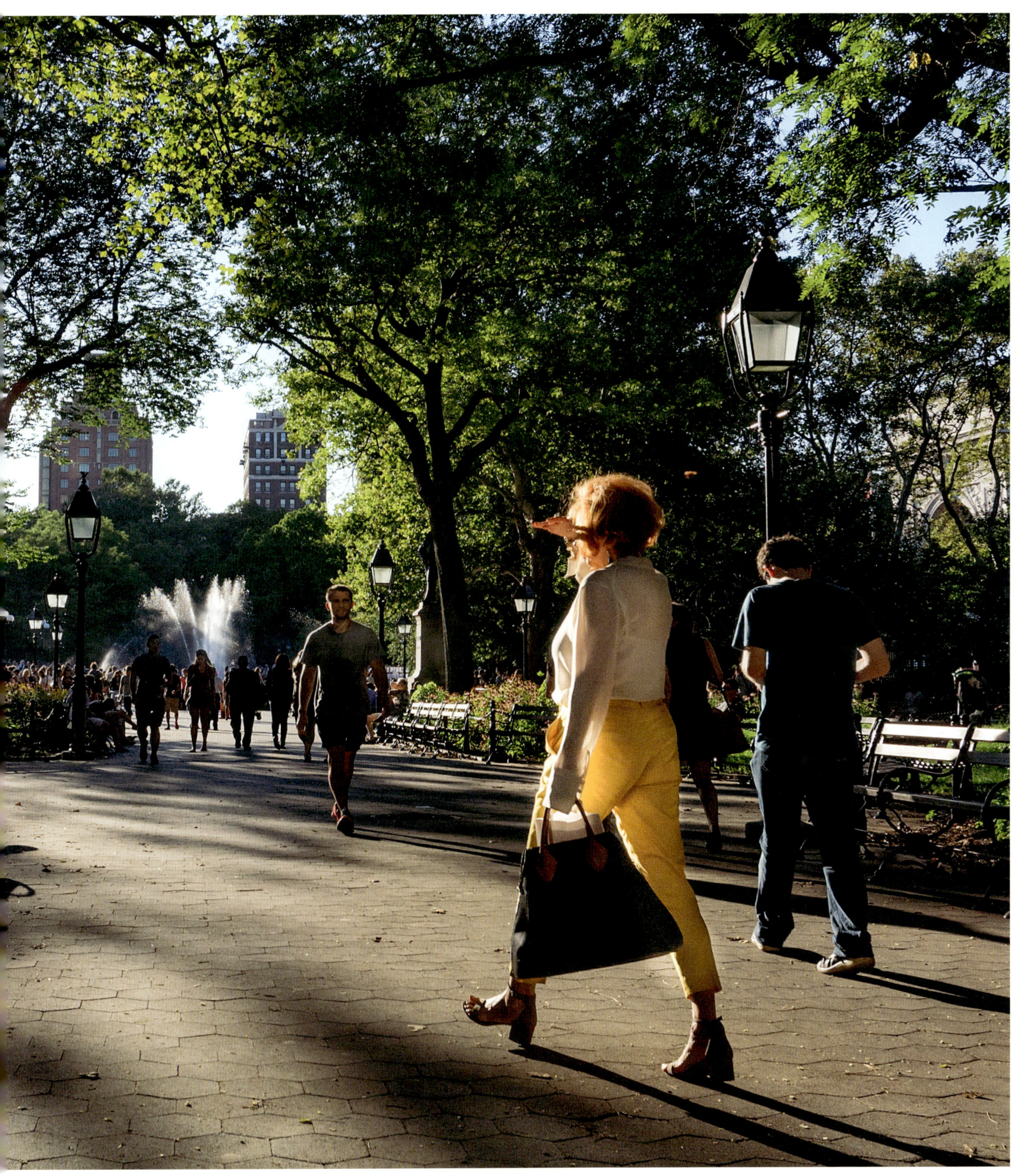

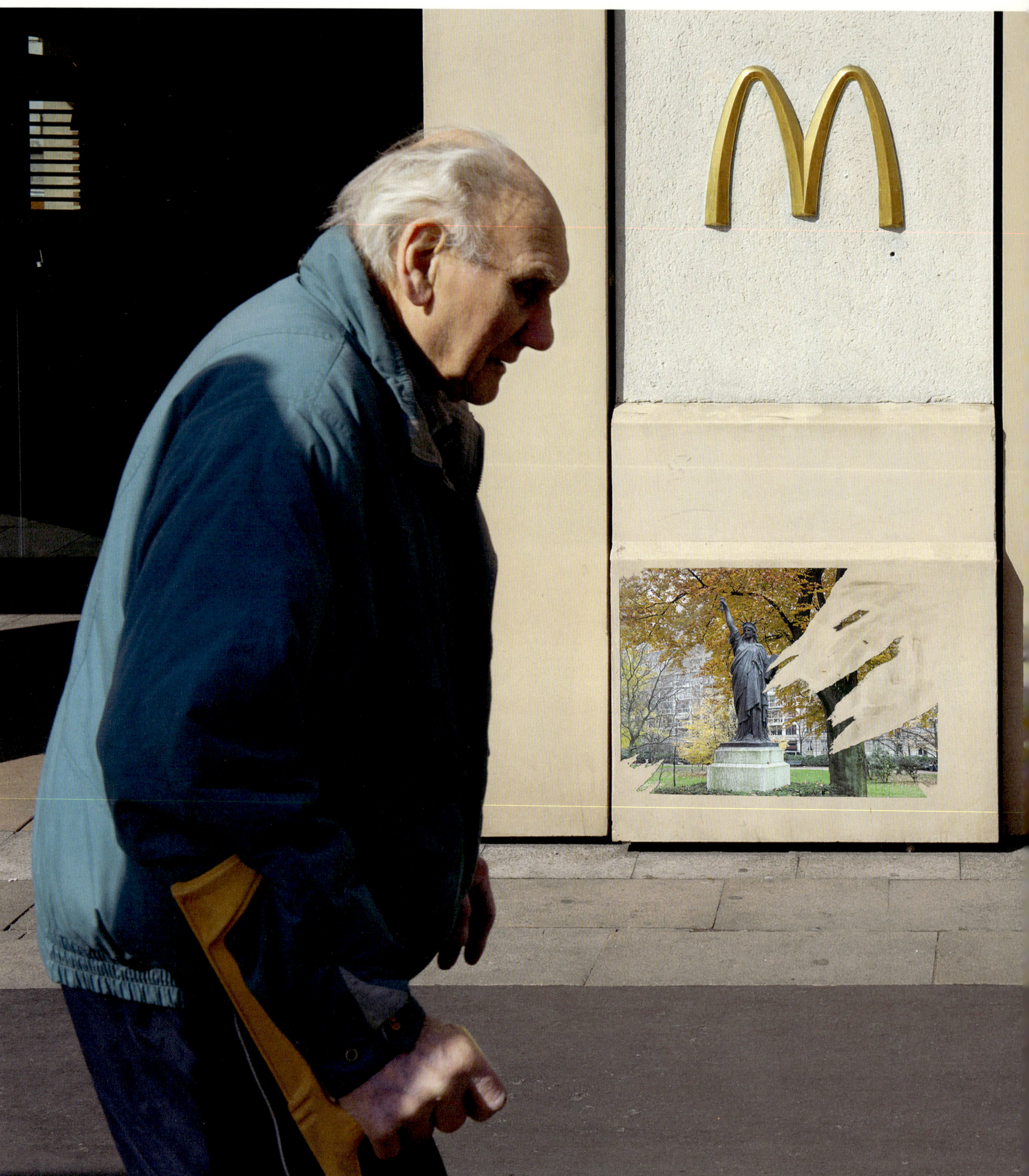

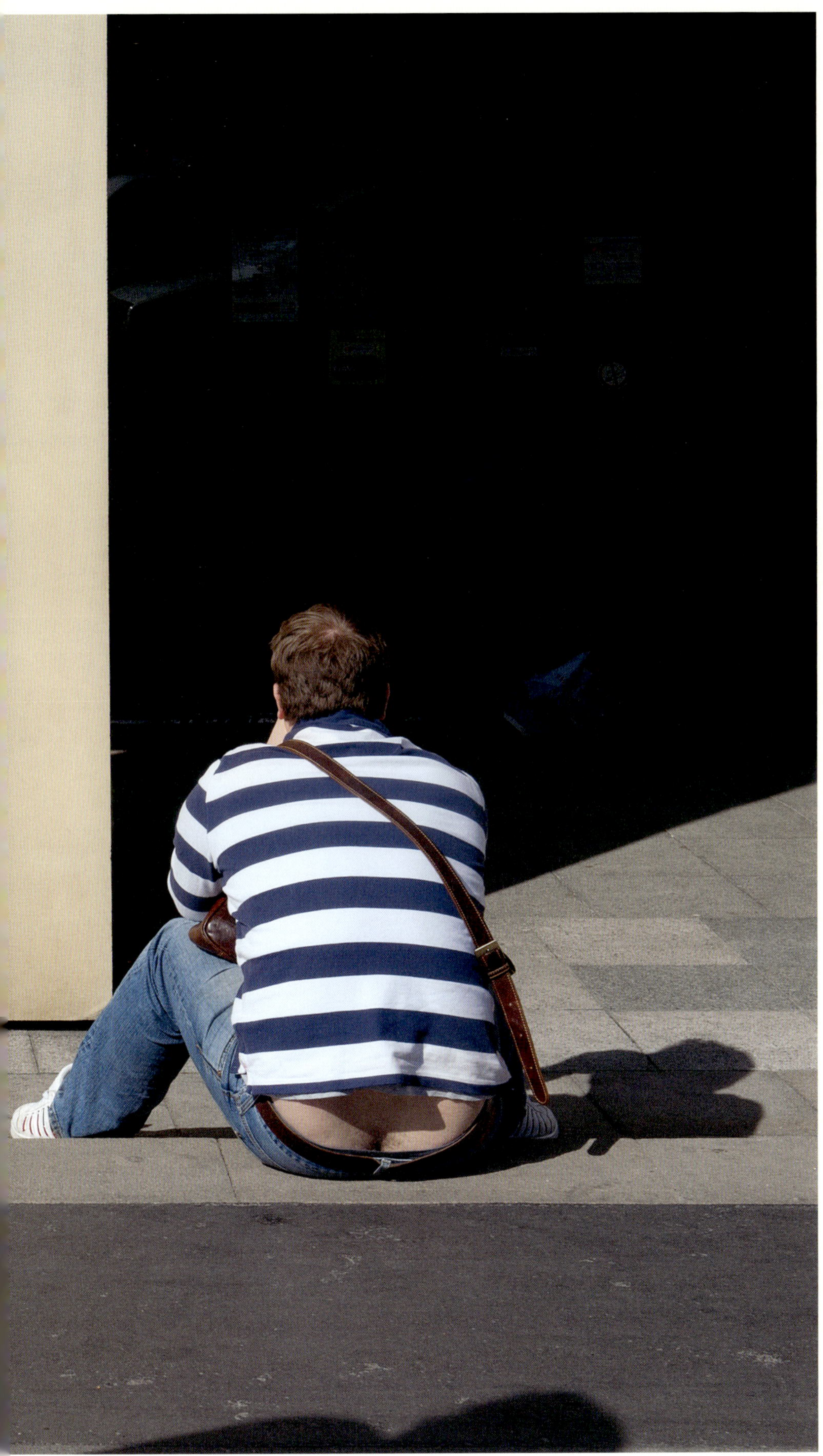

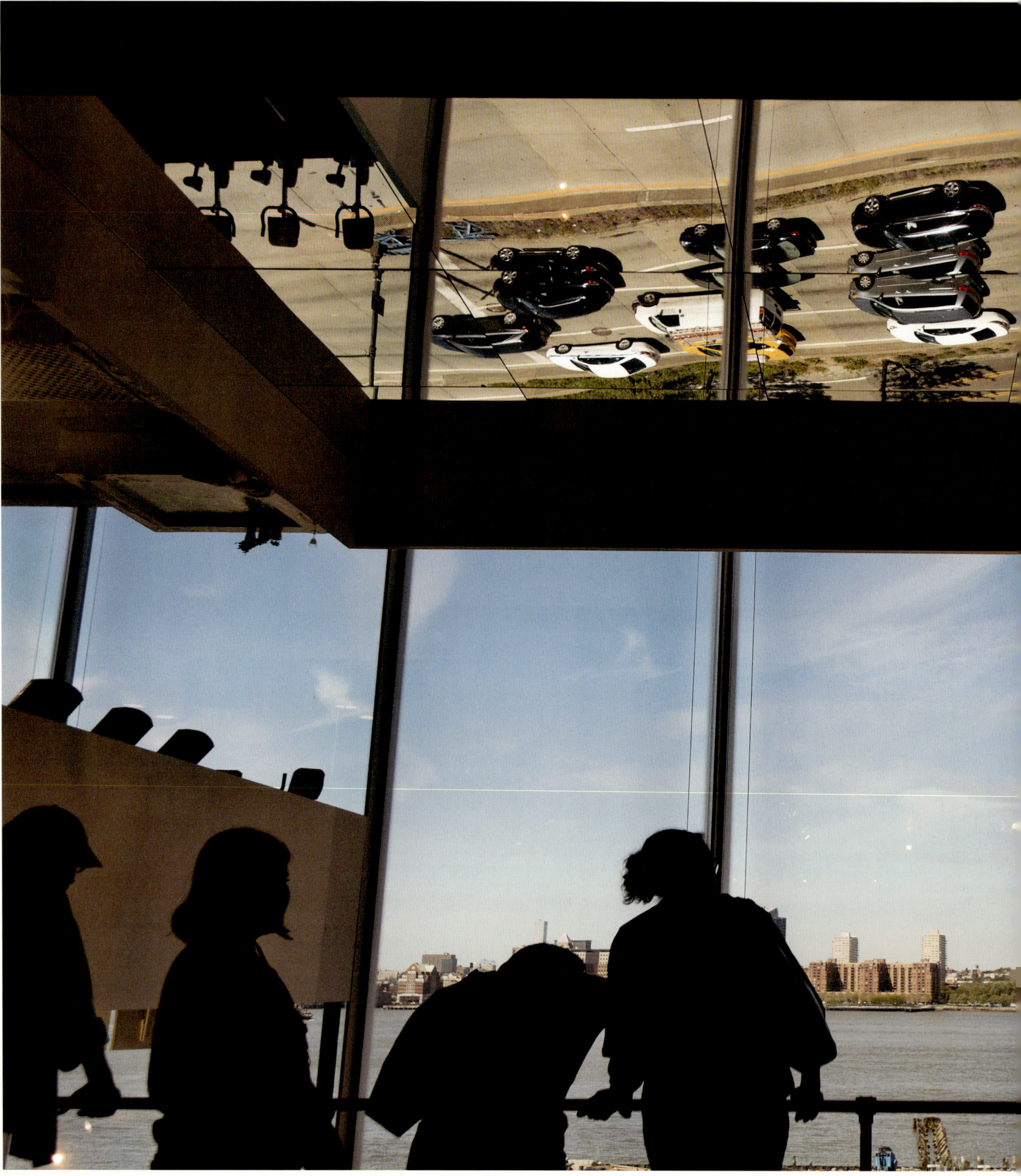

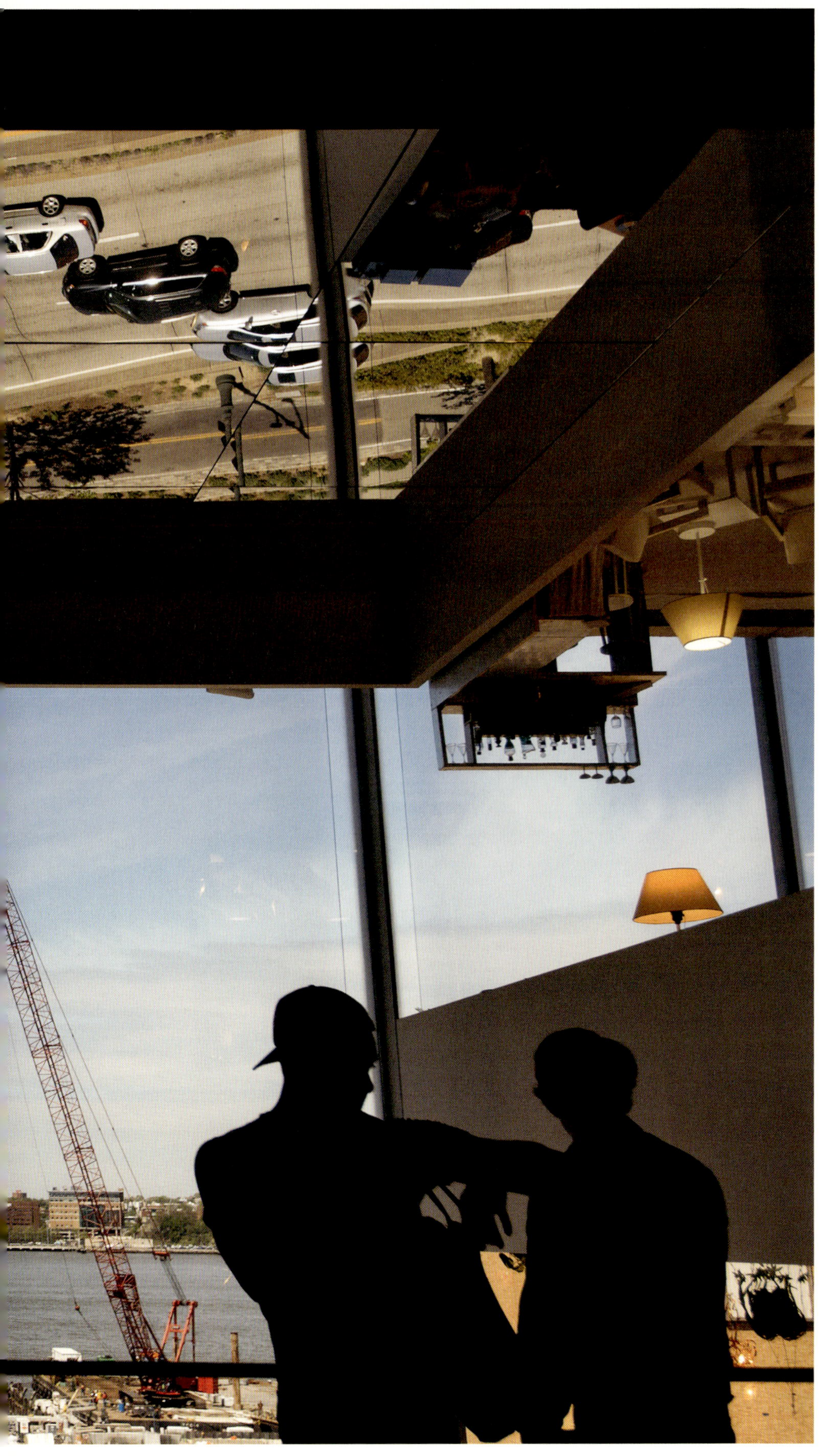

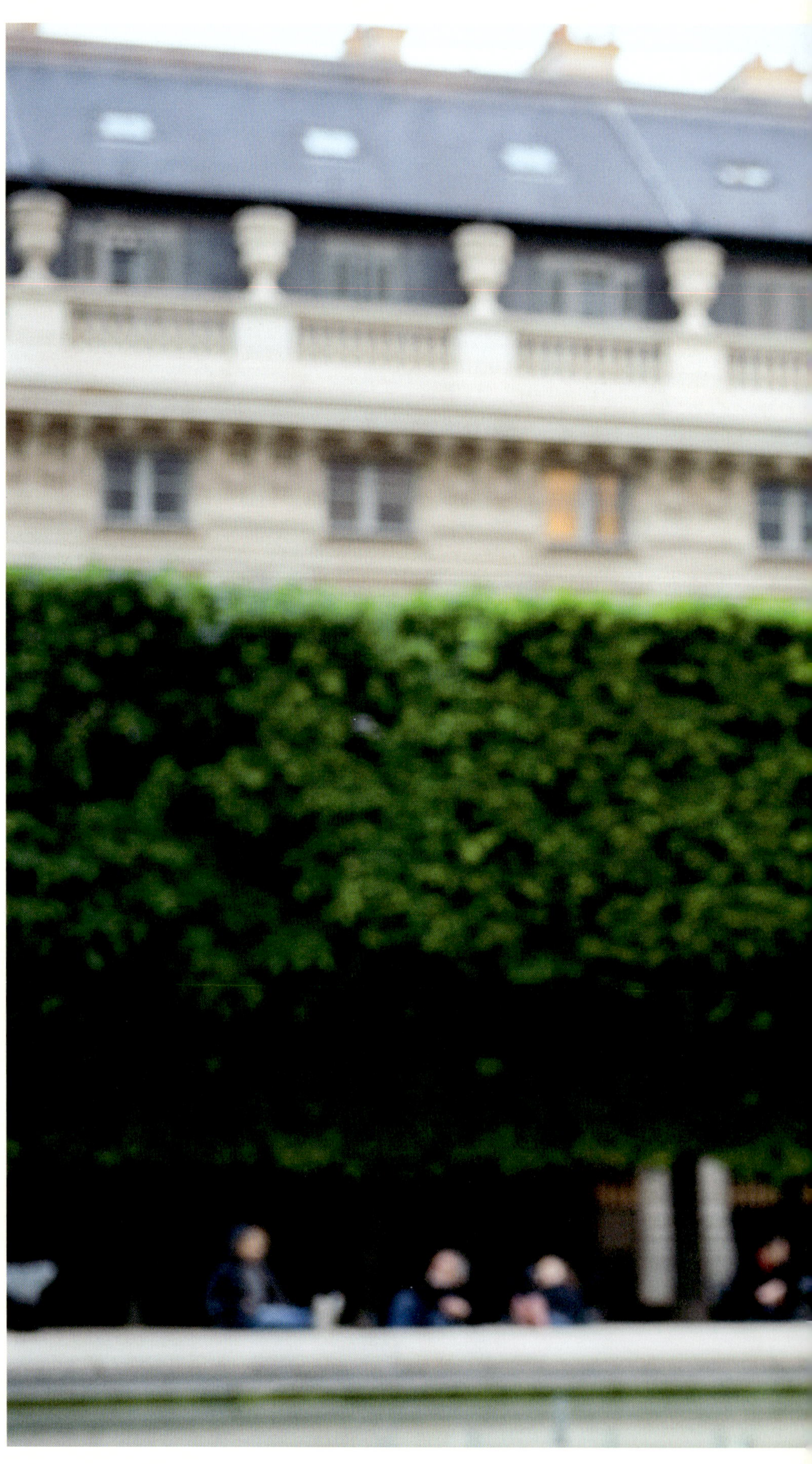

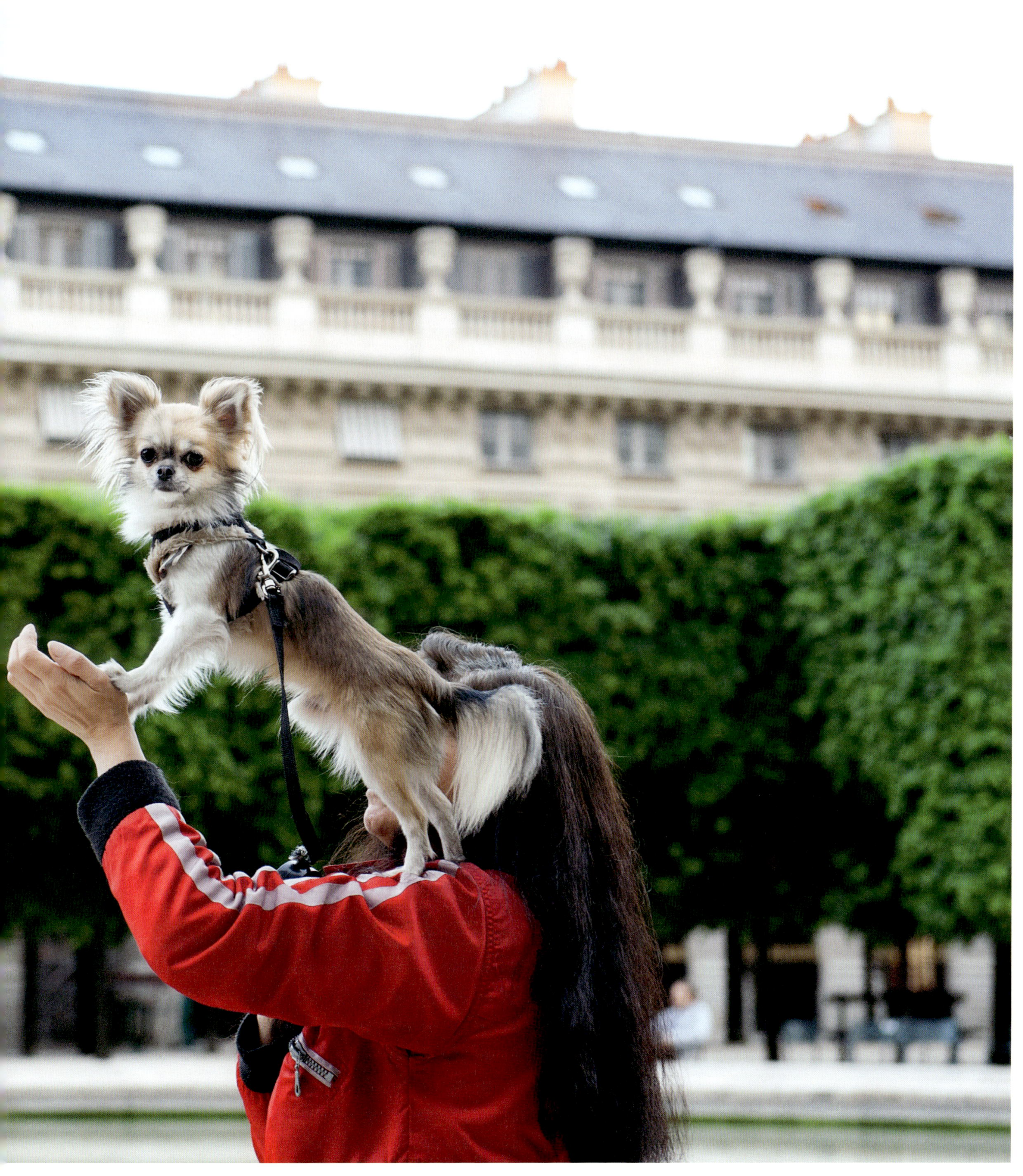

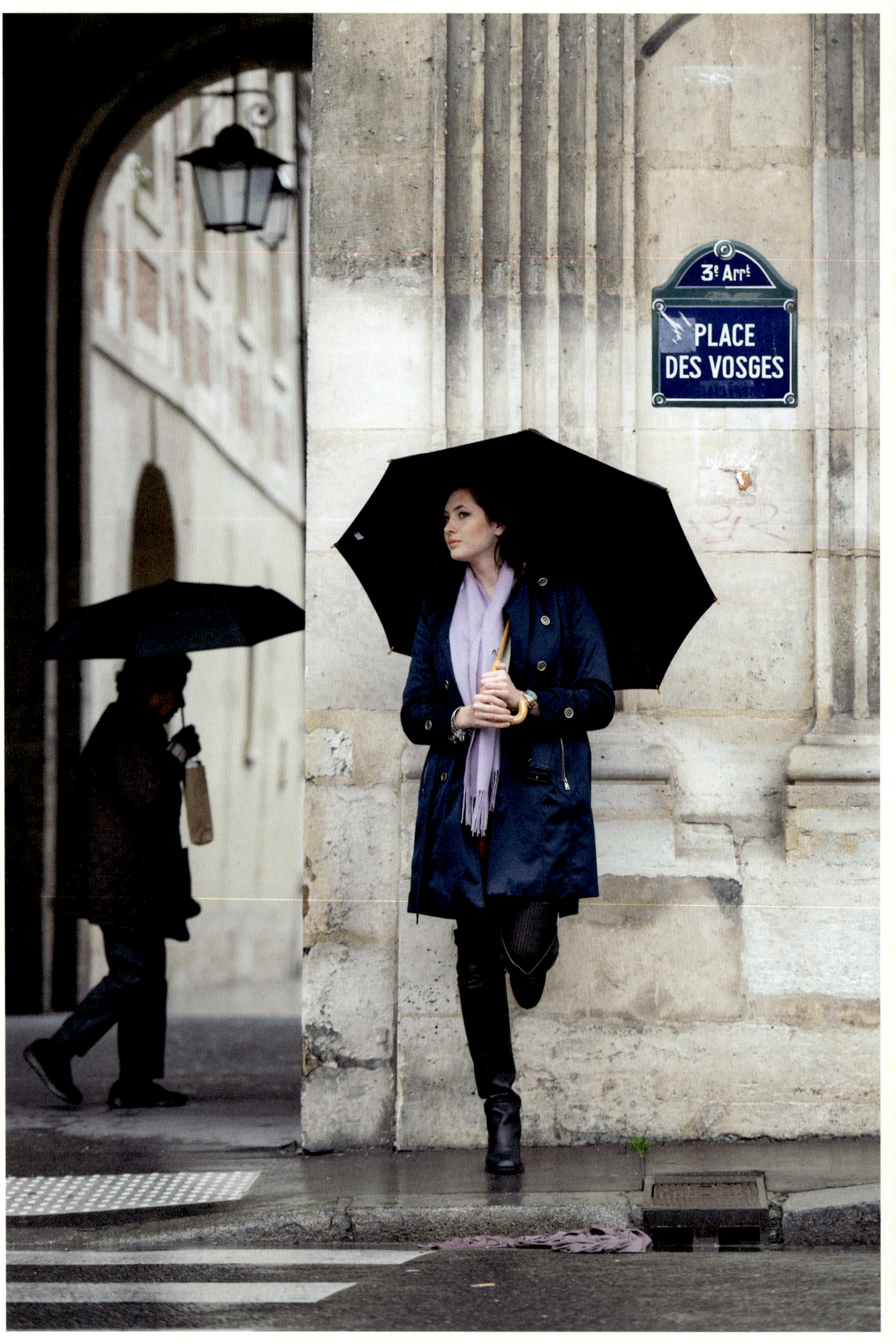

3e Arrt
PLACE
DES VOSGES

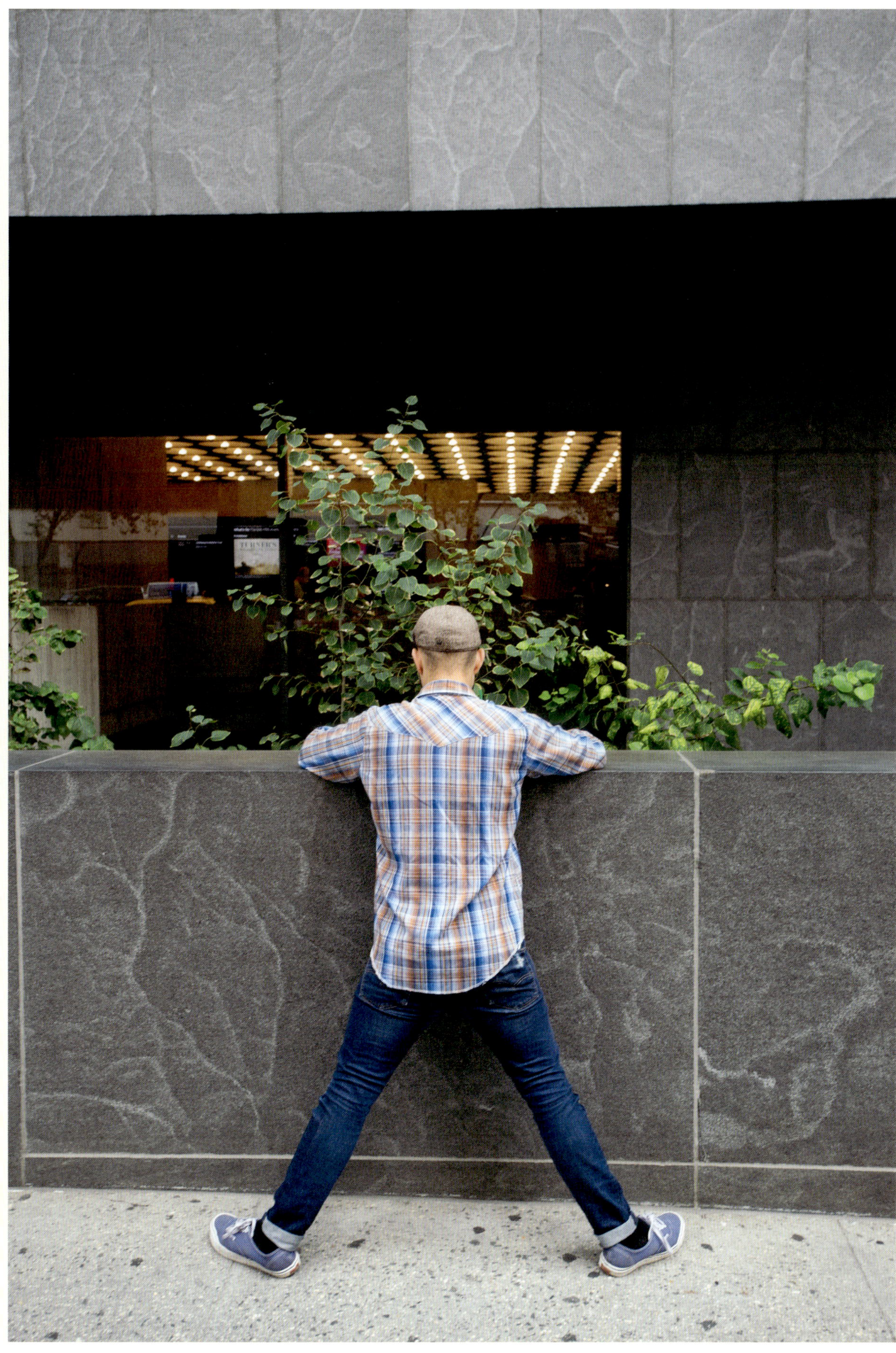

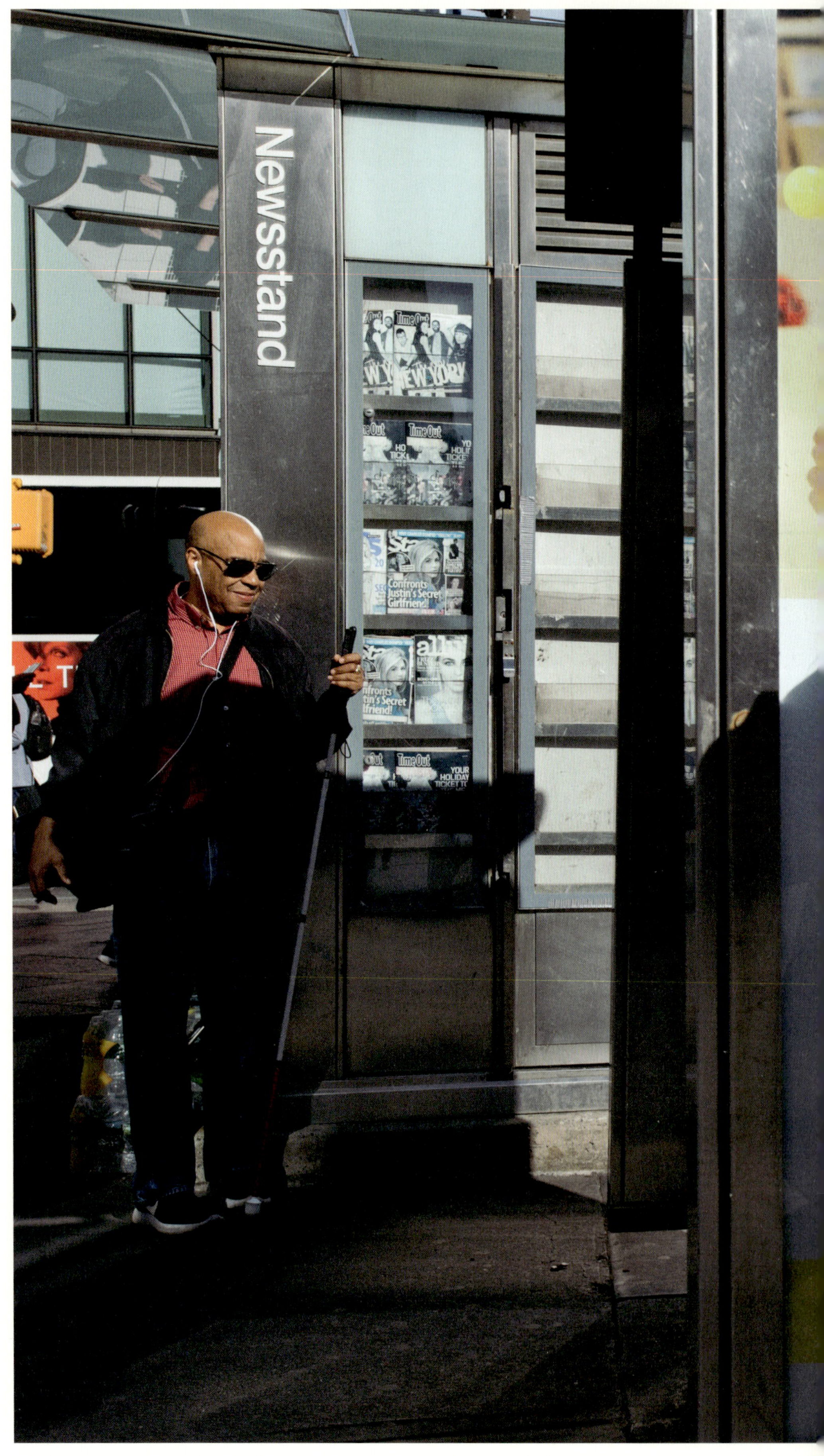

Newsstand

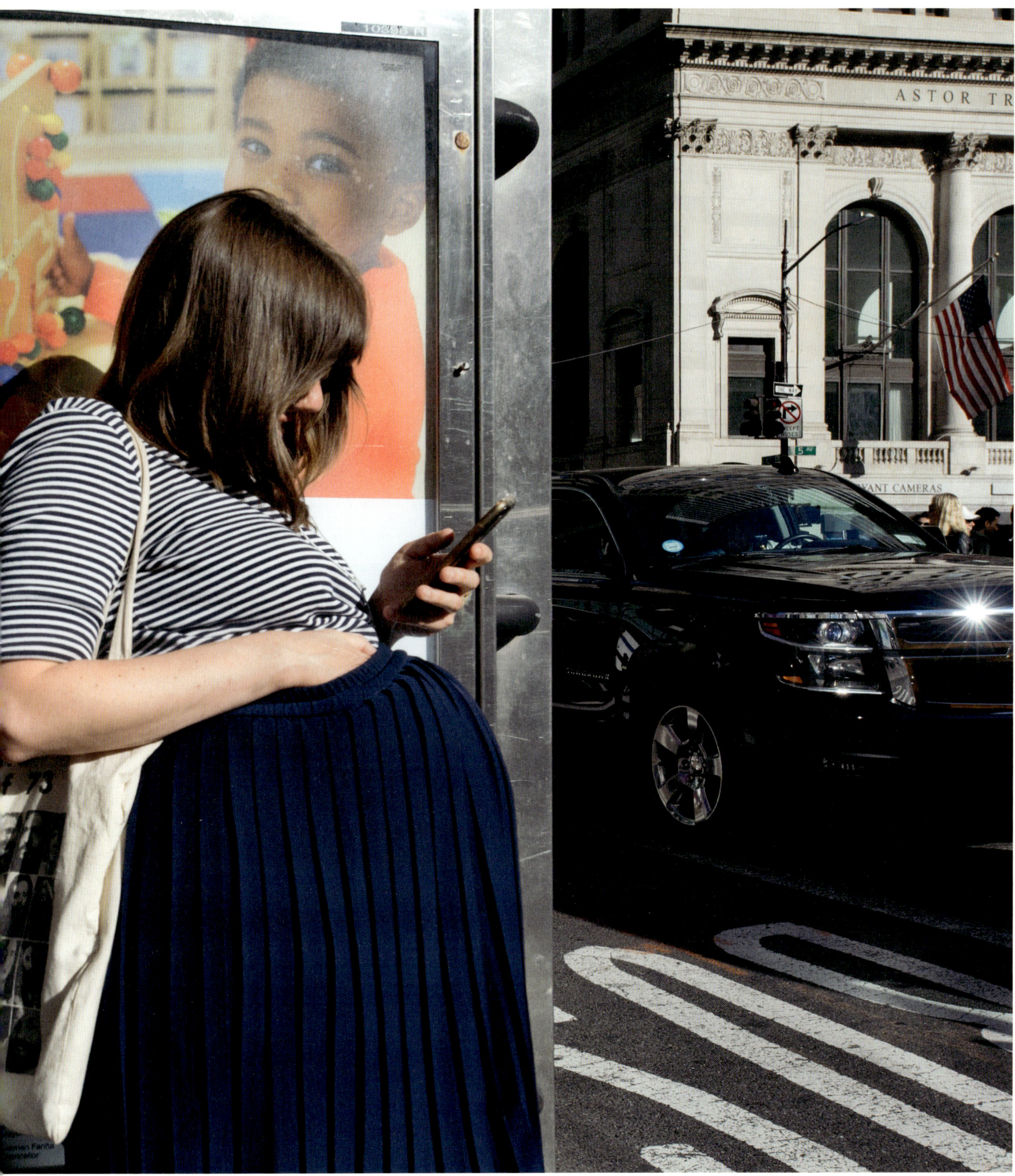

ASTOR TR
YANT CAMERAS
ONE WAY
5 AV

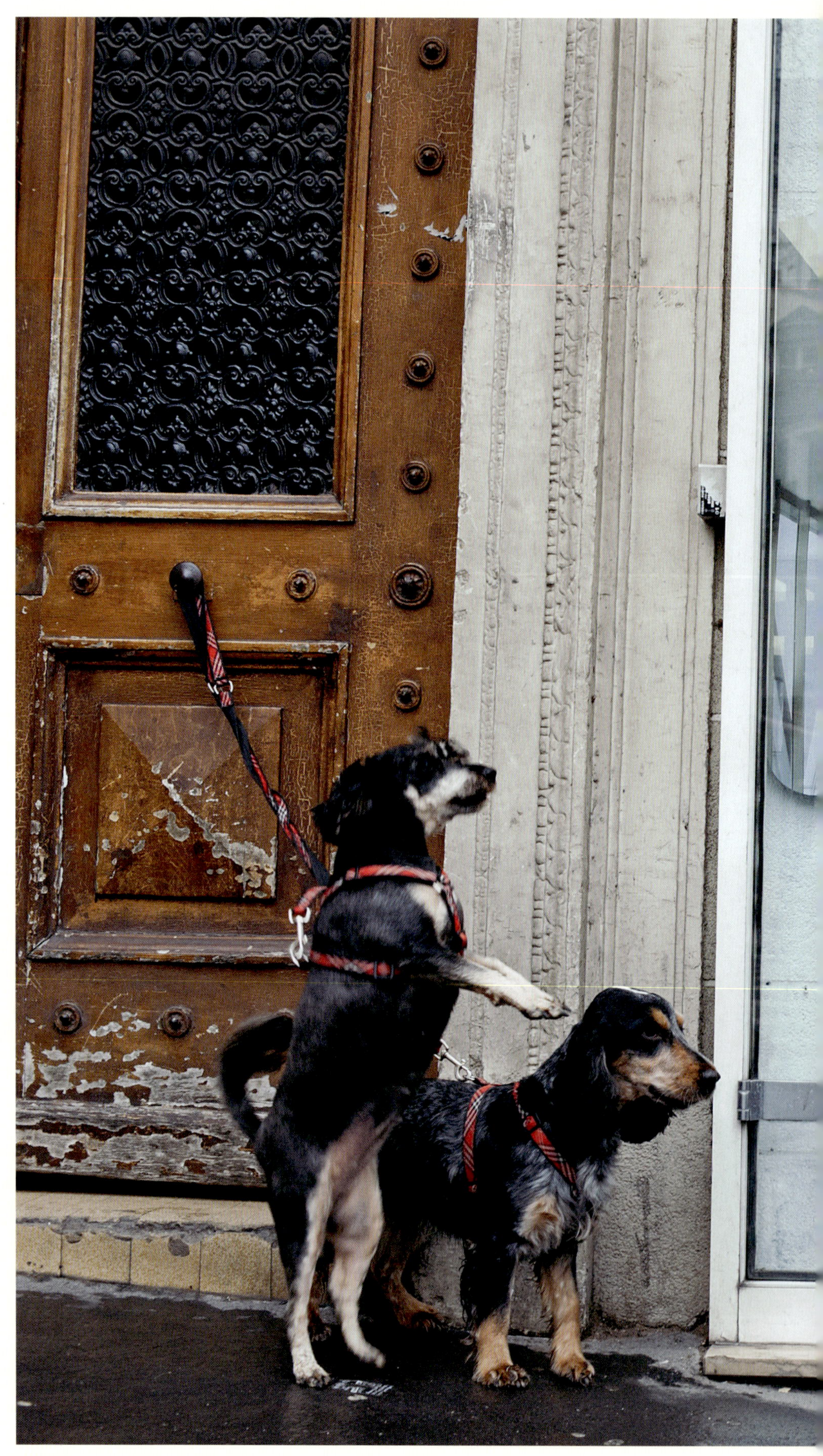

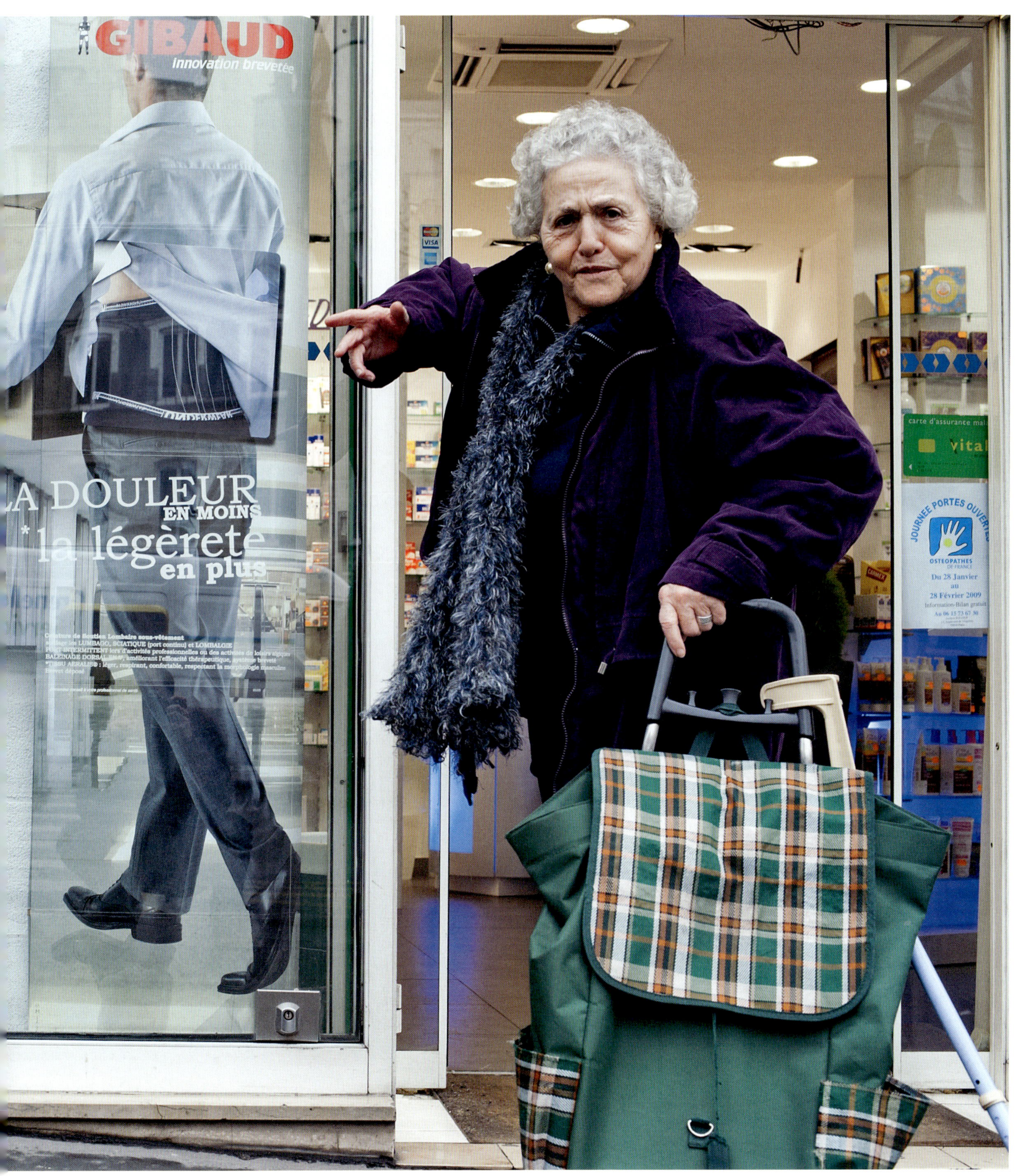
GIBAUD
innovation brevetée
LA DOULEUR EN MOINS
*la légèreté en plus
VISA
carte d'assurance mal...
vital
JOURNEE PORTES OUVERTES
OSTEOPATHES DE FRANCE
Du 28 Janvier
au
28 Février 2009

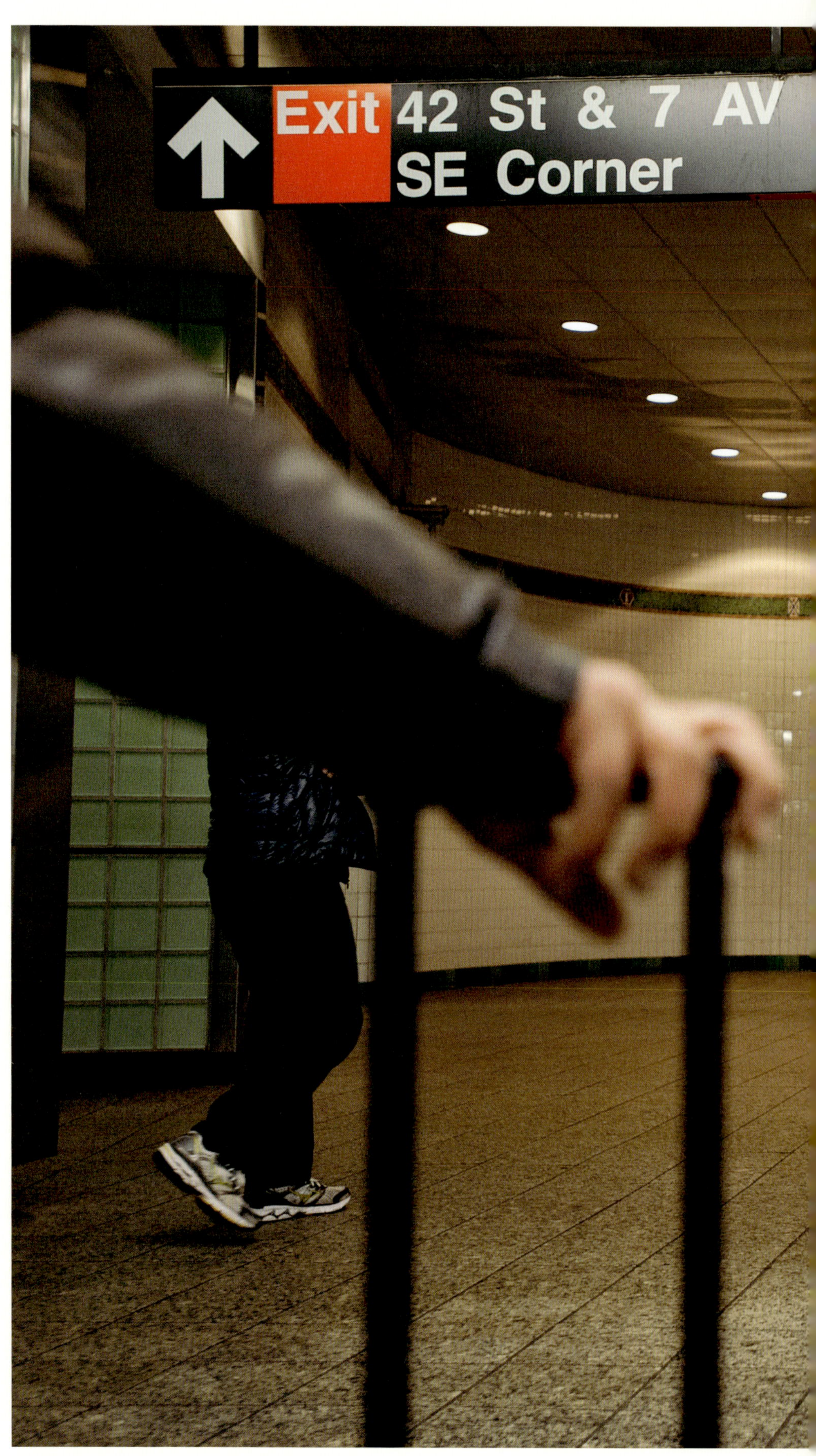
Exit 42 St & 7 AV
SE Corner

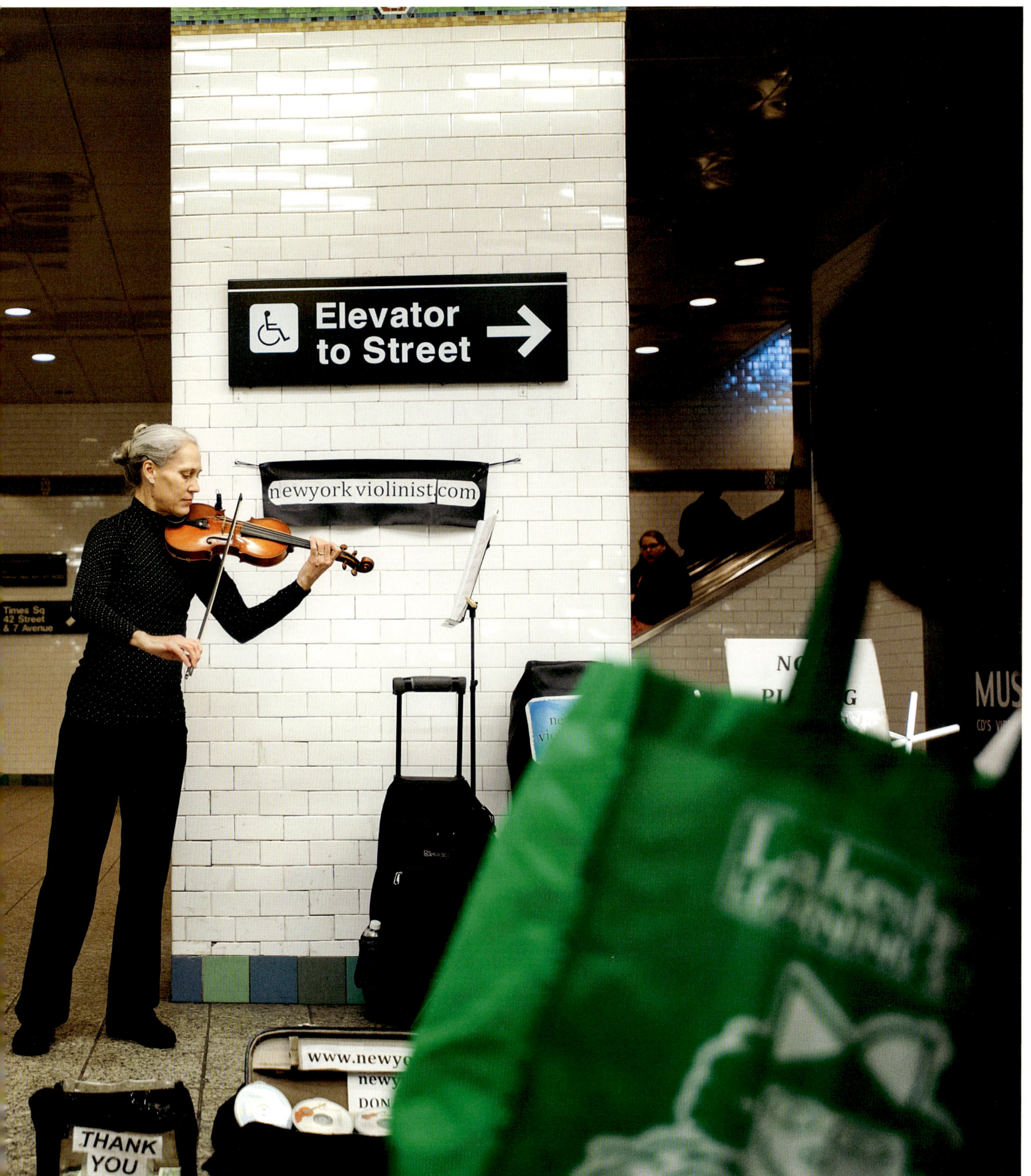

Elevator
to Street
newyorkviolinist.com
Times Sq
42 Street
& 7 Avenue
MUS
CD'S
NO
PL   G
www.newyo
newyo
DON
THANK
YOU

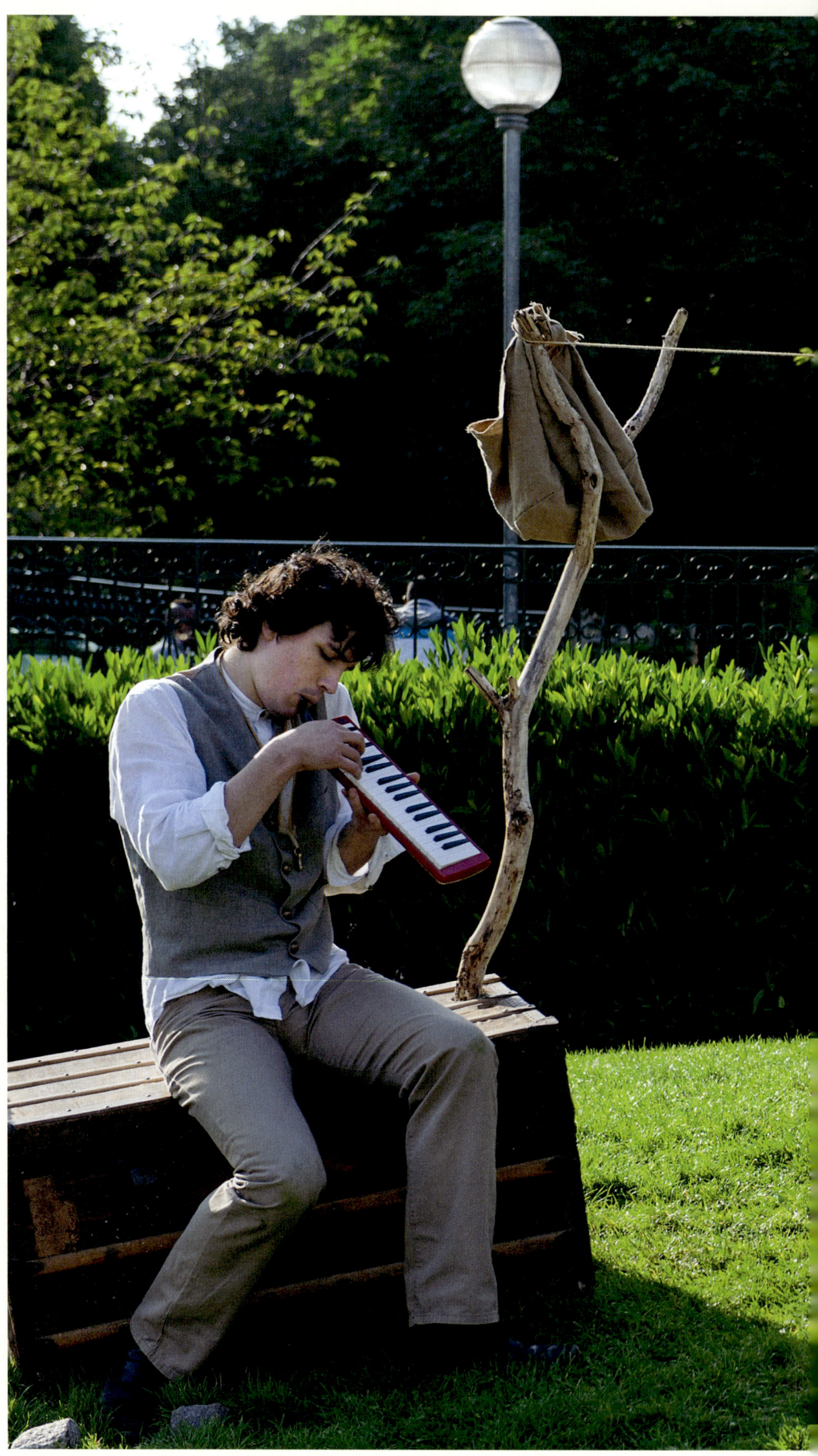

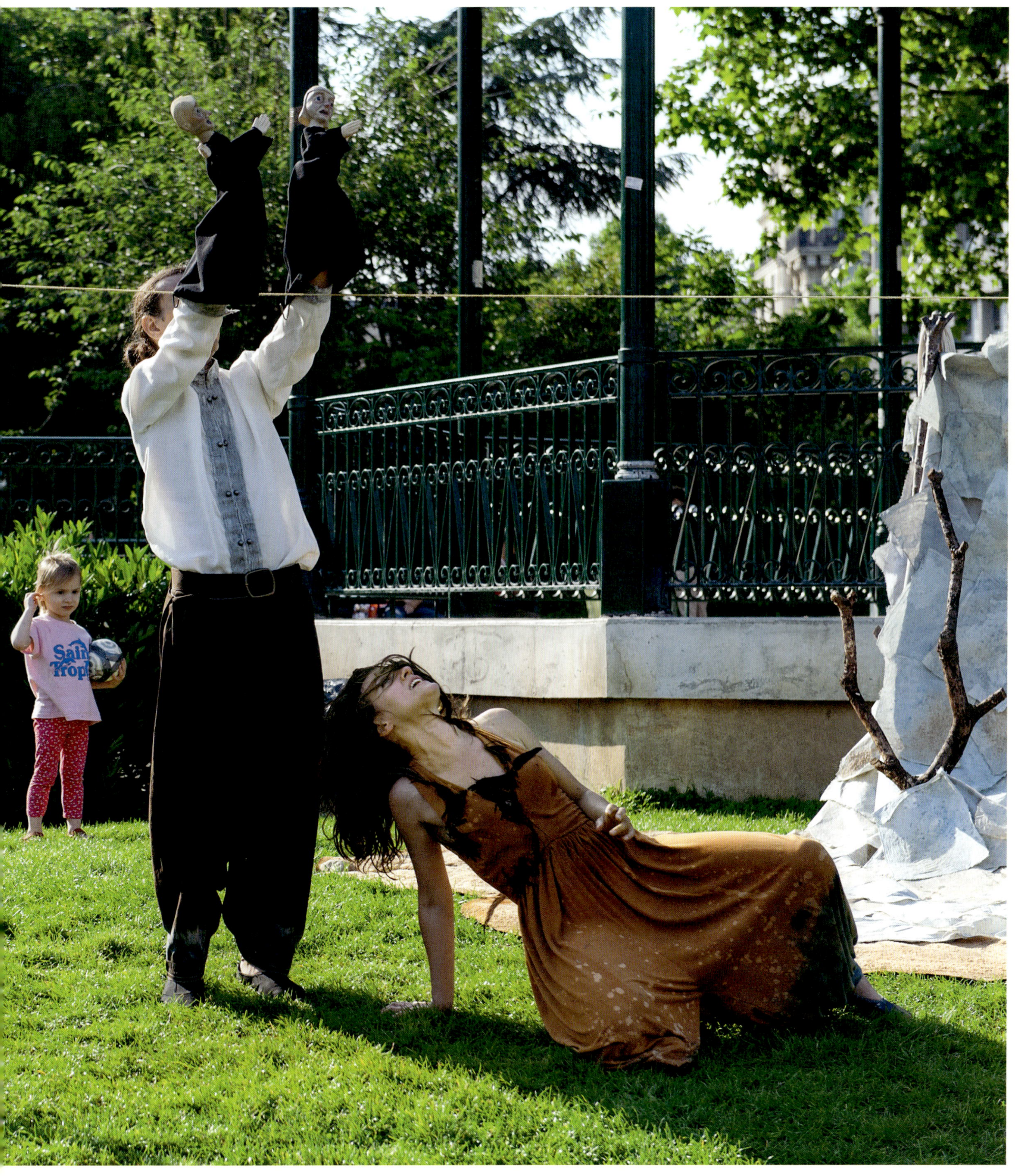

Je suis arrivé en 2004 à Paris comme stagiaire à l'agence VII. Après avoir passé les huit mois précédents à l'école danoise des médias et du journalisme, j'avais décidé de devenir photojournaliste pour pouvoir documenter les dures réalités auxquelles est confrontée l'humanité dans le monde entier. Pendant mon stage, je passais de nombreuses heures à regarder des photos dont beaucoup d'entre elles avaient été prises dans des zones de conflit, du Kosovo au Rwanda. Au fil du temps, je commençais à me demander si documenter la misère du monde par le biais de la photographie servait vraiment à quelque chose.

Pendant mon temps libre, je découvrais la beauté de Paris à pied avec mon appareil photo. Mes longues promenades le long des méandres de la Seine, sous le feuillage coloré du Jardin du Luxembourg en automne ou dans la trépidante rue de Rivoli se transformèrent en excursions thérapeutiques qui m'aidaient à compenser les images en noir et blanc souvent déprimantes que j'archivais chaque jour à l'agence. Plus je marchais, plus je réalisais qu'à Paris, ma nouvelle ville d'adoption, on pouvait faire des photos intéressantes à n'importe quel coin de rue. Me promener dans la ville sans sujet prédéfini ni mission de photographe était pour moi une sorte d'expérience méditative inconsciente que j'appréciais beaucoup. Je commençais à jouer avec les formes, la géométrie, les compositions, les ombres et la couleur. Je découvrais aussi un Paris moins romantique et plus brut, plus éloigné des photos de rues en noir et blanc typiques des années 1940 et 1950. Ernest Hemingway écrivait : « Si vous avez eu la chance d'avoir vécu à Paris en tant que jeune homme, où que vous alliez le reste de votre vie, cette ville reste avec vous, car Paris est une fête qui bouge sans cesse. »

Vers la fin de mon stage à l'agence VII, je montrai une partie de mon travail à Annie Boulat qui dirigeait l'agence de photos Cosmos sur le même palier. Elle trouva intéressant que je passe mon temps à documenter l'animation des rues parisiennes. Je me souviens de son commentaire : « Continue à photographier Paris, car la plupart des photographes parisiens ne veulent pas photographier leur ville. Ils préfèrent photographier des endroits lointains et exotiques ». Cette déclaration me confirma que j'étais peut-être sur la bonne voie et que je ne perdais pas mon temps à capturer visuellement la spontanéité des gens et des endroits que je découvrais. En hommage à l'un de mes compositeurs favoris, George Gerschwin, j'étais effectivement *Un Américain à Paris.* Mes photos d'artistes de rue à Paris Plage ou de gens à la sortie du métro n'étaient pas supposées documenter quelque chose ou raconter une histoire. C'étaient juste des clichés instantanés de beaux instants fugaces pris au hasard du quotidien, et qui semblaient s'imposer soudainement à moi certains jours.

En 2008, je participai à un stage de photographie d'une semaine à New York dirigé par Alex Webb et sa femme Rebecca Norris Webb dont j'admirais les photographies en couleurs depuis des années. Le thème de leur stage était « Trouver sa vision ». Chaque après-midi, nous, les participants, étions libres de photographier n'importe où à New York. Je m'aventurai donc hors de Manhattan, vers les quartiers du Queens ou de Brooklyn, sans cesse à la recherche de compositions intéressantes. Je me rendis vite compte que j'étais devenu un étranger dans mon propre pays. J'avais passé suffisamment de temps en Europe pour que la vie quotidienne aux États-Unis et plus particulièrement à New York me paraisse rafraîchissante et stimulante. C'était un sentiment semblable à celui que j'avais éprouvé lorsque j'avais déménagé à Paris quatre ans plus tôt.

Le stage à New York fut une expérience formidable et à la fin, je commençai à voir certaines similitudes entre les photos que je prenais là et celles que j'avais faites à Paris. Je plaçai les photos les unes à côté des autres et constatai qu'elles s'accordaient bien visuellement. Les rues de New York avaient souvent été photographiées en couleurs, ce qui n'était pas souvent le cas de Paris. Je constatai également que les images que je produisais soulevaient des questions ou évoquaient des problèmes socio-économiques qui concernaient les deux villes. Malgré mon intention de chasser de mon esprit la souffrance humaine pendant mon stage à l'agence à Paris, les injustices et les inégalités étaient omniprésentes dans les rues de ces deux villes. Un jour, j'eus par exemple une longue conversation avec une femme sans abri à Washington Square à New York. Elle avait passé plusieurs années dans la rue et était toxicomane. Elle n'était pas la seule. Je remarquai aussi que certaines photos des deux villes pouvaient caractériser les liens historiques et culturels étroits entre la France et les États-Unis, symbolisés par la petite statue de la Liberté dans le jardin du Luxembourg. Beaucoup de photos étaient elles-mêmes des repères historiques dans ces villes qui, comme des organismes vivants, sont soumises à des changements constants.

Cette semaine dans la Big Apple fut le début d'une relation amoureuse visuelle avec Paris et New York qui dura dix ans et dont le point culminant est cette juxtaposition photographique de mes deux villes préférées. Prendre des photos de rue durant cette période m'a permis de comprendre qui je suis. Cette expérience est peut-être aussi le reflet de mon caractère. Ce type de photographie est un genre particulier intransigeant qui exige de la patience et de la persévérance. Vous êtes à la merci du monde et il n'est pas possible d'organiser ni de prévoir quand ou comment prendre les photos. Chaque moment est différent, c'est pourquoi cet exercice demande différentes techniques photographiques. J'ai remarqué qu'être calme et en paix avec mon environnement et moi-même produisait souvent des photographies intéressantes. Les athlètes utilisent l'expression « to be in the zone » pendant une course ou un match important. Cet état d'esprit est important lorsqu'on photographie des lieux urbains. J'étais peut-être dans un « New York State of Mind », comme le chantait Billy Joel dans l'une de mes chansons préférées. Je pense souvent que ressentir les photos est aussi important que les voir.

Contrairement aux premières années de ma vie à Paris ou à l'époque de la redécouverte de mon pays à travers différents voyages à New York entre 2008 et 2018, je suis aujourd'hui moins enclin à photographier ces deux villes, et peut-être moins motivé. J'ai souvent mon appareil photo avec moi, mais je ressens moins l'urgence de rechercher des photos. Peut-être suis-je devenu un autochtone dans les deux villes qui ressent maintenant le besoin de photographier ailleurs, comme Annie Boulat l'avait souligné en 2004 durant mon stage à Paris. Quoi qu'il en soit, photographier des gens à Paris et à New York fut une expérience interculturelle inoubliable. J'ai toujours été curieux de rencontrer de nouvelles personnes et de découvrir de nouveaux endroits. À New York, je me rappelle avoir bavardé avec un dealer à un coin de rue tranquille dans Harlem, par une fraîche soirée d'automne. Je lui demandai qui étaient ses clients et il me répondit « Dave, ce sont des types de *downtown* comme toi ». Il y avait aussi ce trader qui faisait une pause cigarette devant la bourse de New York. Il m'avait remercié de lui avoir demandé la permission de faire son portrait, ce qui avait donné lieu à une assez longue conversation sur la photographie et sur Paris. À Paris, je me trouvais parmi les manifestants Place de la République après les attentats de Charlie Hebdo le 11 janvier 2015. Des gens avaient escaladé la statue et chantaient la Marseillaise, mais à la fin ils scandaient une phrase où se mêlaient l'humour et la peur : « Mais nous avons peur quand même ». Environ un million et demi de personnes étaient présentes et il était quasiment impossible pour la police de sécuriser la zone.

Une chose est certaine, Paris et New York sont des villes qui font rêver. Comme le chante Alicia Keys dans son tube *Empire State of Mind* en duo avec Jay-Z, New York est « une jungle de béton où se fabriquent les rêves ». Paris n'est pas une jungle de béton, mais plutôt une jungle de vieilles pierres que les gens du monde entier rêvent de visiter au moins une fois dans leur vie.

J'ai pu réaliser l'un de mes rêves : celui de photographier les gens et les endroits extraordinaires de Paris et de New York, mes deux villes préférées.

In 2004, I arrived in Paris as an intern at the VII Photo Agency. After spending the previous eight months at the Danish School of Journalism, I had my mind set on becoming a photojournalist, and the possibility of documenting the harsh realities facing humanity around the world. While at VII I spent many hours each day looking at images, many of which were taken in war zones from Kosovo to Rwanda. Over the course of one year, I began questioning whether or not documenting the world's misery with photography really made a difference.

In my spare time, I decided to discover the beauty of Paris on foot, with my camera. Long walks along the meandering Seine, under the colorful fall foliage of the Luxembourg Gardens, or along the bustling Rue de Rivoli became therapeutic outings which helped counterbalance the often somber black and white images that I archived on a daily basis at the agency. The more I walked, the more I realized that interesting and intriguing photos were to be had on any street corner in Paris, my new home. Wandering around the city was a kind of meditative, unconscious experience that I enjoyed very much, without having any predefined subject or assignment to photograph. I found myself playing with form, geometry, compositions, shadows and color. I also saw a Paris that was less romanticized and grittier, a change from the black-and-white street photographs that we know from the 1940s and 50s. Ernest Hemingway wrote, "If you are lucky enough to have lived in Paris as a young man, then wherever you go for the rest of your life, it stays with you, for Paris is a moveable feast."

Towards the end of my internship at VII, I showed some of my work to Annie Boulat who headed the Cosmos photo agency next door. She liked the fact that I spent time documenting street life in Paris. I remember her commenting, "Keep photographing Paris because most Parisian photographers don't want to photograph their own city. They want to travel to 'exotic' faraway places." This statement gave me confidence that I was perhaps on the right track and not wasting my time visually capturing the spontaneity of the people and places that I encountered. In tribute to one of my favorite composers, George Gershwin, I was indeed 'An American in Paris'. My photos of street performers at Paris Plage (Paris Beach), or of people exiting metro stations were not necessarily meant to document or tell a story. They were perhaps just snap shots of the beautiful fleeting moments that come upon us on a daily basis and seemed to present themselves to me unexpectedly on good days of taking photos.

In 2008, I attended a week long photography workshop in NYC led by Alex and Rebecca Norris Webb, a husband and wife team whose color photography I have long respected and admired. The theme of their workshop was 'Finding your vision'. Each afternoon we, the students, were free to photograph anywhere in NYC. I found myself venturing out of Manhattan, towards the boroughs of Queens or Brooklyn, constantly on the hunt for interesting compositions. I quickly began to realize that I had become a foreigner in my own country. I had spent enough time living abroad in Europe that daily life in the U.S., and more specifically in NYC, was fresh and invigorating. It was similar to the feeling that I had when I moved to Paris four years before.

The workshop in NYC was a great experience, and at the end I began seeing some similarities between the photos that I took there and those already in my archive from Paris. I put some of the photos side by side and noticed that they could visually play with one another. New York's streets had been photographed in color before, but this was not often the case in Paris. I also found myself producing images that asked questions or touched on socioeconomic issues in both cities. Despite my intention to clear human suffering from my mind, while an intern at the photo agency in Paris, such injustices and inequalities were omnipresent on the streets of both of these global cities. For example, one day in Washington Square in NYC I had a long conversation with a homeless lady who had been on the streets for several years and had suffered from an enduring drug addiction. She was not alone. I also noticed that some photos from both cities could mark the strong historical and cultural ties between France and the United States represented by the small statue of liberty in the Luxembourg Gardens. Many photos were historical markers themselves since cities are like living organisms undergoing constant change.

That week in the Big Apple was the beginning of a 10-year long visual love affair with Paris and NYC, which has culminated in this photographic juxtaposition of my two favorite cities. Taking street photographs over this time period has allowed me to understand who I am and is perhaps also a reflection of my character.

This kind of photography is a unique and unforgiving genre that requires patience and perseverance. One is at the mercy of the world and cannot organize or predict when or how to take pictures. Every moment is different and thus requires different photographic techniques. I've found that being calm and at peace with my surroundings and myself often led to interesting pictures. Athletes talk about being 'in the zone' during an important match or during a big race. This state of mind is important when photographing in urban places. Perhaps I was in a 'New York State of Mind', which is one of my favorite Billy Joel songs. I often think that feeling pictures is as important as seeing them.

In contrast to my first years living in Paris or re-discovering my own country through several trips to New York City between 2008 and 2018, I am now less inclined and perhaps less motivated to photograph in these two cities. I often have my camera with me but feel less of an urgency to search for photos. Maybe I have become a local in both places, and now feel the need to photograph elsewhere as Annie Boulat mentioned in 2004 during my internship in Paris. Nonetheless, it was the cross-cultural experience of photographing people in Paris and New York that produced ever-lasting memories. I've always been curious about meeting new people and discovering new places. In New York, I remember chatting with a drug dealer on a quiet street corner in Harlem one crisp fall evening. I asked him who his clients were and he responded, "Dave, they're guys like you downtown." Then there was the trader having a cigarette break outside of the New York stock exchange. He thanked me for asking his permission to take his portrait which then led to a rather lengthy conversation about photography and Paris. In Paris, I was among the protestors at the Place de la République following the Charlie Hebdo shooting on January 11, 2015. People had climbed up the statue and were singing the 'Marseillaise', terminating with a vocal gest of both humor and fear, "But we are scared at the same time." There were an estimated 1.5 million people present and it was nearly impossible for the police to secure the area.

One thing is certain, both Paris and New York City conjure up dreams. As Alicia Keys sings in her hit song 'Empire State of Mind' with Jay-Z, New York is a "concrete jungle where dreams are made of". Paris is not a concrete jungle, but rather an ancient stone one that people around the globe dream about visiting at least once in their lifetime.

One of my dreams has been fulfilled. It was photographing the extraordinary people and places of Paris and New York, my two favorite cities.

2004 kam ich nach Paris, um bei der Fotoagentur VII ein Praktikum zu machen. Nachdem ich die vorange-gangenen acht Monate an der Dänischen Hochschule für Medien und Journalismus studiert hatte, war ich fest entschlossen, ein Fotojournalist zu werden und die grausame Wirklichkeit zu dokumentieren, die die Menschen weltweit ertragen müssen. Bei VII verbrachte ich jeden Tag viele Stunden damit, Fotos anzuschauen, die größtenteils aus Kriegsgebieten, vom Kosovo bis Ruanda, stammten. Im Laufe des Jahres begann ich zu hinterfragen, ob es wirklich notwendig war, das Elend mittels Fotografie zu dokumentieren.

Ich beschloss, in meiner Freizeit das schöne Paris zu Fuß zu erkunden. Natürlich hatte ich meine Kamera immer dabei. Ich machte lange Spaziergänge an der sich durch Paris schlängelnden Seine, unter dem farbenpräch-tigen Herbstlaub im Jardin du Luxembourg oder entlang der belebten Rue de Rivoli. Diese Ausflüge hatten etwas Therapeutisches und waren ein guter Ausgleich zu den oftmals düsteren Schwarz-Weiß-Fotos, die ich Tag für Tag in der Agentur archivierte. Je mehr ich unterwegs war, desto stärker wurde mir bewusst, dass sich an jeder Straßenecke von Paris, meiner neuen Wahlheimat, interessante und spannende Motive finden ließen. Die Spaziergänge durch die Stadt waren eine Art von meditativer, unterbewusster Erfahrung, die ich sehr genoss, ohne dass ich ein festgelegtes Thema oder einen Auftrag für ein Fotoprojekt hatte. Ich begann mit Formen, Geometrie, Kompositionen, Schatten und Farbe zu spielen. Dabei entdeckte ich auch die weniger romantischen und die ungemütlichen Seiten von Paris, was im Kontrast zu den Schwarz-Weiß-Straßenszenen, die wir aus den 1940er- und 1950er-Jahren kennen, stand. Ernest Hemingway schrieb einmal: „Wenn du das Glück hattest, als junger Mensch in Paris zu leben, dann trägst du die Stadt für den Rest deines Lebens in dir, wohin du auch gehen magst, denn Paris ist ein Fest fürs Leben."

Gegen Ende meines Praktikums bei VII zeigte ich einige meiner Arbeiten Annie Boulat, die die Fotoagentur Cosmos leitete, die gleich nebenan war. Sie fand es gut, dass ich meine Zeit damit verbrachte, das Leben auf den Straßen von Paris zu dokumentieren. Ich erinnere mich, dass sie sagte: „Fotografiere Paris nur weiter, denn viele Pariser Fotografen wollen nicht ihre eigene Stadt fotografieren. Sie wollen zu ‚exotischen' entle-genen Orten reisen." Ihre Aussage bestätigte mich darin, dass ich vielleicht auf dem richtigen Weg war und es keine Zeitverschwendung war, die Spontaneität der Menschen und Orte visuell festzuhalten. Um meinen Lieblingskomponisten George Gershwin zu zitieren, war ich tatsächlich ein „Amerikaner in Paris". Meine Fotos von Straßenkünstlern beim Paris Plage oder von Menschen, die aus den Metrostationen kamen, sollten nicht unbedingt etwas dokumentieren oder eine Geschichte erzählen. Sie waren einfach Schnappschüsse der wunderbaren flüchtigen Momente, die wir jeden Tag erleben und schienen sich mir an guten Fototagen unerwartet zu bieten.

2008 nahm ich an einem einwöchigen Foto-Workshop in New York City teil, der von dem Künstlerehepaar Alex und Rebecca Norris Webb geleitet wurde, deren Farbfotografien ich seit Langem respektiert und bewundert hatte. Der Titel des Workshops lautete „Finde deinen Blickwinkel". Wir, die Teilnehmer, hatten jeden Nachmittag frei, um in der Stadt zu fotografieren. Ich verließ Manhattan und fuhr nach Queens oder Brooklyn auf der Suche nach interessanten Kompositionen. Mir wurde bald klar, dass ich nun ein Fremder in meinem eigenen Land war. Ich hatte genug Zeit in Europa verbracht, dass mir der Alltag in den USA, und insbesondere in New York, neu und erfrischend erschien. Ich fühlte mich so ähnlich wie vier Jahre zuvor, als ich nach Paris gezogen war.

Der Workshop in New York war eine tolle Erfahrung, und am Ende erkannte ich einige Ähnlichkeiten zwischen den Fotos, die ich dort gemacht hatte, und jenen, die ich bereits in meinem Archiv in Paris aufbewahrte. Ich legte einige Fotos nebeneinander und stellte fest, dass sie in einen visuellen Dialog miteinander traten. Es gab bereits Farbfotos der Straßen von New York, aber nicht viele von Paris. Ich machte Fotos von Situati-onen, die Fragen aufwarfen oder sozioökonomische Themen in beiden Städten ansprachen. Zwar wollte ich meinen Kopf von dem menschlichen Leid frei bekommen, das ich in der Pariser Fotoagentur als Praktikant gesehen hatte, Ungerechtigkeiten und Ungleichheiten waren jedoch auf den Straßen beider Weltstädte all-gegenwärtig. Beispielsweise unterhielt ich mich eines Tages auf dem Washington Square in New York längere Zeit mit einer seit vielen Jahren auf der Straße lebenden Frau, die schon lange drogensüchtig war. Sie war nicht die einzige. Ich stellte auch fest, dass sich mit einigen Fotos aus beiden Städten die enge historische und kulturelle Verbindung zwischen Frankreich und den Vereinigten Staaten darstellen ließ, die durch die kleine

Freiheitsstatue im Jardin du Luxembourg symbolisiert wurde. Viele Fotos waren historische Marksteine, da die Städte im ständigen Wandel begriffenen lebenden Organismen ähneln.

Diese Woche im „Big Apple" war der Beginn einer zehn Jahre andauernden visuellen Liebschaft mit Paris und New York, die ihren Höhepunkt in der fotografischen Juxtaposition meiner beiden Lieblingsstädte fand. In dieser Zeit hat mir das Fotografieren von Straßenszenen geholfen zu verstehen, wer ich bin und es spiegelt vielleicht auch meinen Charakter wider. Diese Art von Fotografie ist ein besonderes und unbarmherziges Genre, das Geduld und Durchhaltevermögen erfordert. Man ist dem Lauf der Welt ausgesetzt und kann weder den Zeitpunkt, an dem man ein Foto aufnehmen wird, noch die Art der Fotografie festlegen. Jeder Moment ist anders und erfordert daher unterschiedliche fotografische Techniken. Ich habe festgestellt, dass mir oftmals interessante Bilder gelangen, wenn ich mit meiner Umgebung und mir selbst im Reinen war. Athleten sprechen von einem „Tunnelblick", wenn sie ein wichtiges Spiel oder ein großes Rennen absolvieren. Dieser mentale Zustand ist wichtig, wenn man in urbanen Umgebungen fotografiert. Vielleicht war ich voll und ganz auf New York eingestellt, ein Zustand, der in *New York State of Mind*, einem meiner Lieblingssongs von Billy Joel, besungen wird. Ich denke oft, dass es ebenso wichtig ist die Bilder zu fühlen wie sie zu sehen.

Im Gegensatz zu meinen ersten Jahren in Paris oder der Wiederentdeckung meines eigenen Landes durch mehrere Reisen nach New York City zwischen 2008 und 2018 bin ich nun weniger geneigt und vielleicht weniger motiviert, in diesen beiden Städten zu fotografieren. Ich habe oft meine Kamera bei mir, verspüre aber nicht den Drang, nach Fotomotiven zu suchen. Vielleicht bin ich in beiden Orten heimisch geworden und spüre nun die Notwendigkeit, an anderen Orten zu fotografieren, was wohl Annie Boulat 2004 meinte, als ich Praktikant in Paris war. Dennoch war es die interkulturelle Erfahrung, Menschen in Paris und New York zu fotografieren, durch die unauslöschliche Erinnerungen entstanden sind. Ich fand es immer spannend, neue Menschen kennenzulernen und neue Orte zu entdecken. Ich erinnere mich, wie ich an einem kühlen Herbstabend in New York an einer ruhigen Straßenecke in Harlem mit einem Drogenhändler plauderte. Ich fragte ihn, wer seine Kunden seien, und er antwortete: „Dave, das sind Typen wie du aus der Innenstadt." Dann gab es den Aktienhändler, der eine Zigarettenpause vor der New Yorker Börse machte. Er dankte mir dafür, dass ich ihn um seine Erlaubnis bat, eine Porträtaufnahme von ihm machen zu dürfen, was dann zu einem ziemlich langen Gespräch über Fotografie und Paris führte. Nach dem Anschlag auf *Charlie Hebdo* am 11. Januar 2015 schloss ich mich den Demonstranten auf dem Pariser Place de la République an. Einige Menschen waren auf die Statue geklettert und sangen die Nationalhymne. Am Ende sangen sie mit Humor und Angst in der Stimme: „Aber gleichzeitig fürchten wir uns." Es waren geschätzte 1,5 Millionen Menschen zugegen, und für die Polizei war es mehr oder weniger unmöglich, den Bereich zu sichern.

Eines ist sicher, sowohl Paris als auch New York City wecken Träume. Wie Alicia Keys in ihrem Hit *Empire State of Mind* mit Jay-Z singt, ist New York „ein Betondschungel, aus dem die Träume gemacht sind". Paris ist kein Dschungel aus Beton, sondern eher einer aus alten Steinen, von dem die Menschen weltweit träumen, ihn mindestens einmal im Leben zu besuchen.

Einer meiner Träume ist wahr geworden: die außergewöhnlichen Menschen und Orte in meinen Lieblingsstädten Paris und New York zu fotografieren.

Remerciements

J'aimerais tout d'abord remercier mes parents qui m'ont emmené en voyage lorsque j'étais jeune. Ils m'ont appris à être curieux et ouvert sur le monde et m'ont aidé à développer ma passion pour les différentes cultures. Ils m'ont aussi encouragé à faire ce que je voulais dans la vie et à travailler dur pour atteindre mes objectifs. Maman et Papa, je vous aime.

Carole, merci infiniment d'avoir accepté d'écrire la préface de mon premier livre de photographie. Tout comme la mienne, ton âme semble habiter à la fois en Europe et aux États-Unis. Comme tu as vécu la plupart du temps à Paris et à New York, personne d'autre que toi ne pouvait mieux parler de ces deux endroits. Ton joli texte place également mes photos dans un contexte photographique à la fois historique et artistique.

J'aimerais remercier mes professeurs de photographie George Laumann et Robert Nelson au lycée Robinson de m'avoir fait découvrir ce beau média visuel. Depuis mes débuts avec mon premier appareil, un sténopé fabriqué à partir d'une boîte de flocons d'avoine Quaker, en passant par le développement de pellicules Tri-X et d'impressions dans une chambre noire, c'est grâce à eux que j'ai pu développer ma propre vision du monde et mon propre style photographique. Merci à vous George et Robert.

First and foremost I would like to thank my parents who took me traveling at a young age and taught me to be curious about the world and also helped develop my fond interest in learning about different cultures. They also encouraged me to do what I wanted to in life and to work hard to achieve my goals. Mom and Dad, I love you.

Carole, thanks so much for agreeing to write the lead text for my first photo book. Like me, your soul seems to reside in both Europe and the United States. Having spent most of your life living in both Paris and New York City, I cannot think of a better person to reflect on both places. Your lovely prose also puts my photos in both a historical and artistic photographic context.

I would like to thank my high school photography teachers George Laumann and Robert Nelson at Robinson Secondary for introducing me to this beautiful visual medium. Starting with my first photo with a pinhole camera made out of a 'Quaker' oatmeal box and continuing on with developing Tri-X film and prints in the darkroom, it was thanks to them that I was able to develop my own view of the world and my photographic style. Thank you George and Robert.

Zu allererst möchte ich meinen Eltern danken, die mich schon in jungen Jahren auf Reisen mitnahmen und mich lehrten, der Welt neugierig zu begegnen und mir halfen, ein echtes Interesse an unterschiedlichen Kulturen zu entwickeln. Sie ermutigten mich auch, meine beruflichen Wünsche umzusetzen und fleißig daran zu arbeiten, meine Ziele zu erreichen. Mom und Dad, ich liebe euch.

Carole, ich danke dir von Herzen, dass du zugestimmt hast, das Vorwort für mein erstes Fotobuch zu schreiben. Uns verbindet, dass du dich sowohl in Europa als auch in den Vereinigten Staaten heimisch zu fühlen scheinst. Ich kann mir keine bessere Person vorstellen, die sich gedanklich mit beiden Orten auseinandersetzen kann. Deine wundervolle Prosa setzt meine Fotos sowohl aus historischer als auch künstlerischer Sicht in den richtigen Kontext.

Ich möchte auch meinen Lehrern George Laumann und Robert Nelson der Robinson Secondary School dafür danken, dass sie mich mit diesem wunderbaren visuellen Medium in Kontakt gebracht haben. Ich habe mein erstes Foto mit einer Lochkamera aufgenommen, die ich aus einer Schachtel von Quaker Haferflocken gebastelt hatte, und entwickelte dann den Tri-X Film und die Fotos in der Dunkelkammer. Ich verdanke es ihnen, dass ich meine eigene Sichtweise auf die Welt und meinen Stil als Fotograf entwickeln durfte. Danke George und Robert.

David Bacher est un citoyen américain et autrichien qui vit en France depuis 15 ans. Il a obtenu un diplôme d'économie et d'anthropologie à l'université de Virginie puis de photojournalisme à l'école danoise des médias et du journalisme. Le travail de David a été publié entre autres dans le magazine *National Geographic* et ses photos ont été exposées en Europe et aux États-Unis. Il collabore également avec des organisations internationales telles que les Nations Unies. David aime se consacrer à des projets personnels à long terme tels que celui sur lequel il travaille actuellement au Maroc.

Carole Naggar est née en Egypte et a déménagé à Paris lorsqu'elle était très jeune. Elle a passé la plupart de sa jeunesse et de son adolescence à Paris avant de s'installer à New York. Elle partage maintenant son temps entre Paris et New York. Carole est poète, historienne de la photographie, conservatrice et peintre. *Tereska and Her Photographer* (une fiction basée sur une photographie), les livres de photographies Magnum *Le Catalogue Raisonné* et *Saul Leiter: In my Room* sont ses dernières publications. Elle écrit régulièrement des articles en ligne dans *Aperture* et *The New York Review of Books* et dirige la collection *Magnum Photos Legacy Biography* depuis 2014.

David Bacher is an American and Austrian dual citizen who has been living in France for 15 years. He holds a degree in economics and anthropology from the University of Virginia, and a continuing degree in photojournalism from the Danish School of Journalism. David's work has been published in *National Geographic* among several other magazines and his photos have been exhibited in both Europe and the United States. He also collaborates with international organizations like the United Nations. David most enjoys working on long-term personal projects like his current one on Morocco.

Carole Naggar was born in Egypt and moved to Paris at a young age. She spent most of her childhood and young adulthood in Paris and later moved to New York City. She now spends her time in both Paris and New York City. Carole is a poet, photography historian, curator, and painter. Her most recent publications are *Tereska and Her Photographer* (a fiction based on a photograph), *Magnum Photobook: The Catalogue Raisonné* and *Saul Leiter: In my Room*. She is a regular contributor to *Aperture* and *The New York Review of Books* online, and since 2014 she has been Series Editor for the *Magnum Photos Legacy Biography* series.

David Bacher, ein amerikanischer und österreichischer Staatsbürger, lebt seit 15 Jahren in Frankreich. Er hat an der University of Virginia einen Abschluss in Ökonomie und Anthropologie und an der Dänischen Hochschule für Medien und Journalismus einen Abschluss in Fotojournalismus erworben. Davids Arbeiten wurden unter anderem in *National Geographic* veröffentlicht und sowohl in Europa als auch den Vereinigten Staaten ausgestellt. Er arbeitet auch mit internationalen Organisationen wie den Vereinten Nationen zusammen. David arbeitet am liebsten an langfristigen persönlichen Projekten wie dem aktuellen über Marokko.

Carole Naggar wurde in Ägypten geboren und kam als Kind nach Paris. Sie verbrachte ihre Kindheit und Jugend in Paris und zog später nach New York City. Heute lebt sie in Paris und New York. Carole ist eine Poetin, Fotohistorikerin, Kuratorin und Malerin. Zu ihren jüngsten Publikationen zählen *Tereska and Her Photographer* (ein Roman, der auf einer Fotografie beruht), *Magnum Photobook: The Catalogue Raisonné* und *Saul Leiter: In my Room*. Sie schreibt regelmäßig für *Aperture* und die Online-Ausgabe von *The New York Review of Books*. Seit 2014 ist sie Herausgeberin der *Magnum Photos Legacy Biography* Serie.

COLOPHON

Paris/NYC

I would like to thank Silvia and Lois and their very talented team at Edition Lammerhuber — Birgit, Johanna and Martin. Your keen eye for editing pictures and your creative graphic design, together with your knowledge of color management and the entire printing process, made this book possible. Thank you Sophie, Nathalie, Felix and Hannelore for translating and editing the texts into three languages. *David*

Book concept Lois Lammerhuber, David Bacher
Photography David Bacher
Authors Carole Naggar, David Bacher

Translations and Proofreading Hannelore Schatz (English),
Sophie Dandres, Nathalie Maupetit (French), Felix Mayer (German)

Art director Lois Lammerhuber
Graphic design Martin Ackerl, Lois Lammerhuber, David Bacher
Typeface LAMMERHUBER by Titus Nemeth
Digital post production Birgit Hofbauer
Project coordination Johanna Reithmayer

Print and binding Print Alliance HAV Produktions GmbH, Bad Vöslau, Austria
Paper Luxo Art Samt new, 170 g/m²

Managing director EDITION LAMMERHUBER Silvia Lammerhuber
EDITION LAMMERHUBER Dumbagasse 9, 2500 Baden, Austria
edition.lammerhuber.at

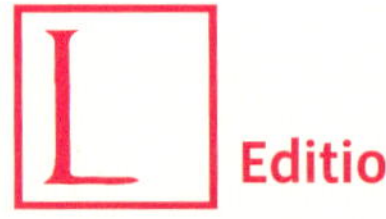

Edition Lammerhuber

Copyright 2019 by EDITION LAMMERHUBER ISBN 978-3-903101-65-4

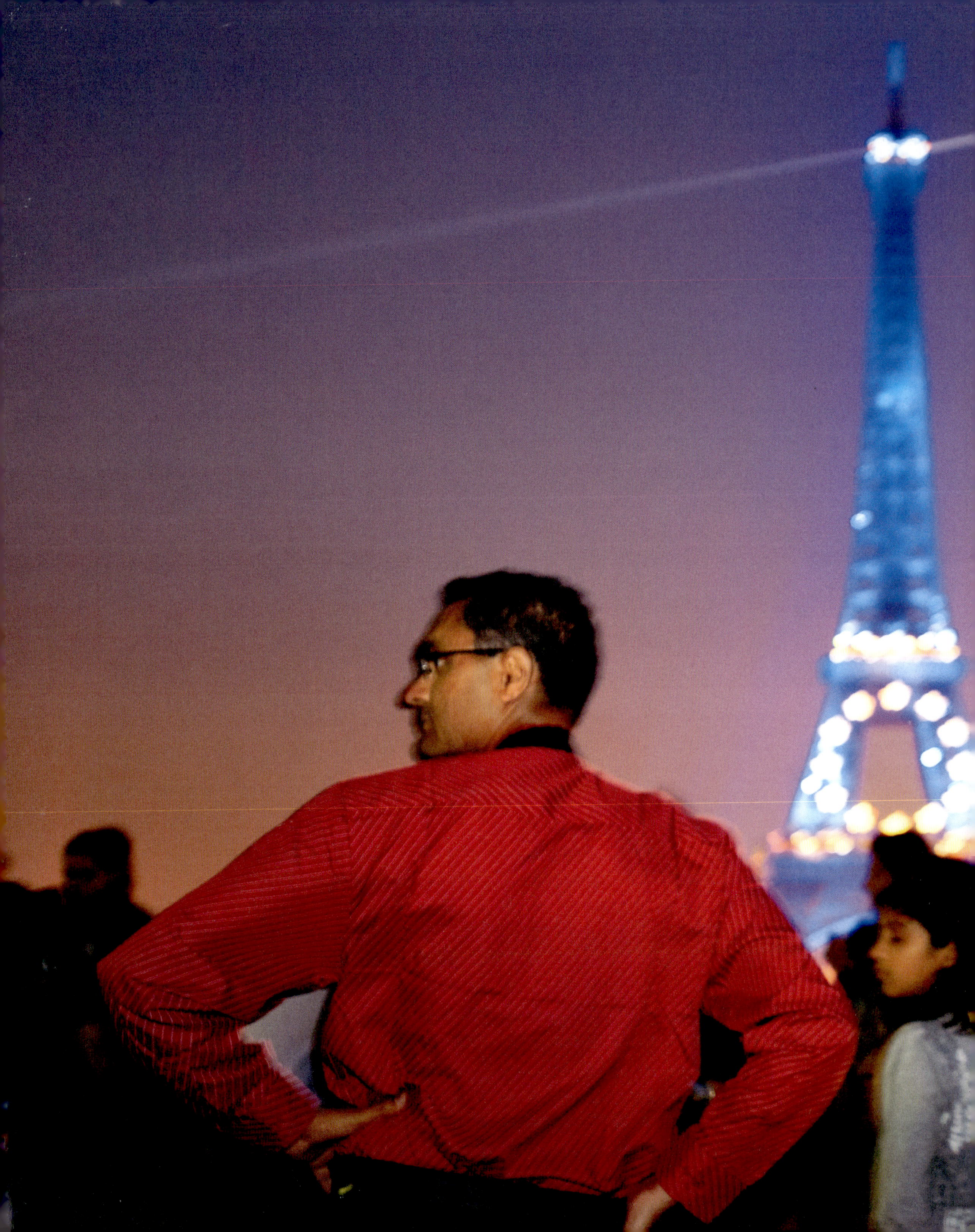